Pro HTML5 Performance

Jay Bryant
Mike Jones

Pro HTML5 Performance

ISBN-13 (pbk): 978-1-4302-4524-7

ISBN-13 (electronic): 978-1-4302-4525-4

President and Publisher: Paul Manning
Lead Editor: Ewan Buckingham
Technical Reviewer: Jeffrey Johnson
Editorial Board: Steve Anglin, Ewan Buckingham, Gary Cornell, Louise Corrigan, Morgan Ertel, Jonathan Gennick, Jonathan Hassell, Robert Hutchinson, Michelle Lowman, James Markham, Matthew Moodie, Jeff Olson, Jeffrey Pepper, Douglas Pundick, Ben Renow-Clarke, Dominic Shakeshaft, Gwenan Spearing, Matt Wade, Tom Welsh
Coordinating Editor: Mark Powers
Copy Editor: Thomas McCarthy
Compositor: Bytheway Publishing Services
Indexer: SPi Global
Artist: SPi Global
Cover Designer: Anna Ishchenko

Distributed to the book trade worldwide by Springer Science+Business Media New York, 233 Spring Street, 6th Floor, New York, NY 10013. Phone 1-800-SPRINGER, fax (201) 348-4505, e-mail orders-ny@springer-sbm.com, or visit www.springeronline.com.

For information on translations, please e-mail rights@apress.com, or visit www.apress.com.

Apress and friends of ED books may be purchased in bulk for academic, corporate, or promotional use. eBook versions and licenses are also available for most titles. For more information, reference our Special Bulk Sales–eBook Licensing web page at www.apress.com/bulk-sales.

Any source code or other supplementary materials referenced by the author in this text is available to readers at www.apress.com/9781430245247. For detailed information about how to locate your book's source code, go to www.apress.com/source-code.

Contents at a Glance

Contents

Foreword

I've written thousands of pages of technical documentation. For all that, I've never written anything I think is more important than this book. Mike and I have described a paradigm of web development that has the potential to revolutionize the profession. As we say repeatedly throughout the book, if all web developers were to adopt the methodology we describe, they would get more done in less time. If even a significant portion of web developers adopted it, together we and they could accelerate the creation of content across the entire World Wide Web. A lot of content still hasn't hit the Web, and a lot of applications haven't even been imagined because the data to drive them aren't there yet. If we web developers can just speed up the process of getting content onto the Web, we can speed up the creation of life-changing applications for people all over the world.

Mike and I don't claim that the methodology we present is new. In fact, we give the source where Mike first found the idea. Also, we suspect that it's been independently discovered a number of times. However, until now, no one has documented it with explicit examples accompanying it. We wanted to change that—and I think we've done so successfully. Again, we hope to see wide adoption of the paradigm, less to sell books (writing a book doesn't pay all that well, in fact) than to empower our fellow web developers and thereby ultimately make things better for people who visit web sites—in other words, everyone.
Is it arrogant to think we could have that kind of impact? You be the judge. *We* felt we ought to try.

Jay Bryant

About the Authors

 **Jay Bryant** occupies a space between two distinct fields: writing and programming. For more than two decades, he has been trying to help software developers better their game in writing for General Electric, Motorola, Dell, and other companies and programming for the New York Times Group and MorningStar, among other firms, as well as for various state agencies. If you're curious about his career, look him up on LinkedIn.

 **Michael Garrett Jones** has over 15 years of web development experience. He has worked in leadership development positions for Microsoft, Dell, Johnson & Johnson, Citi, and other companies. Michael has created distinctive patterns to implement high-performing, intuitive front-end APIs, and he's done work that's upheld design intentions to pixel perfection across an e-commerce site second only to Amazon.

During his freelance career, Michael's created over 60 sites. His work ranges from logo creation through company branding to a fully realized web presence.

Having a graphic design background, Michael was reluctant to tailor his output to fit the clunky layout options available in the early web days. Spending professional and personal time learning how the Web works has allowed him to be uncompromising in implementing his design aspirations.

With an out-of-the-ordinary perspective that comes from having been on both sides of the web development world of design and coding, Michael's been able to develop very efficient patterns, patterns that offer visitors and developers alike a great experience.

About the Technical Reviewer

 **Jeff Johnson** has been working on the web for more than a decade and currently heads Studio and a Half, a web design company based in Midland, TX. He holds a B.S. in Computer Science from the University of Texas of the Permian Basin and can recite the script of the first *Back to the Future* movie in its entirety.

Jeff, who launched his first computer-related business while still in high school, calls technology and entrepreneurship his truest loves—after his employee-wife, Veronica, of course. When not crafting code, Jeff can be found mentoring high school boys who share his affinity for *Stargate* and his aversion to sports. The highlight of his year is spending several weeks in Russia, where he works with teenaged orphans at a summer camp.

Acknowledgments

We thank the members of the UIF Team for their expertise, from which we learned so much, and for their trust and support in implementing our unusual patterns. From the leadership down, all the team members really worked at getting along with us and with each other; together they acted as one to meet the many interesting challenges we threw at them.

The following people on the UIF team should be singled out for special thanks:

Eric Hexter
Won Lee
Matt Hinze
Jason Cavaliere
Raj Kaimal

Finally, of the folks at Dell, we especially thank Thom Phipps, who led the team that created the underpinnings of the UIF.

On the book side, we thank Jeff Johnson, our technical reviewer. In addition to doing the testing to ensure that our assertions were correct, Jeff had a number of good ideas that we incorporated into the book. Ewan Buckingham, our Development Editor, also deserves a shout-out for steering us clear of several minefields and for pointing out how to fix the train wreck that was the first draft of one particular chapter. Finally, we thank Mark Powers, our Coordinating Editor, for all his help with managing the huge number of document files and image files that go back and forth between all the players and through several versions before a book emerges at the end of the process. All of them are thorough, pleasant, and professional people, and we appreciate their work.

PART 1

Introduction

This book deals with creating high-performance web sites. Its focus is large and high-volume sites. We met while working for a company whose web site has upwards of 50,000 pages and gets more than 80,000,000 visitors a month (many more during the holiday shopping season). The advice the book gives, however, applies equally to smaller sites, sites that don't get nearly as much traffic. Regardless of the site's complexity or traffic load, everyone wants good performance, after all.

We discuss three kinds of performance in the book:

- client-side (that is, browser) performance
- server-side and network performance
- developer performance

As this list implies, we cover how to get the best possible page load times, how to limit HTTP requests and bandwidth usage as much as possible, and how developers can reuse content. In the book's last two-thirds, we detail a system whereby developers can create reusable components and then use them to build pages. That technique is our ultimate lesson in how to boost developer performance. While we address making reusable components and building pages from them, we continue to focus on providing advice and techniques, supported by code samples, for maximizing client-side and server-side performance.

Along the way, we offer techniques for solving some of the trickier web development problems, such as fashioning tabs that can be individually addressed and leaders that always render correctly. We also show how to create visual interest with CSS, through the use of some lesser-known CSS selectors, including the :before and :after pseudo-selectors.

In other words, we've created a book about performance and then laced it with other tips and tricks. We hope you enjoy it and find some of the techniques presented in it useful.

CHAPTER 1

■ ■ ■

Introduction

Not long ago, while interviewing candidates for job openings, we discovered some appreciable knowledge gaps in the performance and scalability areas among our fellow developers. While many developers were fully versed in their server-side language of choice, they seemed to have no more than an anecdotal level of learning in HTML5 and CSS3. (By "anecdotal level," we mean they'd seen examples of HTML5 and CSS3—or perhaps had read a synopsis of the new aspects of HTML5—and drew conclusions from those patterns but missed some of the deeper meaning behind them.) In other words, we found a lot of people who could tell us how to do something but not why they'd want to do that something. More importantly, they didn't know how their favored techniques could make code perform better or reduce the time it took them to get work done. Seeing in this situation a great opportunity to help fellow developers elevate their front-end game, we decided to write this book.

The two of us met while working for a Fortune 50 company second only to Amazon in e-commerce business. In other words, we got to see what did and didn't work at the high end of the scale. In addition, we were on a team tasked with writing a framework to be used across the company's site, a site consisting of tens of thousands of pages. Also, we were starting from scratch during a conversion to MVC. So while our code had to perform extremely well for each visitor (to the tune of 80 million visitors a month), it also had to be efficient enough to meet the needs of many teams across the company— literally dozens of client teams.

The things we hope to pass on in this book derive from the lessons learned in that endeavor and from the unique perspective our experience provided: a deeper understanding of HTML5/CSS3 performance and, hopefully, some game-changing patterns that will elevate your front-end skills to the next level. We'd like to think we might even see a paradigm shift in web development, at least for large and complex sites.

A Live Site with Working Code Examples

In order to get the concepts and techniques we cover in this book across to as many readers as possible, we created a live site that has the working code examples shown in the book, as well as a responsive e-commerce POC. You can find the sample site at http://www.clikz.us

Figure 1-1 shows our sample site.

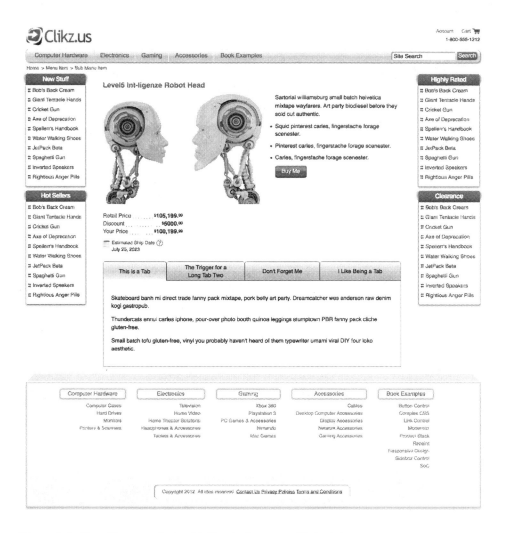

Figure 1-1. The clikz.us web site (© iStockphoto.com/Ociacia)

What to Expect

Let's be very clear about what this book is and isn't. "HTML5" is such a loaded term that it can be misleading, especially when it's in a book title. The term can mean a wide variety of things above and beyond its technical meaning, which is just a particular (and as of 2012, the latest) version of HTML. It is also used to describe any number of new technologies being introduced by browser makers: support for CSS3, native audio and video, Canvas, WebSockets, App Cache, Local Storage, Index Databases, File API, and Geolocation, among others.

While all of these things are exciting and well worth getting to know, this book focuses on the following areas:

- Understanding how browsers (modern and legacy) process code and how to use that knowledge to your advantage.

- Delivering extremely high performance HTML5 (in the sense of the latest version of HTML), CSS3, and JavaScript; the JavaScript cover mostly provides a fallback for browsers that don't support HTML5 and CSS3.

- Showing you new patterns and tricks to add to your cookbook, patterns and tricks that answer a lot of e-commerce and generic site needs in a way that delivers a great experience to your visitors and makes your job as a front-end developer more enjoyable and efficient;

- Integrating server-side logic into truly powerful and versatile front-end results.

- Giving you a unique perspective on developing front-end code that maximizes what each technology has to offer and cleanly separates concerns so your code scales well and has longevity.

Defining High Performance

We've defined four areas to focus on when it comes to performance. We started with the traditional definition of performance as it relates to page load, but then we found more performance gains, leading to the following kinds of performance:

- page-load times
- browser performance
- network performance
- developer performance

Page-Load Times

Most people associate web site performance with page-load times. That's a reasonable perspective, since slow page loads generate frustration and increased bounce rates (visitors leaving the site). Also, with Google now offering page rank based in part on page load time, you've got all the incentive you need to pay attention to this definition of performance.

Browser Performance

Modern browsers really focus on performance. From faster JavaScript engines to optimized parsing algorithms to complex animations handled by CSS—it's a whole new ball game out there. As a result, if you're code isn't optimized to take advantage of these advances, you could be missing out on some significant performance gains.

Network Performance

Bandwidth is an expense every company wants to control and ultimately limit as much as possible. We show techniques that reduce bandwidth while still making pages that look just as good (if not better) and that render at least as quickly on visitors' browsers.

Developer Performance

We think we speak for most developers when we say we don't like continually rewriting a bunch of similar code and, worse, having to maintain it month after month and year after year. In that spirit, we share techniques and approaches that let you reuse code in a surprising number of circumstances. At their heart is the concept of starting with clean, flexible HTML5 as a content container and then leveraging CSS for what it does best, visual presentation of that content.

We also share approaches to segregating code for maximum reuse and a minimum of name clashing. Not only does this approach help if you're the only developer, but it really shines if you're on a team of people working on a site.

Besides making for a less repetitive and so happier day, the resulting performance yields a great bonus: the time saved and reduction of code used to express a wide variety of presentation goals let you gold-plate (i.e., optimize, make more robust and bulletproof, and otherwise improve) your code. This is often the step that gets missed in high-demand work environments. We all tell ourselves we'll come back later and really optimize our code, but we rarely get the opportunity.

As we point out later in the book in talking about the button control, it may seem like a lot of extra code for a button, until you realize you'll never have to make another button—*ever*.

Responsive/Adaptive Design

We also cover responsive/adaptive design techniques. This is the idea of your site adapting or responding to different devices (smart phones, tablets, etc.). We include these techniques in a book about performance to introduce the "one code base" concept. Instead of writing one site for a smart phone and another for a tablet, you write your code once and have it adapt. This is a big developer performance gain, both for the first version and for subsequent maintenance.

Grid Systems

CSS grid systems are all the rage these days and for good reason: A grid system can save a lot of time and many headaches. We give you the lowdown on grid systems and show you how to use one to reduce the CSS you'll need and how it can be fully leveraged, in conjunction with responsive design, to really speed up development and make your pages more consistent and less error-prone.

A Deeper Understanding of CSS

We hope that, by the end of this book, you'll have a deeper and clearer idea of what CSS does and why. We present some advanced techniques; you might be surprised by the power they give you. We also show you ways to take advantage of modern CSS techniques while adapting gracefully to older browsers. As developers, we want to help you take advantage of all the performance enhancements and power of CSS3! However, we still want to provide good experiences for visitors who use older browsers. We'll show you how to do both in the same code base.

PART 2

■ ■ ■

Performance Basics

This section of the book addresses our development methodology, how to boost page-load times (client-side performance), our use of Responsive Web Design, and the web reuse pattern. Basically, we're setting context so that the rest of the book makes sense.

We cover how separation of concerns is useful to front-end developers, why we embrace progressive enhancement, and why we think you should embrace it, too. We also cover how a browser loads a web page, because it's hard to talk about client-side performance without understanding how browsers render pages.

Then we cover basic performance guidelines that apply to all pages. As already mentioned, we cover how to improve page-load times and, to a lesser extent, how to minimize strain on the network by using as little bandwidth as possible. We also address why page-load time matters. Then we discuss each of the individual guidelines, including the long pole in the tent: reducing HTTP requests. If we succeed in teaching nothing else, we hope at least to show you how to limit fetching things from the server.

Next, we address Ethan Mercotte's excellent technique: Responsive Web Design. We discuss how to use media queries, flexible images, and flexible grids to create pages that look good on almost any device. In addition to simply resizing elements and images, we add content as displays get larger.

Note that we don't advocate taking away content as displays get smaller; rather, we embrace the Mobile First paradigm and start with the smallest device we intend to support. Embracing progressive enhancement involves giving visitors with better devices a better presentation. We want you to think in terms of adding to a minimal (but still good) presentation rather than subtracting from a complete presentation.

This part explores one of our core concepts: reusing content for multiple presentations. We call each alternate presentation of the same content a treatment. Using the same HTML structure, we apply different sets of styles. Finally, we show how we rely on CSS nesting and on the fact that CSS fails silently (that is, without error messages to the visitor) to get the presentations we want.

CHAPTER 2

■ ■ ■

Development Principles

Having found a few principles to be helpful, we use them repeatedly throughout the book (and throughout our work outside the book, of course). These principles underlie everything we're going to say in the book. Consequently, we thought we should delineate them here, before we move on to the chapters that deal with more specific topics. The following sections show the design and development principles that we embrace:

- Code for Modern Browser Performance
- Use CSS to Manage Boundaries
- Embrace Progressive Enhancement
- Embrace Separation of Concerns

These principles let us achieve the best possible performance for the people who visit our sites, for ourselves, and for our colleagues when we work on large development teams. Some of these principles (especially using CSS to manage boundaries) also let us avoid some of the biggest cross-browser headaches.

Code for Modern Browser Performance

If you want to be a performance ninja, you must understand how browsers work (at least in broad strokes). Only then can you know where the bottlenecks are and optimize around them. Figure 2-1 shows a flowchart illustrating the journey of your code (HTML & CSS) into the final rendered version that your visitor sees in the browser.

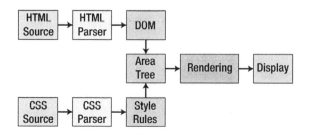

Figure 2-1. Code being processed by a browser

First, the HTML gets parsed into a DOM Tree, a.k.a. Document Object Model (DOM). That's one reason why the first thing a browser does when it encounters a page is download the page's HTML content. The other reason is that the HTML contains the references to all the other resources (style sheets, scripts, images, and so on) that define the page. Then a second tree is created by combining the DOM and the style rules (which are generated from CSS, both supplied by you and those native to the browser) into a Render Tree (or in Firefox a Frame Tree). From this Render Tree, the browser starts displaying or painting your elements onto the screen. This painting starts in the upper left and flows left to right and top to bottom.

You can gain performance in two ways:

- Reduce the number of elements in the HTML.

- Limit redrawing.

Reduce the Number of Elements in the HTML

By reducing the number of HTML elements (which have to be first parsed into the DOM and then later into the Render Tree), you can let the browser more quickly get to the Display endpoint (shown in Figure 2-1). The easiest way to reduce HTML elements is not to use them to achieve style goals and to use the smallest amount of HTML you need to reach those design goals.

Remember the principle of Separation of Concerns, which we'll cover in detail later in this chapter. Let HTML contain content, and let CSS contain presentation. Doing so increases client-side performance and, with its being easier to maintain, developer performance.

Limit Redrawing

While reducing the number of elements in your HTML helps, limiting the number of times that a browser has to redraw (or repaint, as the operation is sometimes known) an element is often a bigger help. Web developers force redrawing to happen by changing the DOM or changing the styles of elements that have already been displayed.

The performance cost of a change depends on the scope of the change. Modern browsers are designed to repaint only what is necessary. So while making a change to an element's position or inserting a new element can cause an extensive redraw (because it affects sibling elements), a style change to a background color causes a redraw of only that element (and its child elements).

You should consider two issues when making changes to the DOM or restyling elements. The first issue is the depth of the change within the DOM. The deeper in the DOM tree, the more isolated the change; so you should make your changes as far down the tree as possible. The second and more important issue is that, if you're going to make several changes to the DOM, make them all at once rather than one at a time. Because of that second issue, CSS can be your best friend when modifying the DOM.

For example, if you wanted to change an element's width, background color, and text color on a double-click, you might use JavaScript similar to that shown in Listing 2-1.

Listing 2-1. JavaScript That Creates Multiple Redraw Events

```
<a href="javascript:;" id="example">I'm an Example</a>
<script>
  var example = document.getElementById("example");
  example.ondblclick = function() {
    example.style.backgroundColor = "red";
    example.style.width = "200px";
    example.style.color = "white";
  }
```

```
</script>
```

In this example, we're setting the styles for the element one at a time. First, the script sets the background color to red (forcing a redraw), then sets the width to 200px (forcing a second redraw), and then sets the text color to white (forcing a third redraw). And while you could certainly still use JavaScript in a number of ways to combine those style changes into one call, the easier and more maintainable way is to use JavaScript to set a CSS class that includes all those properties. Doing so combines all the style changes into one redraw. Listing 2-2 shows an example of restyling that forces only one redraw to happen.

Listing 2-2. JavaScript That Creates a Single Redraw Event

```
<style>
  .dblClick {
    width: 200px;
    background: red;
    color: white;
  }
</style>
<a href="javascript:;" id="example">I'm an Example</a>
<script>
  var example = document.getElementById("example");
  example.ondblclick = function() {
    example.className = "dblClick";
  }
</script>
```

Finally, you should put CSS (including references to external style sheets) in the head element and put scripts at the bottom of the body element. Because the browser can start to render elements before it has completely parsed the HTML, putting CSS in the head ensures those elements are styled correctly. More importantly for performance, you don't want elements to have to be redrawn because you put a style declaration after the element it rendered. Also, it's a bad visual effect to see items shifting about unintentionally. Also, because browsers have to evaluate JavaScript files, putting them at the beginning of the HTML can delay rendering of your visual elements and give the visitor the perception of a slower page load.

We'll cover putting CSS at the top and putting JavaScript at the bottom in the next chapter. We'll also talk about some other ways to avoid redraw events in the next chapter.

Use CSS to Manage Boundaries

As we'll discuss in greater detail later in this chapter in the section entitled "It's All Just Boxes", a browser renders a web page as a series of boxes, and those boxes often contain other boxes. Consequently, we can say that a browser's natural rendering model is boxes within boxes. Knowing that, it's wise to arrange your layout to work with rather than against the box-within-a-box rendering model that browsers implement.

To make the most of this box-within-a-box implementation, the good thing to do is arrange each element or group of elements such that it is fully contained within a box. Conversely, the bad thing to do is have things sticking out of your boxes. We'll illustrate both the good and the bad practice with an example.

First, let's define what we're doing. We want to create an article stack that includes an image to the left of the article text and a headline above the article text and that lets the article text extend vertically to any height. We call it a "stack" because it stacks elements on the page. Figure 2-2 shows an example of the desired output.

Chrome's Evil Twin Brother

The logo is darker because they couldn't make it look right with a goatee.

Figure 2-2. Our target output

Listing 2-3 shows the HTML that provides the content for this article stack.

Listing 2-3. The HTML Behind Our Article Stack

```
<article class="browserArticle">
  <h1 class="subTitle accentColor1">Chrome's Evil Twin Brother</h1>
  <span class="evilChromeLogo"></span>
  <p>The logo is darker because they couldn't make it look right with a goatee.</p>

</article>
```

Listing 2-4 shows a set of CSS rules that would create a box and place all the content within the box with the relationships we want to have.

Listing 2-4. CSS to Put Our Article Stack in a Box

```
.browserArticle
{
  /* We set the position: relative so the absolutely positioned
     element within uses this box to position itself */
  position: relative;
  width: 200px;
  padding-left: 48px;
  /* We set a minimum height in case there's not enough content to make the box big enough
     to house the image. We use the height of the image plus 3 for the top offset. */
  min-height: 39px;
}

.subTitle
{
  font-size: 18px;
}

.evilChromeLogo
{
  background: url(images/evilChromeLogo.png) no-repeat 0 0;
  height: 36px;
  width: 38px;
  position: absolute;
  left: 0;
  top: 3px;
  z-index: 1;
}
```

```
.accentColor1
{
  color: #1C70AD;
}
```

The key style in Listing 2-2 is the .browserArticle rule. It specifies a width of 200 pixels and no height, giving us a box 200 pixels wide that will extend to the height of its content. It also specifies a left padding value of 48 pixels. We'll use that 48 pixels as the place to put our image. The .evilChromeLogo rule, in addition to specifying the background image and its height and width, uses the position: absolute rule and the left: 0 rule to put the image on the box's left margin. In this fashion, we've created a box that contains all of its content within its boundaries. That way, we don't have to think about what might happen to any content that goes outside the boundaries, because that never happens.

Now let's look at one wrong way to create the same layout. We're still using the HTML in Listing 2-3 as our source of content. Listing 2-5 shows one variety of poor practice for laying out our article stack.

Listing 2-5. *Flawed CSS for Our Article Stack*

```
.browserArticle
{
  position: relative;
  width: 200px;
  margin-left: 48px;
  /* Removed paddingleft setting */
}

.subTitle
{
  font-size: 18px;
}

.evilChromeLogo
{
  background: url(images/evilChromeLogo.png) no-repeat 0 0;
  height: 36px;
  width: 38px;
  position: absolute;
  left: -48px;
  top: 3px;
  /* Removed z-index setting */
}

.accentColor1
{
  color: #1C70AD;
}
```

Most of this listing is identical to Listing 2-4. We've highlighted the changes in bold. We're still creating a 200-pixel-wide box, putting our text in the box, and putting the image to the left of the text. The difference is that we're now putting the image outside the box. The browserArticle class specifies a left margin rather than left padding. The "evilChromeLogo" class specifies a left value of –48 pixels (and that negative number is the value that should set off alarm bells for you).

13

The trouble is that a margin is outside the box of the element that defines the margin. Padding is within the box of the element that defines the padding. Consequently, while both of these rulesets work on modern browsers, the ruleset in Listing 2-5 is more likely to encounter inconsistencies on older browsers. As we discuss in the next section, "Embrace Progressive Enhancement," you don't want to give any visitors a bad experience, even if they are using archaic software.

We also find that it's more natural (Mike says, "It just feels right") to define the box for the entire article stack and then set "left: 0" to put the image on the left margin. The intent of the code is clearer, and the code is more maintainable than the negative offset approach.

This example illustrates our belief that markup should

- Express its intent clearly (that is, embrace Meaningful Markup), which helps the people we work with know what we're doing.

- Work for as many browsers as possible, which saves the trouble of writing and maintaining additional cross-browser code.

- Be easy to create and maintain, which empowers both ourselves and our team members later in the code's life cycle.

- Be modular, which enables reuse.

We should explain the reuse goal a bit more. If you write code that can be independent of context, it can be reused, because it's not bound to any given setting. Consider the example of a Buy button. It's an interface element with a particular purpose (enabling a purchase), but it might appear in a number of different contexts (such as a product details page, a product listing page, and a special offers page). Making that Buy button modular lets us plunk it down anywhere we want a Buy button without having to tinker with it in each place. Also, because we're not doing any funky tricks with boundaries, any given module is more likely to play nice in different situations. We have found that reaching for reuse lets us get a lot done in a hurry, once we take the time to set up the code for reuse in the first place.

It's not always easy to identify places where your code has wandered away from these goals. The trick is to watch for anything that makes neighboring boxes overlap, including negative offsets to the left or positive offsets to the right.

Embrace Progressive Enhancement

Progressive enhancement is the practice of having a base design of your site that's acceptable on all browsers and then adding enhancements for increasingly modern browsers (that is, progressively). Starting with CSS/HTML fundamentals lets us have a site that works on all browsers and gives us the opportunity to enhance it greatly with HTML5 features for browsers that support those features. Listing 2-6 shows an HTML element that forms the basis for a simple example.

Listing 2-6. An HTML Element for a Simple Example of Progressive Enhancement

```
<div class="someClass"></div>
```

Listing 2-7 shows the CSS (which illustrates the progressive enhancement) to style the div element shown in Listing 2-6.

Listing 2-7. The CSS to Style Listing 2-6 via Progressive Enhancement

```
.someClass
{
```

```
  width: 100px;
  height: 100px;
  background-color: #2067f5;
  background-image: -webkit-gradient(linear, left top, left bottom, from(#2067f5), to(#154096));
  background-image: -webkit-linear-gradient(top, #2067f5, #154096);
  background-image: -moz-linear-gradient(top, #2067f5, #154096);
  background-image: -ms-linear-gradient(top, #2067f5, #154096);
  background-image: -o-linear-gradient(top, #2067f5, #154096);
  background-image: linear-gradient(to bottom, #2067f5, #154096);
}
```

Here we have a div that will make a 100 × 100 pixel box. The background of that div now has some progressive enhancements in the CSS. Every browser can understand the first background declaration: background-color: #2067f5. Now if your site's visitors happen to view this code on a browser that understands one of the next six declarations, they would see not only a blue box but one with a nice gradient to it. In essence, everyone gets a blue box, but some visitors get a nicer blue box.

A number of tools exist to help with creating the various browser-specific settings. One that we use is http://css3please.com

Figure 2-3 shows the result of the someClass style in the Chrome browser.

Figure 2-3. The someClass Style example in chrome

As you can see, it makes a gradient from a medium shade of blue down to a darker shade of blue.

Using Feature Detection to Drive Progressive Enhancement

With HTML5, never has progressive enhancement been more pronounced. Browsers that support HTML5 provide a great deal of functionality that we can use for very little overhead because they're native to the browser. With HTML5, rather than send JavaScript Files to the browser, we simply specify new markup options and CSS3 and have the browser do the fancy work for us. However, for the time being, a lot of the great functionality of HTML5 will instead have to be done with scripts on older browsers so that we can get the same functionality on all browsers, whether they support HTML5 or not.

Enter feature detection. By using feature detection, we can switch to the more native and thus better performing features that get handled in the browsers. This is done with a mix of Boolean switches in JavaScript, to detect the features the browser supports, and CSS, to provide an alternative implementation when a feature is not supported. A browser will ignore (rather than throw an error for) a CSS selector or property it doesn't understand. Thus, we can put in CSS3 progressive enhancements, and IE8 (for example) will ignore them (see Listing 2-7).

Before we talk more about feature detection, let's consider a common alternative. Many sites try to detect which browser each visitor uses and present a page optimized for that browser. Let's say, for example, that we detect a visitor using IE8 and offer some non-HTML5 alternative functionality. While workable in theory, this approach turns out to be a huge burden in practice. As browsers and versions proliferate, maintaining a version of a site quickly becomes very expensive. Adding yet more overhead, browsers like Chrome and Firefox have been versioning quickly, and, in the case of Chrome, auto-updating. So tying code to a specific version of a browser becomes even more unmanageable. Worse still, sites that try this strategy soon find that the developers do nothing but maintain all those browser-specific versions and never embrace new technologies that can create a better visitor experience and ultimately a more profitable web site. And none of the preceding addresses the issue of spoofing the User Agent, which further complicates the picture.

Consequently, we strongly recommend using feature detection rather than browser-specific versions of your web site. That way, you can detect whether the features you need are available and, if so, use them or, if not, present an attractive alternative to that visitor. Since few sites use every available feature, you can focus on just the few features you need, which makes for much more maintainable code and ensures that each visitor sees an attractive web site.

At the time of writing, we believed the best way to implement feature detection was to use the Modernizr open-source library. You can find the Modernizr project at `http://www.modernizr.com/` and download it from `http://www.modernizr.com/download/`

Modernizr works by testing whether a feature is available using JavaScript; it then adds a class to the body tag either noting it's available or not available (that is, the class `canvas` or `no-canvas` is added). You can also check its availability with JavaScript (that is, `if(Modernizr.canvas){ do something }`). However, each one of the tests it runs has a performance cost; while it's very slight, each test still takes time. So another great thing about Modernizr is that you can choose just those features you want to detect when you download the Modernizr script files. For example, if you know your web site doesn't use the `canvas` element, you can uncheck the canvas options.

For more information on using Modernizr, consult the Modernizr documentation at `http://modernizr.com/docs`

Embrace Separation of Concerns

As we mentioned in Chapter 1, one kind of performance to consider is developer performance. Provided they won't make the experience worse for site visitors, things you can do to improve the performance of the web developers often more than pay for the time needed to adopt a new methodology. Embracing separation of concerns is one of those things. Those familiar with MVC will have heard "separation of concerns" quite often, but the expression's roots go back to 1974.[1] If you haven't heard about the idea before, it's separating functions into logical areas so they're less fragile and easier to understand. Indeed, we assert not only that separation of concerns in web development leads to code that is less fragile and easier to understand but that it also increases browser performance because separating out style to CSS is faster than using HTML or JavaScript to control the appearance. In the front end, HTML, CSS, and JavaScript constitute the critical trio.

In times past it was common to use an overlapping combination of HTML, CSS, and JavaScript as a solution to any problem—a technique lovingly (or not so lovingly) called DHTML. Figure 2-4 shows this overly interwoven relationship.

---

1   Edsger W. Dijkstra, "On the role of scientific thought," in Edsger W. Dijkstra, *Selected Writings on Computing: A Personal Perspective* (New York, NY: Springer-Verlag, 1982), pp. 60–66. ISBN 0-387-90652-5.

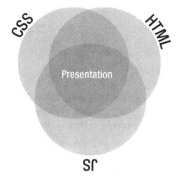

Figure 2-4. Overly interwoven web development concerns

Before web developers began to embrace separation of concerns, we'd use HTML tables as design elements, use JavaScript to generate large portions of the HTML, and otherwise do whatever seemed useful at the time. This approach was so pragmatic in character that it was only maintainable if the page had been written within the previous month or so; otherwise, we wouldn't be able to remember how it worked and would have to figure out the code all over again.

A more logical and maintainable approach is to let each part of the trio do what it does best. And while the three must overlap each other, it's possible (and definitely desirable) to have them overlap in a way that makes reading and maintaining code much easier and faster. Figure 2-5 shows this better relationship of the three concerns.

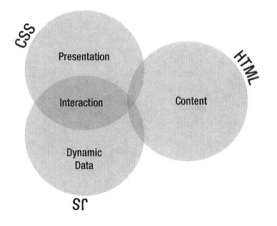

Figure 2-5. A better separation of concerns

HTML

HTML is the owner and the source of the content. You can then use CSS and JavaScript to interact with that content. You'll notice it does overlap CSS slightly; you have to have enough contact between the distinct elements in the HTML and the rules in the CSS to enact your design goals.

CSS

CSS is the master of presentation. For presentation purposes, CSS offers the best performance, especially if you're mindful of using the correct selectors (which we'll get to in Chapter 3). In addition to the existing benefits of CSS, CSS3 lets you reduce your dependency on images to assist in presentation of rounded corners, drop shadows, complex gradients, and other effects. You can also leverage SVG in your CSS to create some stunning effects. CSS3 also lets us create a great deal of interaction without reaching for JavaScript or other technologies that would normally handle menu fly-outs or other animation effects in your website. And while you still need to use JavaScript with browsers that don't support CSS3 for the animation, you can use feature detection to only use that JavaScript when necessary. As Figure 2-4 shows, CSS can lessen the dependency on JavaScript to define interaction.

JavaScript

JavaScript is the king of dynamic data. For one thing, it's the crucial part of AJAX. It overlaps HTML, because it can feed HTML into the browser (usually generated from a database interaction). Formerly also the king of interaction, JavaScript now has a new partner in the fight for user input, namely CSS (as noted in the preceding paragraph). In addition to being able to offload a lot of mouse interaction functionality, including hovers and clicks, CSS can also handle animation functionality, which used to be the exclusive purview of JavaScript.

Let's consider an example of interaction: making the text appear when visitors hover over the title or the icon. Figure 2-6 shows the initial state (before the user moves the mouse over the title or the icon).

 Chrome's Evil Twin Brother

Figure 2-6. *Interaction example initial state*

When visitors hover over the title or icon, the description appears when the mouse slides down, as shown in Figure 2-7.

 Chrome's Evil Twin Brother

The logo is darker because they couldn't make it look right with a goatee.

Figure 2-7. *Interaction example during the interaction*

We created this effect by using the pseudo hover class on the "browserArticle" class. Normally we would use JavaScript, such as jQuery's $(".browserArticle").slideDown() and $(".browserArticle"). slideUp(), to get the "slide out" effect. But we can use native modern browser functionality and call a transition defined in the "browserArticle" class (transition: all 0.5s ease-in-out;) that says if there are any changes (the all part), attempt to express them as a transition (animation) to happen over .5 seconds with an easing of ease-in-out. So when we have a hover set up to make the height 45 pixels, it displays a nice transition. And to keep in line with progressive enhancement, the description still appears on older browsers (such as IE 7 and 8), just without the animation effect. Listing 2-8 shows the modified CSS that makes the animation work.

Listing 2-8. *CSS for slide-out animation*

```css
.browserArticle
{
  position: relative;
  width: 200px;
  height: 45px;
  padding-left: 48px;
  overflow:hidden;
      -webkit-transition: all 0.5s ease-in-out;

        -moz-transition: all 0.5s ease-in-out;

         -ms-transition: all 0.5s ease-in-out;

          -o-transition: all 0.5s ease-in-out;

            transition: all 0.5s ease-in-out;
}

.browserArticle:hover
{
  height: 110px;
}

.subTitle
{
  font-size: 18px;
  margin-top:0;
}

.evilChromeLogo
{
  background: url(images/evilChromeLogo.png) no-repeat 0 0;
  height: 36px;
  width: 38px;
  position: absolute;
  left: 0;
  top: 3px;
}

.accentColor1
{
  color: #1C70AD;
}

.description:hover
{
  height: 50px;
}
```

Whenever possible, we prefer to offload interaction functionality to CSS because browsers can use their native code to handle it, which enables better performance. Also, getting the same functionality from CSS often requires less code than the JavaScript equivalent.

Summary

In this chapter, we've covered some helpful information for improving performance—for the people who visit our sites, for ourselves, and for our teammates. In particular, we looked at

- How a browser loads a web page.

- How to use CSS to keep areas of a page from trampling each other and to reduce cross-browser nastiness.

- How to use progressive enhancement to provide every visitor with a good experience.

- How to use the concept of separation of concerns to make our code easier to develop and maintain.

We're certain that as you use these techniques, you'll find your own ways to further refine them and match them to your working model, just as we have done. We hope that once you've done so, they'll provide you with the same powerful benefits that they've given us.

In the next chapter, we'll cover more specific ways to improve page load times (that is, performance from the visitor's point of view).

CHAPTER 3

■ ■ ■

Performance Guidelines

Our experience and research have let us create a set of performance guidelines that we keep in mind when working on web sites. As it happens, we find that our guidelines mostly match those of Yahoo and Google and other companies that do best-in-breed web development.

With one exception, we believe these rules can make any web site better. They may help high-content, high-traffic sites more than sites with less content and traffic, but even personal web sites benefit from good performance. The exception in these guidelines is the use of a Content Delivery Network (CDN). A CDN makes sense if you have enough content and traffic to make it economically viable and doesn't make sense otherwise.

■ **Note**   None of the rules presented in this chapter are specific to HTML5 or CSS3 or any other particular technology. However, in a book about performance, we would be remiss in not presenting this information.

Why Page Load Time Matters

In addition to wanting to provide the best possible experience for the people who visit their sites and desiring simply to do the best work they can, web developers have another very good reason to concern themselves with page load times. In April 2010, Google started including how quickly a page loads as a factor in its search rankings.[1] Pages that don't rank high attract fewer customers to those web sites, and sales suffer accordingly. WebSiteOptimization.com pulled together the results of a number of studies and came to the following conclusion:

> *Google found that moving from a 10-result page loading in 0.4 seconds to a 30-result page loading in 0.9 seconds decreased traffic and ad revenues by 20% (Linden 2006). When the home page of Google Maps was reduced from 100KB to 70–80KB, traffic went up 10% in the first week, and an additional 25% in the following three weeks (Farber 2006). Tests at Amazon revealed similar results: every 100 ms increase in load time of Amazon.com decreased sales by 1% (Kohavi and Longbotham 2007).*
>
> WebSiteOptimization.com[2]

---

1   Source: http://googlewebmastercentral.blogspot.com/2010/04/using-site-speed-in-web-search-ranking.html.
2   Source: http://www.websiteoptimization.com/speed/tweak/psychology-web-performance/.

In our minds, a 1% drop in sales for every 100 milliseconds is a huge impact. Clearly, page load time must be a key concern for web developers.

The Guidelines

Each of the following sections describes a particular guideline (in order of impact on page load time):

- Make Fewer HTTP Requests
- Use a Content Delivery Network (CDN)
- Avoid Empty `src` or `href` Attributes
- Add Expires Headers
- Compress Components with GZIP
- Put CSS at the Top
- Put JavaScript at the Bottom
- Avoid CSS Expressions
- Remove Unused CSS
- Minify JavaScript and CSS
- Minimize Redrawing

Make Fewer HTTP Requests

Making fewer HTTP Requests is the shining star in the constellation of performance guidelines. It's a complex topic, so we've split it into the following individual bits of performance guidance:

- Understand Parallel Connections
- Combine Resource Files
- Use Image Sprites

Understand Parallel Connections

We've observed that the idea of making fewer HTTP requests often gets overlooked even though it's the single biggest performance gain from which most sites would benefit. Developers focus on the complexity of the back end and fail to realize that much of the loading bottleneck is in the browser. Because the developers of web sites can't control what browsers do but *can* control what their own servers and databases and code do, they naturally focus on what they can control. That's good, right up until the developers fail to account for how browsers work. Then it's a problem. Figure 3-1 illustrates this perception problem.

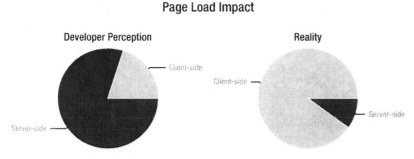

Figure 3-1. *Page load impact: Developer perception vs. reality*

The browser-side restriction that developers often fail to consider is how many resources a browser can load at a time. The HTTP 1.1 specification says, "A single-user client SHOULD NOT maintain more than 2 connections with any server or proxy." In recent years, most browsers have exceeded this suggestion. Many browsers currently support four parallel connections, while a few support six. IE8 varies its connections by the client's bandwidth, from two connections for a dial-up connection to six connections for a broadband connection.

Nothing brings a point home like an illustration, so let's consider an example. Figure 3-2 shows the loading of apple.com (through http://www.webpagetest.org/).

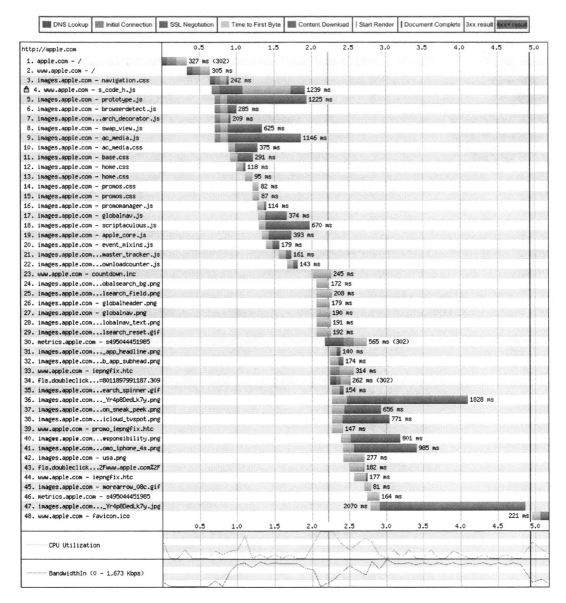

Figure 3-2. Loading the resources for Apple.com

Notice that the HTML loaded in 327 milliseconds. In other words, the text content of a page comes down very quickly. Then notice that the other files (mostly images from images.apple.com) arrived in groups. That grouping pattern is the direct result of the number of parallel connections the browser can open. It's a bit like a railroad marshaling yard. At a busy yard, there are a lot of trains but only a few outbound tracks. Consequently, the dispatchers have to send the trains in groups rather than all at once. Large web sites have the same problem.

You can put resources into multiple hosts (such as www.apple.com and images.apple.com, in the example shown in Figure 3-2.) However, that practice improves performance only up to a point, as the cost of additional DNS lookups leads to rapidly diminishing returns.

Combine Resource Files

The result of the parallel connection problem is that bigger files are better files. We know that sounds like wild heresy to some developers, but it's true. For a long time, we worked to make resources smaller. We remember the days of 1200-baud modems and dial-up connections, when watching the images come in was a sort of progress bar for the page. However, times have changed, and the vast majority of people have fast Internet connections. With our modern infrastructure, any given file isn't likely to strangle the browser. Consequently, fewer big files are better than more small files. Going back to our marshaling yard example, if we can put more cars on each train, we can get more goods down the same tracks. (As an aside, railroads have long sought to get more cars per train. Jay is a bit of a railroad historian, among his other hobbies.) The same holds true for files and parallel connections.

Also, each HTTP request has at least some overhead, both in time and in bandwidth. Consequently, if you can combine your resources such that you need fewer HTTP requests to render a page, you gain that much more rendering speed for the site's visitor.

The sum of all these considerations is that you should combine your content into fewer files. If possible, combine multiple CSS style sheets into a single file and multiple JS files into a single file. When different pages use different CSS and JS files, combining them such that each page gets a single CSS file and a single JS file can be an issue. However, you can solve that issue by using a build script that runs each time you modify your CSS and JS files. Such a build script would determine the files used by each page, create the required unique files, and add the needed link elements to each page. Dynamic content can still benefit from such a build system if the dynamic pages share a common set of CSS and JS files.

Another strategy is to combine the CSS and JS files on the fly when you deliver the page. Given that this step will require processing, it won't be as fast as using prebuilt files. If your web site is complex enough, though, it may still be a better choice than using many separate files.

Finally, another strategy is to deliver a CSS file that's common to all pages and then, as your visitors hit each page, deliver another CSS file specific to that page. Given that mastheads and footers and other large areas often remain the same from page to page, this strategy can make for easier maintenance and still provide a great deal of benefit, both for the company serving up the page and for the site's visitors. The company saves the bandwidth and other overhead of delivering the contents of the common CSS file over and over, and the visitors get better performance. For very large sites, this final strategy often represents a good compromise between maintainability and performance.

Use Image Sprites

Image sprites are really just combined image files. They offer a handy way to achieve the goal of combining small files into larger files and delivering content more quickly over the browser's relatively low number of parallel connections.

Most sites use a collection of images across the site's pages. One way to reduce HTTP requests is to put all those common images into a single image (an image sprite). Then, every time you need one of those images, you refer to the sprite and specify a set of coordinates within the sprite. So put all your logos, custom bullets, navigation hints, and other common image collateral in a single image and use that image across all your pages.

An interesting technique for gaining a bit of performance is to group sprites by color range and then save each sprite file such that it uses only the colors in that range. This technique makes each sprite file smaller. It's especially effective for sites that use a restricted palette of colors. For example, if your company's logo is red and gray, the firm's marketing people may have created a bunch of images that use the company color scheme for navigation and other purposes. In that case, you might gain substantial size savings by having a file for those images and restricting the color range to red and gray.

If you have lots of common image collateral, you may need more than one image sprite, even if you don't separate by color range. Also, if different parts of your company maintain separate parts of the common image collateral (perhaps one group maintains the navigation images while another maintains the logos), you may want to have separate files.

One of the questions that came up (from our technical reviewer, Jeff Johnson) while we were writing this chapter was, when is a sprite file so large that it should be split? It's a good question, because there's definitely a point at which one big file is more of a problem than two smaller files. However, that point varies because of a number of factors, such as how many other HTTP requests a client requires to fully load your site, whether the site uses a CDN, and even which browser a visitor uses. Consequently, we can't give a hard and fast answer. We can only tell you that, if you think your page load times might benefit from splitting large sprite files into smaller sprite files or combining smaller files into larger files, establish some metrics and a way to monitor those metrics, and then try them. As with a lot of other things in web development, there's not a single best way. Often, we have to test to find the answer that works for a given situation.

As a rule of thumb and a good starting point, though, holding down HTTP requests trumps other concerns. Consequently, if you can, combine all those commonly used images into just a few images. Ideally, get them into a single image. Then use offsets to display the right part of the image. Figure 3-3 shows a sprite from google.com.

Figure 3-3. *Sprite from Google.com*

To use this sprite, we created a div that uses a class and then defined the matching CSS class, which specifies the details of the image we want. Listing 3-1 shows the div element.

Listing 3-1. *A div for an Image from a Sprite*

```
<div class="arrowPrev"></div>
```

Listing 3-2 shows the CSS class.

Listing 3-2. *CSS for a Sprite*

```
.arrowPrev
{
  width: 22px;
  height: 25px;
  background-image: url(googlesprite.png);
  background-position: -6px -13px;
  background-repeat: no-repeat;
}
```

The CSS specifies the sprite, the width and height of the viewport that contains the image within the sprite, and the starting point (the actual offset) of the image. It also specifies that the image should not repeat.

The result is the previous arrow, as shown in Figure 3-4.

Figure 3-4. *Result of using a sprite*

Another great benefit of sprites is that loading just one image from a sprite puts the entire sprite into the browser's cache. Because every subsequent use of the sprite doesn't need to fetch an image, many HTTP connections can be saved. In the example from Google, this one sprite, with its 60 smaller images, can save as many as 60 HTTP connections. That's an enormous performance gain.

You can find a number of different web sites that can you help you work with sprite files. In the past, we have used http://www.spritecow.com and http://www.spritebox.net

Use a Content Delivery Network (CDN)

A content delivery network has many servers strategically placed to create a web that covers the world. So someone in Austin or in Paris who visits your site has a short hop to get to its assets. The catch is these files don't change easily, so you should use them only for assets that don't change much—assets such as images, fonts, JavaScript libraries, Media, and so on. Putting all that static content close to the user can really speed up performance.Conversely, content that has to be dynamic should usually be served from a single location. Even for large companies, the effort required to sync database transactions across geographically separated servers is rarely worth the effort. The timing issues alone often give network engineers fits. So most web businesses should keep purchases, logins, and other data-dependent transactions at a single location.

One of the tricks in working with a CDN is the practice of prepending a timestamp to files. In this way you have a unique file and don't have to worry about an obsolete file being cached on the CDN servers dished out to your visitors. When you make file updates with a new timestamp, you will have to update your referring code, too. It can seem like a hassle if you're working on small to midsized sites, so you'll have to judge if a CDN is appropriate for your project. It does add cost and wouldn't make sense if your website, say, supported a local business or was geographically isolated.

■ **Note**   If a content delivery network won't help you, then it's not really the second-best performance tip. We left it here, though, because, if you do need one, a CDN is second only to lowering the number of HTTP requests in boosting page-load performance.

Avoid Empty src or href Attributes

The pattern that we've seen is to create an img element with an empty src attribute and then dynamically assign the value of the src attribute during page load with JavaScript. The trouble with this is that elements always get evaluated before scripts get run (especially if you put your scripts after everything else, as we recommend later in this chapter). Consequently, the browser tries to evaluate that empty attribute and creates an HTTP request to do so.

A similar pattern and problem appears for href attributes, usually in anchor elements. Sometimes, developers want to use an anchor element as a trigger for a JavaScript-based interaction. The trouble is that, if the href attribute is blank, the browser sends an HTTP request to the server when the user triggers the interaction. That doesn't affect page load time, but it does create needless traffic on the servers, wasting bandwidth and potentially slowing delivery for all visitors. The simple fix for this problem is to set the value of the href attribute to a JavaScript command that does nothing. Listing 3-3 shows an example of this fix.

Listing 3-3. *Fixing an Empty href Attribute*

```
<a href="javascript:;" class="triggerName">Trigger</a>
```

However, just using an empty JavaScript command is not the best solution. A better one is to provide a description (which appears in the status bar when the user hovers over the link) and block the href from being evaluated. Listing 3-4 shows how to do it.

Listing 3-4. *Creating a Descriptive href Attribute*

```
<a href="#Something_Descriptive" id="triggerName">Trigger</a>
<script>
$("#triggerName").click(function(e){
        e.preventDefault(); //This cancels the link capability and doesn't call the href.

        // The rest of your code
})
</script>
```

Now the site's visitors get a hint before committing to doing something, and href isn't creating a wasteful HTTP request.

We should point out that our approach to this problem differs when we have a separate presentation for visitors who have turned off or otherwise have no access to JavaScript. In those cases, we use an actual link.

We should also point out that empty src and href attributes can cause errors, too. If you track state in the request headers (whether through cookies or some other mechanism) and send an empty attribute, you can lose track of the state. At that point, you have a good chance of frustrating visitors, who will quickly take their business elsewhere or be hopping mad if they have no choice but to use your site.

Of course, you also want to write to your log files every time you catch an empty attribute. If you get a lot of them, you definitely want to find out why it happens and fix it.

Add Expires Headers

You should add an `Expires` header to all your static components (images, stylesheets, scripts, flash, PDF, and so on). Adding an `Expires` header with a date far in the future lets your static content be cached by browsers. Listing 3-5 shows a typical Expires header.

Listing 3-5. A Typical Expires Header

```
Expires: Wed, 1 Jan 2020 00:00:00 GMT
```

Consequently, when those visitors return, their browsers won't have to fetch the static content for subsequent visits and they'll have a much faster loading time. Of course, adding `Expires` headers does nothing for first-time visitors or people who clear their cache between visits. On the other hand, it doesn't do them any harm and it does benefit at least some visitors. In fact, since people tend to visit the same sites over and over, it may improve the experience for most visitors.

The downside to setting `Expires` headers far in the future is that you have to rename the files on which you set the `Expires` headers. Returning visitors will have cached your assets, and you want them to have your updated assets. Consequently, you'll need a versioning scheme of some sort. One interesting way to do this is to incorporate a datestamp into your file names. For example, your base style sheet might be named `base20120303.css`. The interesting thing about adding datestamps to files is that you can instantly see the history of changes in your version control system. If you feel that adding datestamps makes the file names too long, you can use a simple version number that indicates the number of times the file has been revised. For example, if you have revised your base style sheet 13 times, it might be named `base13.css`.

For a good example of how to set the `Expires` header, look at the `htaccess` file from `http://www.html5boilerplate.com` (which we use in Chapter 6, too).

Compress Components with GZIP

The HTTP/1.1 specification introduced the `Accept-Encoding` header, which can indicate that the content in the HTTP request is compressed. Such a header appears in Listing 3-6.

Listing 3-6. An Accept-Encoding Header

```
Accept-Encoding: gzip, deflate
```

As you can see, that header specifies two kinds of compression. GZIP is more common, because it is the most effective compression scheme available. According to Yahoo's "Best Practices for Speeding Up Your Web Site" page, GZIP reduces the size of a response by about 70%.[3] A study by an engineer at Intel[4] revealed savings of as much as 90% for some file types (text scored highest), but Yahoo's 70% is probably a better average for all file types.

Compression reduces the time required to fetch a compressed resource, which improves the experience for visitors. It also reduces bandwidth, which saves money for the company serving the page (and may save visitors money if they haven't paid for unlimited bandwidth from their ISP or mobile carrier).

---

3   Source: `http://developer.yahoo.com/performance/rules.html#gzip`.
4   Source: `http://software.intel.com/en-us/articles/http-compression-for-web-applications/`.

The one problem with compression is that there are still a few browsers (and, more rarely, proxies) that mishandle it. For that reason, you need to add a Vary field to the header, so that those browsers and proxies can negotiate for uncompressed content. Adding the Vary field to the header is done with an instruction in the header, as shown in Listing 3-7.

Listing 3-7. Adding a Vary Field to a Header

```
Header set Vary *
```

■ **Note**   Depending on the web server, how you set headers and the fields in them varies tremendously. What we've shown is the output that needs to appear in the HTTP header rather than any particular set of code for setting it.

You should compress any content that's textual by nature. That means you should compress your HTML, CSS, scripts, XML, JSON, and anything else that's really just text. Images and PDF files should not be compressed, as compression should be part of their storage format. If someone did make an uncompressed image or PDF file (it's possible, at least for PDF), the remedy is to fix the file, not to compress that kind of content.

The reason you don't want to compress images and PDF files is that they can actually get bigger when you compress them. The compression engine can't actually make the resource smaller, but because it still has to add its own control codes, the file gets larger. Consequently, you shouldn't compress *everything*.

Put CSS at the Top

If your page contains style information, put that information at the top (in the head element). To avoid redrawing, many web browsers won't start rendering a page until the browser has all the style information. Consequently, if your style information is at the bottom of the page, these browsers load everything before starting to render anything. Your poor site visitors sit there looking at a white screen for a long time, and, as a consequence, many will find somewhere else to visit.

Large sites and slow connections exacerbate the problem. The more content a page has, the more imperative it becomes that style information come before content. There are still some people using dial-up, and we ought to do what we can to make their web experience as pleasant as possible. Also, many people (including the authors of this book) do a fair bit of web surfing on mobile devices, and many places still have relatively slow performance for mobile connections. We certainly don't want to lose the business of mobile visitors, so we need to let them see at least some content while the rest of the content loads. Consequently, we want to put CSS at the top of the page.

Interestingly, the fact that many browsers load all the style information before rendering anything also argues for combining a page's external CSS into a single file. Fetching multiple files over the network is naturally slower than fetching a single file. Since we want the user to see at least something as quickly as possible, we ideally want just one fetching of the style content.

Put JavaScript at the Bottom

Scripts block parallel downloads. In other words, when the browser is downloading a script, it's not downloading anything else. If your scripts are at the top of the page, you've blocked the ability to show the user part of the page while the rest of the page loads.

You can potentially use the DEFER attribute in a script element to let the browser know that it can download other content while it downloads this script. Doing so has two problems, though. The first is that not all browsers honor the DEFER attribute. The second is that the contract for using the DEFER attribute is that any script with that attribute does not use document.write. Consequently, you can't use the DEFER attribute with scripts that do use document.write. (Later in this chapter, when we talk about why rearranging the DOM isn't a good idea, we'll see why avoiding document.write is a good idea.)

By putting all your scripts at the end (just before the body element's closing tag), you've in essence deferred script loading until the end and so handily avoided the problem of blocked parallel downloads altogether. Also, you won't have to rely on a Ready event to ensure that elements are available, because all of your elements will be ready before any of your scripts run.

Avoid CSS Expressions

Internet Explorer supported CSS expressions for versions 5, 6, and 7. Other browsers never supported them.

A CSS expression lets a style be dynamically set when the page is loaded. Listing 3-8 shows a CSS expression (from Microsoft's Dynamic Properties web page).

Listing 3-8. *A CSS Expression*

```
object.style.left=(document.body.clientWidth/2) - (object.offsetWidth/2);
```

That expression tries to center an element. You can achieve the same effect with the CSS shown in Listing 3-9.

Listing 3-9. *A Replacement for a CSS Expression*

```
.center {
  margin-left: auto;
  margin-right: auto;
  width: 200px;
}
```

When minified (which we'll get to later in this chapter), the regular CSS is shorter than the CSS expression, so there's not much point to this particular CSS expression.

The downside to CSS expressions is that they generally get evaluated far more often than their authors intend. Ideally, they would be evaluated only when the page is rendered (including when the page is refreshed). However, they are often reevaluated when the user scrolls up and down the page or just moves the mouse around. Many users (we've heard numbers in the 80% range)[5] "look with their mouse", which means that wherever on the page their eyes go, their mouse follows. Imagine how much mouse movement that is if someone is reading an article. Because CSS expressions are reevaluated when the mouse moves, the expression may be evaluated thousands of times (we've seen references to tens of thousands) while the page is in the browser. That's really going to strangle performance for the poor site visitor.

Remove Unused CSS

In most browsers (so far as we know, all of them, in fact), the browser's styling engine evaluates the CSS rules to find a match for each element. In doing so, it has to work through all the CSS rules. Consequently, if a style sheet has any unused rules, it's causing more work for the styling engine for no gain. Removing

---

5   M. C. Chen, J. R. Anderson, and M. H. Sohn, "What can a mouse cursor tell us more? Correlation of eye/ mouse movements on web browsing," *Proceedings of Computer Human Interaction (CHI)* (2001): 280–81.

unused rules also makes the CSS file smaller, which allows the browser to more quickly fetch it and saves bandwidth.

It can be tempting to make a single stylesheet for an entire site and use it even when some pages don't use all the rules in the stylesheet. However, doing so is usually a mistake because those pages won't load as quickly as they will if the unneeded rules aren't present.

Of the existing solutions for this problem, our favorite is to make a stylesheet that contains rulesets common to all pages and then have other stylesheets for each area (or even page) on the site. For example, all pages might include a style sheet called `all.css` or `base.css`, while the pages related to buying a product might include an additional stylesheet called `product.css` or `buy.css`.

Another solution is to make a separate stylesheet for each unique combination of CSS rules used by your site's pages. Depending on your development environment, you may be able to create these files with a build or other server-side script. Given that most large web sites create pages dynamically, the system that creates the pages needs logic to determine which style sheet to use.

Still another solution is to build style sheets dynamically as pages are requested. The downside to that is the additional processing required on the server side and the need to generate the same file names such that the stylesheets can be cached by browsers.

Finally, a developer can make a style sheet for each unique combination of CSS rules by hand and remember when to use each one. However, anything that relies on human memory is so unreliable that we'd rather take the performance hit of using the same stylesheet for every page.

Minify JavaScript and CSS

"Minifying" is removing all nonfunctional characters from source code. With JavaScript and CSS, you should remove all whitespace (including newline characters) whose removal won't break the code, all block delimiters that won't break the code, and all comments. In other words, ruthlessly strip any character that doesn't absolutely have to be present to make the code work. Minifying code makes for faster loading and lower bandwidth usage.

We prefer to use a minifying tool to do our minifying for us. Humans are prone to mistakes, either removing something that shouldn't be removed or leaving in things that can be removed. Also, by using a tool, we can be as verbose as we like, including comments for our fellow developers and making the source files easy to read, and still trust that we'll get good performance because of our minifying tool.

One final benefit of a minifying tool (it's an optional setting in most minifiers) is being able to replace all the variable names with very short names and otherwise replace long things with short things, which i provides another substantial saving in file size. The downside is that the content is very difficult to understand—and much more error prone if a change is made to it in that state—after that kind of replacement. That's OK, though, provided you are maintaining source files as verbose files and then minified only for each release or only when delivered to your site's visitors.

We use Yahoo's YUI Compressor to minify our CSS and JavaScript. You can get it at http://developer.yahoo.com/yui/compressor/.

To provide a fair-sized example, we've repeated Listing 2-2 in Listing 3-10.

Listing 3-10. An Example of "Chatty" CSS

```
.browserArticle
{
  /* We set the position: relative so the absolutely positioned
     element within uses this box to position itself */
  position: relative;
  width: 200px;
  padding-left: 48px;
```

```
    /* We set a minimum height in case there's not enough content
       to make the box big enough to house the image. We use the
       height of the image plus 3 for the top offset. */
    min-height: 39px;
}

.subTitle
{
    font-size: 18px;
}

.evilChromeLogo
{
    background: url(images/evilChromeLogo.png) no-repeat 0 0;
    height: 36px;
    width: 38px;
    position: absolute;
    left: 0;
    top: 3px;
    z-index: 1;
}

.accentColor1
{
    color: #1C70AD;
}
```

Listing 3-11 shows the same CSS snippet after it's been minified.

Listing 3-11. An Example of Minified CSS

```
.browserArticle{position:relative;width:200px;padding-left:48px;min-height:39px}.subTitle{font-
size:18px}.evilChromeLogo{background:url(images/evilChromeLogo.png) no-repeat 0 0;height:36px;wi
dth:38px;position:absolute;left:0;top:3px;z-index:1}.accentColor1{color:#1C70AD}
```

Listing 3-10 has 678 bytes. Listing 3-11 has 341 bytes. That's a saving of 337 bytes, or just about half. This example may be an extreme case, due to the presence of the large comments in the original. However, minifying is still a good idea, even when the savings are not as dramatic.

We'd like to thank the folks at http://freeformatter.com for creating an online implementation of the YUI compressor. It's handy for a quick check of how something compresses, and we used it to make the sample shown in Listing 3-11.

Minimize Redrawing

We find page redrawing to be highly aggravating, and we think most other people do, too. Ever try to click a link, only to have the browser choose that moment to redraw the page and discover that you've clicked nothing or, worse, the wrong link? That's annoying, and it's a good thing for web developers to avoid. Here's a set of guidelines for minimizing the number of times a browser has to redraw your pages in order to properly render them:

- Specify Dimensions for Images

- Use Tables Only for Tabular Content
- Specify a Character Set
- Don't Rearrange the DOM

Specify Dimensions for Images

You should specify dimensions for img elements. When a browser is creating its area tree, it sets aside an area for each element. If you don't specify the dimensions of an img element, the browser is likely to guess wrong at first and then correct its mistake after it has downloaded the image. When it corrects its initial guess, it has to redraw the page to properly place the element. You can avoid that redraw by providing dimensions.

Use Tables Only for Tabular Content

Among the many other reasons to use tables only for content that is tabular in nature (rather than as a layout device) is that tables often force a redraw as the browser renders them. As browsers receive each row, they often try to progressively layout tables. When a row with content that requires different column widths or row heights appears, the previous rows have to be redrawn. That's not usually too much trouble if the site developers have used table elements only for tabular content. However, when developers use tables (and especially tables within tables, as in many poorly coded sites), whole sections of the page can "jump" from one place to another as the page loads. That can be very jarring for visitors to the site.

Specify a Character Set

Most browsers (but not IE6, 7, and 8) buffer a portion of the page until they find the character-set definition. They do so because the character set is a big factor in rendering the page. A different character set can mean an entirely different appearance from what the browser would render with its default character set. Consequently, you can make most browsers start to show content to your site's visitors more quickly—much more quickly than if you don't—by specifying the character set as the first child of the head element within the HTML.

The only thing worse than not specifying a character set is specifying one so late in the HTML that the browser finds the character set definition after it has started rendering with its default character set. In those cases, unless the developer is lucky enough to have specified the same character set as the browser's default set, the browser throws away its current rendering and begins to redraw the page.

Don't Rearrange the DOM

Rearranging the DOM often forces the browser to redraw the page. Usually, the browser works out the DOM pretty quickly, as loading the HTML file is the first thing a browser does (though it may load other resources specified within the HTML file at the same time). Consequently, any script that adds elements to or removes elements from the DOM is likely to cause the browser to redraw at least part of the page. Also, moving an element within the DOM really amounts to removing it from one location and adding it another, which is even worse than just adding or removing elements.

If you must rearrange the DOM for some reason, avoid inserting one node at a time when you have a group of nodes to insert. For example, if you wish to insert a list, don't add the list (ul or ol) element and then add each of its children (li). Each insertion forces a redraw, so adding a list with two items forces three redraw operations. Instead, create a string that contains the HTML for the list you want to insert, and then insert that string all at once. That way, you force just one redraw operation.

A similar principle applies to dynamically setting style on an element. Don't set each style element in your JavaScript. Instead, create a class with all the necessary style information, and then set the class on the element. Again, you get one redraw operation rather than multiple redraw operations.

You really should avoid modifying the DOM at all. However, if you must (we've been forced into it, too, so we know it happens), do it in such a way that you're not repeatedly forcing redraw operations.

Further Reading

Among the many sources of information about HTML and CSS performance optimization, we find the following to be the most useful:

- http://developer.yahoo.com/performance/rules.html
- http://code.google.com/speed/page-speed/docs/rendering.html

Summary

This chapter presented a number of things you can do to optimize page load times for visitors to your web sites. The following items are simple changes that you can make quickly (if you haven't already):

- Put CSS in the head element.
- Put JavaScript below the body element.
- Specify dimensions for images.
- Specify a character set.

Of course, if you have a lot of pages, even simple changes can be a lot of work, just because of the repetition.

If you're in a position to make larger, more systemic changes, try the following improvements (if you haven't already made them):

- Make fewer HTTP requests by:
  - Combining your resource files.
  - Using image sprites.
- Avoid empty src or href attributes.
- Compress components with GZIP.
- Avoid CSS expressions.
- Use efficient CSS selectors.
- Make JavaScript and CSS external.
- Minify JavaScript and CSS.
- Minimize redrawing.

Finally, we strongly recommend a periodic review of web pages while thinking about how a browser loads a page. No one can keep that in mind all the time, because, as developers, we're always bumping into some weird little problem that requires our undivided attention. Consequently, stopping to do a page-load review every once in a while is a good idea. If you're part of a team, pass around the guidelines and get the whole team involved.

CHAPTER 4

■ ■ ■

Responsive Web Design

In keeping with our trend of pointing out techniques that enhance web developer performance, possibly one of the biggest time-savers for developers is the idea of "One Codebase". Essentially, it's the idea of being able to use the same code to deliver an experience to desktop browsers, tablets, and mobile devices.

Traditionally, if you wanted to have a mobile representation of your website, you'd create a separate site that was customized to the form factor and interaction models of a targeted device or devices. Generally speaking, these separate sites would be quite different in code structure and, if you worked for a big company, might be created and maintained by specialized developers who work in the mobile space.

Then, in 2008, W3 created a specification for CSS3 media queries. The various browsers implemented support for media queries more or less quickly, and now we have the option to have our website adapt to the form factor of the visitor's display without server logic, redirects, or complex JavaScript. Media queries constitute one of a set of techniques that together create responsive web design.

Before we go farther, we need to give credit where credit is due. Ethan Marcotte coined the term "responsive web design" in a great article on A List Apart. You can find that article at http://www.alistapart.com/articles/responsive-web-design/.

Responsive Web Design

We can let our websites adapt to the devices they're being viewed on instead of sending visitors with different devices to different sites. One obvious incentive for creating a single site instead of creating a separate site for each device is development time. But let's also consider the quickly changing landscape of devices consuming our sites. Whether we are talking about screen dimensions for a new model of tablet, smart phones, or web capable TV or about a new form factor entirely, such as a car interface, we'd be caught in an endless game of catch up if we tried to constantly adjust the code base for each new device. To see some of the stunning variety of screen sizes, take a look at Morten Hjerde's work at http://sender11.typepad.com/sender11/2008/04/mobile-screen-s.html. From 2005 to 2008, he collected statistics on over 400 devices. Imagine how many more have been introduced since then. Thanks to this plethora of devices, we find that it's far more manageable to change a layout by screen size rather than per device (or even per type of device).

So what does responsive design look like? For a great example check out http://www.bostonglobe.com. Open the *Boston Globe*'s web site in a desktop browser, and make the browser's width smaller. You'll see the content resize to fit the new browser dimensions. As the browser gets smaller, you'll see what a tablet would see and finally what a smart phone would see.

The workhorse of this approach is CSS3's Media Queries. However, by adding techniques for resizing images and the concept of a flexible grid, you can really supercharge your One-Codebase approach. The rest of this chapter examines how to create a responsive web page.

CSS3 Media Queries

W3C says, "A media query consists of a media type and zero or more expressions that check for the conditions of particular media features.". While that's quite illuminating, let's get into a little more detail.

CSS3 can tell you the screen width of the browser window. You don't have to run any JavaScript or do server side detection. And to make it even better, the CSS responds in real time to changes in the browser width. So if your visitors resize their browsers, the CSS automatically adjusts.

In other words, you can enact different CSS rules based on browser width. Listing 4-1 shows an example.

Listing 4-1. Style Element That Includes Media Queries

```
<style>
body
{
  width: 960px;

}


/* Tablets and small desktop browsers */
@media only screen and (min-width: 768px) and (max-width: 991px)
{
  body
  {
    width: 700px;
  }
}
</style>
```

In Listing 4-1, we have a default body width of 960 pixels. However, if the browser window width is between 768 and 991 pixels, we override the default body rules with our new media query–defined width of 700 pixels.

This ability offers a very powerful hook that you can use to customize your presentation—and everyone knows that CSS is the king of presentation—to any screen size range. Not only does this technique work in styling your content, but it also enables you to use it to choose what content sections to display. For example, you might have a right column on your desktop site that has tertiary information that, while informative, may not be crucial for a visitor using a tablet or a smaller mobile device. So you can add a `display:none` property to the ruleset for your tertiary content at those sizes and not worry about it being offscreen or causing unwelcome scroll bars.

In addition, you have the option to display a different navigation scheme to mobile visitors—one that's closer to native application navigation. A common oversight when converting a desktop site to a mobile format is forgetting how the user holds the device. So having navigation at the bottom allows users to use their thumbs to navigate. While it may not always be feasible to fit your navigation scheme at the bottom, a viable alternative is to use a list at the top. Whether you choose top or bottom navigation, you need to avoid using side navigation because of the reduced horizontal real estate and in order to reduce misclicks by errant thumbs. (Your trusty authors both have big hands, by the way, so they really notice this kind of problem.)

Let's look at a slightly more complex example. The following are four design intentions to enable our faux site to fit a desktop browser, a tablet browser, and a mobile browser in both tall and wide orientation.

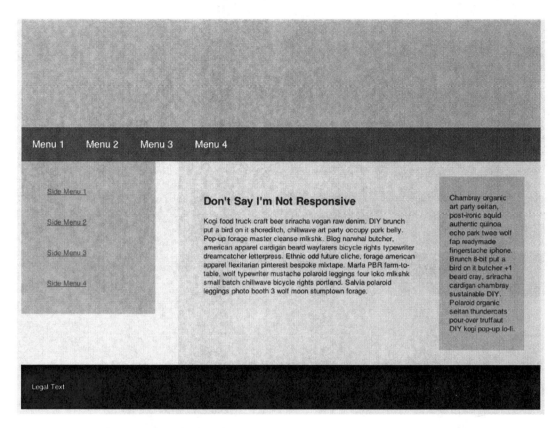

Figure 4-1. Our faux site on a desktop browser

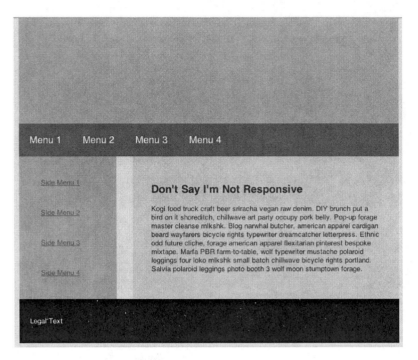

Figure 4-2. *Our faux site on a tablet*

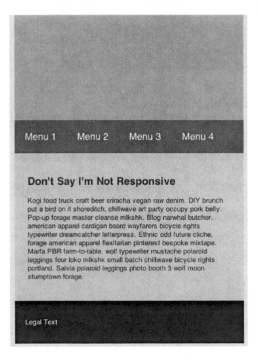

Figure 4-3. *Our faux site on a mobile phone held horizontally*

Figure 4-4. Our faux site on a mobile phone held vertically

Now let's see how media queries change the following HTML into the four design intentions on the fly.

■ **Note**   If you want to test the Mobile Tall intention, make sure to use a browser other than Firefox. It won't trigger the smallest viewport in the desktop browser.

The HTML

Listing 4-2 shows the HTML source for our faux web site.

Listing 4-2. The HTML for Our Faux Web Site

```
<!DOCTYPE html>
<html lang="en">
  <head>
  </head>
```

```
<body>
  <header class="heroWrap" ></header>
  <nav class="mainNav clearfix">
    <ul>
      <li>
        <a href="">Menu 1</a>
      </li>
      <li>
        <a href="">Menu 2</a>
      </li>
      <li>
        <a href="">Menu 3</a>
      </li>
      <li>
        <a href="">Menu 4</a>
      </li>
    </ul>
  </nav>
  <div class="bodyWrap clearfix">
    <nav class="sideNav">
      <ul>
        <li>
          <a href="">Side Menu 1</a>
        </li>
        <li>
          <a href="">Side Menu 2</a>
        </li>
        <li>
          <a href="">Side Menu 3</a>
        </li>
        <li>
          <a href="">Side Menu 4</a>
        </li>
      </ul>
    </nav>
    <div class="contentWrap">
      <section class="contentSection">
        <h1>Don't Say I'm Not Responsive</h1>
        <p>
            Kogi food truck craft beer sriracha vegan raw denim. DIY brunch put a bird on it
shoreditch, chillwave art party occupy pork belly. Pop-up forage master cleanse mlkshk. Blog
narwhal butcher, american apparel cardigan beard wayfarers bicycle rights typewriter
dreamcatcher letterpress. Ethnic odd future cliche, forage american apparel flexitarian pinterest
bespoke mixtape. Marfa PBR farm-to-table, wolf typewriter mustache polaroid leggings four loko
mlkshk small batch chillwave bicycle rights portland. Salvia polaroid leggings photo booth 3
wolf moon stumptown forage.
        </p>
      </section>
      <section class="tertSection">
        <p>
```

Chambray organic art party seitan, post-ironic squid authentic quinoa echo park twee wolf fap readymade fingerstache iphone. Brunch 8-bit put a bird on it butcher +1 beard cray, sriracha cardigan chambray sustainable DIY. Polaroid organic seitan thundercats pour-over truffaut DIY kogi pop-up lo-fi.

```
        </p>
      </section>
    </div>
  </div>
  <footer class="pageFooter">
    <p>
      Legal Text
    </p>
  </footer>
</body>
</html>
```

The CSS

Listing 4-3 shows the CSS file for our faux web site. Note the media queries towards the bottom of the file (each preceded by a comment reflecting its intended target).

Listing 4-3. The CSS File for Our Faux Web Site

```
.heroWrap {
  background: #82BEFF;
  min-height: 200px;
}
.mainNav {
  background: #4B6E93;
}
.mainNav li {
  float: left;
  padding: 20px;
}
.mainNav a {
  color: white;
  text-decoration: none;
  font-size: 18px;
}
.sideNav {
  float: left;
  background: #DDB14B;
  width: 20%;
  padding: 3%;
}
.sideNav li {
  padding: 20px;
}
.sideNav a {
```

```css
    color: #4B6E93;
  }
  .contentWrap {
    float: right;
    width: 64%;
    background: #D6D6D6;
    padding: 3%;
    min-height: 200px
  }
  .contentSection {
    width: 64%;
    padding: 3%;
    float: left;
  }
  .tertSection {
    width: 20%;
    padding: 3%;
    float: right;
    background: #82BEFF;
  }
  .pageFooter {
    background: black;
    padding: 20px;
    color: white;
  }

  /*    Default Layout: 992px. */

  body {
    width: 960px;
    margin: 0 auto;
    background: rgb(232,232,232);
    color: rgb(60,60,60);
    -webkit-text-size-adjust: 100%; /* Stops Mobile Safari from auto-adjusting font-sizes */
  }

  /* Tablet Layout*/

  @media only screen and (min-width: 768px) and (max-width: 991px) {

    body {
      width: 712px;
    }
    .tertSection {
      display: none;
    }
    .contentSection {
      float:none;
      width: auto;
    }
  }
```

```css
/* Mobile Layout */

@media only screen and (max-width: 767px) {

  body {
    width: 252px;
  }
  .tertSection {
    display: none;
  }
  .sideNav {
    display: none;
  }
  .contentWrap {
    width: auto;
    float: none;
  }
  .contentSection {
    float:none;
    width: auto;
  }
}
/* Wide Mobile Layout*/

@media only screen and (min-width: 480px) and (max-width: 767px) {

  body {
    width: 436px;
  }
}
```

All the magic happens in the @media sections. However, as you can see, it's relatively simple and brief CSS to get a pretty robust skeleton working. Of course, your actual CSS probably targets more elements, but this sample lets you see the power this technique offers.

Flexible Images

Now that you have your layout and text treatments adjusting to the device being used by your visitor, it's time to deal with the images. You could again lean on CSS to resize the images for you. This would indeed work; however, you'd be downloading the desktop-size image to the mobile device. This is far from an optimal experience, especially if the mobile user is in a low-bandwidth situation. Additionally, you should be good guys: don't push your visitors toward their data caps (and extra fees from their ISPs) any more than you must.

That being said, you might find yourself in a situation where you don't have the option to institute a server-side solution (this great solution is described later on). In that case, there's a better client-side approach that works independently and makes the server-side solution very effective. We'll start with the client-side approach.

The CSS Way

A technique created by Richard Rutter uses the simple CSS property 'max-width' to do the heavy lifting. Listing 4-4 shows just how simple it is.

Listing 4-4. Setting the max-width Property for an Image.

```
img {
  max-width: 100%
}
```

Honestly, it's that simple. The only trick is not to declare a height or width in the image tag or in CSS. What happens is that the image appears at its original size and then reduces to its containing-element width if the container goes below the original image size. It's like magic.

■ **Note**   One issue with the CSS way is that you have to factor in IE6's to IE8's lack of 'max-width' support by using a conditional statement and setting the width property to 100%.

```
<!--[if lt IE 9]>img { width: 100%;}<![endif]-->
```

Also, this technique doesn't save bandwidth, because it does not change the size of the image file.

The Simple Server-side Solution

The server-side way to do this is to have multiple versions of the same image and provide the image that fits the device each visitor uses.

This clever approach was created by the Filament Group, the people responsible for building the BostonGlobe.com responsive site. As a kindness to other web developers, they've created the files you'll need to successfully use this approach and stored them at https://github.com/filamentgroup/Responsive-Images. The single (but significant) limitation to this solution is that it works for Apache web servers only. However, with some reverse engineering, you can probably implement a similar solution in other server environments.

You have to do a little extra work to make sure you have a smaller mobile-friendly image for every full-sized desktop browser image you've got in your site. Then it's a relative breeze to start using this solution. Listing 4-5 shows what a responsive image looks like.

Listing 4-5. A Responsive Image Element

```
<img src=" images/running-sml.jpg?full= images/running-lrg.jpg" />
```

So you'll include the smaller image path before the query and the larger image as the value for "full" in your query string. Since you still use the max-width technique from the CSS way described in the preceding section, it sizes perfectly, but now you're resizing a much smaller image and not forcing the visitors with mobile devices to download huge images. That's some mobile goodness.

If you wonder what happens under the hood, here's how it's explained on the git page:

As soon as rwd-images.js (I think they meant: responsiveimgs.js) loads, it tests the screen width, and if it's large, it inserts a BASE element into the head of your page, directing all subsequent image, script, and stylesheet requests through a fictitious directory called "/rwd-router/". As these requests reach the server, the .htaccess file determines whether the request is a responsive image or not (does it have a ?full query parameter?). It redirects responsive image requests immediately to their full size, while all non-responsive-image requests go to their proper destination through a URL rewrite that ignores the "/rwd-router/" segment.

Scott Jehl, github comment

Clever as it is, there are additional caveats. If a nonsupported browser requests the image, it gets both images. Presently, this solution supports Safari (desktop, iPhone, iPad), Chrome, Internet Explorer (8+), Opera, and Firefox 4. Also, if JavaScript is disabled in the browser, the visitor using a desktop gets the mobile-sized image. And while neither of these is desirable, they're still better than nothing and so are smart degradation decisions.

Flexible Grids

In the responsive web design example presented earlier in the chapter (in Listings 4-2 and 4-3), we used responsive design to achieve four design intentions. The CSS achieved this goal by detecting screen width and using that value to decide which layout to use. As you watch it work (by changing the size of a browser window), it makes big shifts in each layout. The downside of this approach is that you're locking in the layout for screen resolutions that may not perfectly match. This may be acceptable if you're targeting, let's say, an iPhone, but you're not future-proofing your site as well as you could.

Enter flexible grids. You can learn more about using CSS-based grids at http://960.gs/. We won't get into the CSS nitty-gritty, but we will give you an overview of CSS-based grid systems.

Basically, flexible grids allow the creation of a number of imaginary columns and of gutters between those columns. Suppose the content lines up with a 12-column grid, as shown in Figure 4-5.

Figure 4-5. A 12-column grid with gutters

47

Predefined classes that fit perfectly on the grid of columns can be set on the elements. The classes are something like "colOne", "colTwo", on to "colTwelve". To be clear, we want to point out that "colOne" doesn't refer to the first column. It refers to an element that is one column wide, which might very well be in column 10 or elsewhere. Similarly, column 2 refers to an element that is two columns (including the gutter between the columns) wide and might cross any two columns.

Then if you wanted a div that occupied the entire width of the page, you'd create an element such as the one shown in Listing 4-6.

Listing 4-6. *A div Element That Crosses the Whole Grid*

```
<div class="colTwelve"></ />
```

The result would be something similar to Figure 4-6.

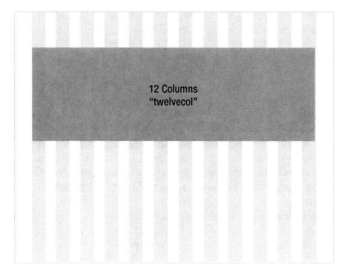

Figure 4-6. *A div that crosses all the columns in a grid*

Similarly, if you wanted to have three equal columns (with gutters between them), you'd create elements similar to those shown in Listing 4-7.

Listing 4-7. *Three Equal Columns in a Grid*

```
<div class="colFour"></div>
<div class="colFour"></div>
<div class="colFour"></div>
```

The result would be something similar to Figure 4-7.

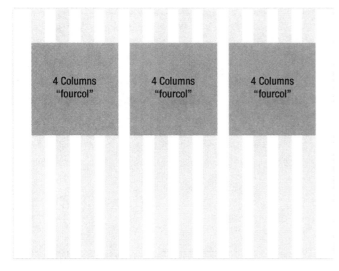

Figure 4-7. Three equal columns with gutters

Adding Flexibility

A fine example of a flexible grid system can be found at `http://cssgrid.net/`. That grid system is based on percentages. Consequently, the grid flexes to the size of the window. Now all the `div` elements you created with the class of "colFour" scale with the browser width. Then you can use the Media Queries to change assets as needed when certain width criteria are met. Later in the book, you'll see how to use the 1140 CSS grid to implement a bit wider grid that still scales well for small devices. You can find the 1140 CSS grid at `http://cssgrid.net`.

Summary

If you implement responsive web design instead of predefined layouts, your site flexes to the size of the browser. There are some downsides to the approach. You have to be comfortable with a certain loss of control when it comes to pixel perfection, as your design must necessarily be more flexible in its constraints. You can overcome this with a clever approach in your design. To do so, you would define elements that don't have fixed widths (rather, widths are percentages if you need widths at all) and change the size of your fonts as the display changes. That way, something as simple as a title isn't suddenly a huge multiline block because your visitor happens to be using a device with a small display. However, it does take more time to develop and test. But the reward for that work is a truly adaptive website. Again, to see a great example of an adaptive site, take a close look at `http://www.bostonglobe.com`.

As we develop our sample e-commerce site throughout the second half of the book, we'll use responsive web design as one of the underpinnings of the site, so you'll see these techniques later.

CHAPTER 5

■ ■ ■

Understanding the Web Reuse Pattern

When Mike first started working for one of the five largest e-commerce sites in the United States, he came up with a development approach that led to a faster development cycle and a much faster update cycle (or decreased maintenance time, to put it differently). This site has a lot of products and many ways to display all those products, depending on where a visitor is in the site (searching versus browsing by category versus browsing by price, and so on).

Initially, Mike identified 14 different product design intentions. Since the site was being built on an MVC platform, the developers had made 14 different views (an MVC view is an HTML snippet with server-side logic embedded through a special syntax), one for each intention (also known as a treatment). Creating one view per treatment is a common approach to the problem. For one thing, one view per treatment maps clearly (enabling communication within and between development teams and between development and design teams). For another thing, it seems, at least in the beginning, to enable rapid development.

Unfortunately, creating one view per treatment swiftly turns out to be a bad paradigm (an antipattern, in the parlance of many developers). As soon as you need to change some aspect of the elements that comprise the various treatments, you suddenly have to change many views rather than one view. For example, if the business stakeholders decided to add something, Mike had to change 14 views. Aside from the pain of doing the same thing 14 times (and what developer doesn't hate repetition?), the odds of missing something go up quickly. It's far too easy to make the change in 13 places rather than 14 and end up with a bug somewhere.

Before we show you how to avoid that mess, we'll first show the problem in detail. Figure 5-1 shows the design variations that Mike identified (with all the company and product information removed, of course).

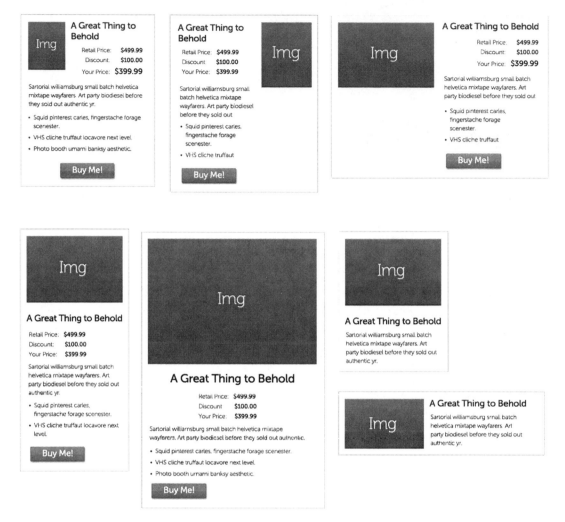

Figure 5-1. *Design variations*

When Mike examined these design intentions, he couldn't help noticing that they all had similar items that needed only to have their layouts changed. He quickly realized that this was a job for CSS, not for a bunch of separate views.

■ **Note**　Mike would like to give credit to Nicole Sullivan, who went through a similar process when she reorganized Facebook's content and discovered that a large amount of it fell into a few patterns. Her description of that process (available in a number of places on the web) very much inspired Mike's work on this similar problem.

Mike found similarities across the various design intentions. Figure 5-2 shows the similarities by color-coding them.

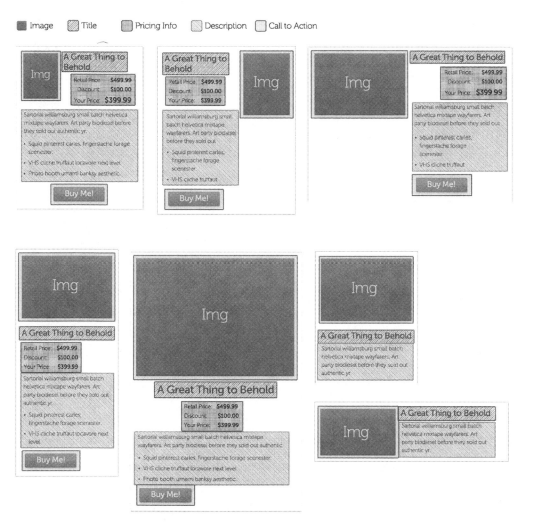

Figure 5-2. Similarities across designs

As you can see, all of these design intentions share an image, a title, and a description. Further, a large majority also share pricing info and a call to action button. Instead of creating different snippets of HTML to reuse throughout our large and high-bandwidth e-commerce site, we created a dynamic master product stack that contained all the elements (image, title, pricing info, description, and call to action). Then we put conditional statements around each element so we could control whether it got rendered in the HTML being pushed down to the customer's browser. We insert a CSS class in the parent element to effect our design intentions. We weren't overly strict about it. If a new product stack treatment that didn't fit in our existing pattern came along, we always had the option to create another view. That being said, after a year and a half, during which we were asked for numerous changes and six additional treatments, we had to create only one additional view (for a switchable feature that we thought was outside the bounds of our product stack view).

So let's look at some code. Listing 5-1 shows (a simplified version of) the HTML behind a product stack.

Listing 5-1. The HTML for a Product Stack

```html
<section class="productStackWrap" >
  <img class="psImage" src="images/image.jpg" />
  <article class="psArticleWrap">
    <h1 class="psTitle">Title</h1>
    <ul class="psPriceWrap">
      <li>
        <span class="spLabel">Label</span><span class="spAmount">Price</span>
      </li>
      <li>
        <span class="spLabel">Label</span><span class="spAmount">Price</span>
      </li>
      <li>
        <span class="spLabel">Label</span><span class="spAmount spTotalPrice">Price</span>
      </li>
    </ul>
    <div class="spDescriptionWrap">
      <p>Description</p>
      <ul class="descBulletsUL">
        <li>Bullets </li>
      </ul>
    </div>
    <button class="psCTA">
      Button
    </button>
  </article>
</section>
```

While you could copy and paste the skeleton and fill in the text and image path manually, the much more efficient route would be to use the server-side solution of your choice and fill the product stack dynamically. At the top-five company where Mike and Jay met, the solution was the Microsoft MVC framework. This is where the maintenance side really gets a performance boost, because now we're just adjusting one piece of code that will update all of our product stacks.

Because we were using Microsoft MVC, our view was in .NET MVC Razor code (which is really just HTML with certain codes embedded in it). However, any similar server-side language (such as JSP or PHP) should allow accomplishment of the same task, since all we do is set some variables and use some logic to decide which bits of HTML to include in the final page that goes down the pipe to the customer.

We're going to create some variables in the view for demonstration purposes, but you'd usually be filling these from a database or model. Also, for the sake of clarity, we're going to keep logic out of the pricing info. Listing 5-2 shows the Razor code for a product stack.

Listing 5-2. Razor code for a Product Stack

```razor
@{
  var Treatment = "psTreatmentA1";
  var Title = "A Great Thing to Behold";
  var ImagePath = "images/image.jpg";

  var RetailPriceAmt = "$499.99";
  var DiscountAmt = "$100.99";
  var YourPriceAmt = "$399.99";
```

```
  var Description = "Sartorial williamsburg small batch helvetica mixtape wayfarers. Art party
biodiesel.";
  var showPricingWrap = true;
  var showDescBullets = true;
  var showButton = true;

}
<section class="productStackWrap @Treatment" >
  <img class="psImage" src="@ImagePath" />
  <article class="psArticleWrap">
    <h1 class="psTitle">@Title</h1>
    if(showPricingWrap){
    <ul class="psPriceWrap">
      <li>
        <span class="spLabel">Retail Price:</span><span class="spAmount">@RetailPriceAmt</span>
      </li>
      <li>
        <span class="spLabel">Discount:</span><span class="spAmount">@DiscountAmt </span>
      </li>
      <li>
        <span class="spLabel"></span>Your Price:<span class="spAmount spTotalPrice">@
YourPriceAmt </span>
      </li>
    </ul>
    }
    <div class="spDescriptionWrap">
      <p>Description</p>
      if(showDescBullets){
      <ul class="descBulletsUL">
        @foreach(Bullet bullet in Model.Item1)
        {
          <li> @bullet.bulletText</li>
        }
      </ul>
      }
    </div>
    @if(showButton){
    <button class="psCTA">
      Button
    </button>
    }
  </article>
</section>
```

The Boolean logic lets us ship only the necessary code for our particular treatment so that we don't have the overhead of shipping unnecessary code and then hiding it with CSS. With this method, we gain a lot of flexibility in the patterns this code can match.

Best of all, by simply adding a class name to our section element with the class: "productStackWrap", we can express a wide variety of design intentions. Keep in mind that we're using the same HTML for each of these CSS transforms.

■ **Note**   We're leveraging CSS nesting to accomplish our heavy lifting. We're relying on CSS failing gracefully. That is, if the browser's CSS rendering engine doesn't understand something in our CSS, it will ignore it (so long as it's syntactically correct). We use CSS nesting a lot.

Listing 5-3 shows an example of CSS nesting.

Listing 5-3. *Example of CSS Nesting*

```
.child {
  font-weight: normal;
}
.parent .child {
  font-weight: bold;
}
```

If there's an element with the class of child that has an ancestor with a class of parent, then the element to which child applies is bold. If not, child retains its font-weight: normal Property. By setting the class of parent" as an ancestor of child, we can control font weight for various elements.

Now let's get back to styling product stacks for multiple designs. Listing 5-4 shows the base CSS that all the treatments share.

Listing 5-4. *Base CSS for All Product-Stack Treatments*

```
/* Shared Product Stack Rules */
.productStackWrap {
  position: relative;
  font-size: 14px;
  margin: 40px 0;
  border: 1px solid #999;
  padding: 20px;
}
.psTitle {
  font-size: 21px;
  font-weight: 700;
  margin: 0 0 5px 0;
}
.psPriceWrap {
  padding: 0;
}
.psPriceWrap li {
  list-style: none;
  padding: 2px 0;
}
.spLabel {
  display: inline-block;
  width: 75px;
  text-align: right;
  padding-right: 3px;
}
.spAmount {
```

```
  display: inline-block;
  width: 75px;
  text-align: right;
  font-weight: 700;
}
.spTotalPrice {
  color: green;
}
.spDescriptionWrap p {
  line-height: 150%;
}


.psCTA {
  background: green;
  color: white;
  padding: 5px 0;
  width: 120px;
  display:block;
  border: 0;
  text-align:center;
  font-size: 20px;
  text-shadow: 1px 1px 1px #666666;
  -webkit-border-radius: 5px;
  -moz-border-radius: 5px;
  border-radius: 5px;
  -moz-background-clip: padding;
  -webkit-background-clip: padding-box;
  background-clip: padding-box;
  background: #92c436; /* Old browsers */
  background: -moz-linear-gradient(top,  #92c436 0%, #97c64b 50%, #80c217 51%, #7cbc0a 100%); /*
FF3.6+ */
  background: -webkit-gradient(linear, left top, left bottom, color-stop(0%,#92c436), color-
stop(50%,#97c64b), color-stop(51%,#80c217), color-stop(100%,#7cbc0a)); /* Chrome,Safari4+ */
  background: -webkit-linear-gradient(top,  #92c436 0%,#97c64b 50%,#80c217 51%,#7cbc0a 100%); /*
Chrome10+,Safari5.1+ */
  background: -o-linear-gradient(top,  #92c436 0%,#97c64b 50%,#80c217 51%,#7cbc0a 100%); /*
Opera 11.10+ */
  background: -ms-linear-gradient(top,  #92c436 0%,#97c64b 50%,#80c217 51%,#7cbc0a 100%); /*
IE10+ */
  background: linear-gradient(top,  #92c436 0%,#97c64b 50%,#80c217 51%,#7cbc0a 100%); /* W3C */
  filter: progid : DXImageTransform.Microsoft.gradient( startColorstr='#92c436', endColorstr='#7c
bc0a',GradientType=0 ); /* IE6-9 */
}
.descBulletsUL li {
  padding: 4px 0;
}
```

To get the base product-stack HTML to look like our first design intention, we'll add the class psTreatmentA1 to the parent element. Of course, that's incomplete. We'll complete the listing for each treatment as we get to that treatment. Please bear with us, and we'll show how the treatments use the base treatment shortly. Figure 5-3 shows the result.

Figure 5-3. *Product-stack treatment A1*

Listing 5-5 shows the CSS for treatment A1.

Listing 5-5. *CSS for Treatment A1*

```
/* Treatment A1 */
.psTreatmentA1
{
  width: 310px;
}

.psTreatmentA1 .psImage
{
  width: 80px;
  height: 112px;
  float:left;
}

.psTreatmentA1 .psTitle
{
  margin-left: 100px;
}

.psTreatmentA1 .psPriceWrap
{
  margin-left: 100px;
}

.psTreatmentA1 .psCTA
{
```

```
  margin: 0 auto;
}

.psTreatmentA1 .psPriceWrap
{
  text-align: right;
}
```

Similarly, we can add the class "psTreatmentB1" to rearrange the content to match another design. Figure 5-4 shows the result.

Figure 5-4. *Treatment B1*

Listing 5-6 shows the CSS for treatment B1.

Listing 5-6. *CSS for Treatment B1*

```
/* Treatment B1 */
.psTreatmentB1
{
  width: 190px;
  padding-right: 156px;
}

.psTreatmentB1 .psImage
{
  width: 116px;
  height: 151px;
  position: absolute;
  right: 20px;
```

```
    top: 20px;
}

.psTreatmentB1 .psPriceWrap
{
  text-align: left;
}
```

Again, we can add the class "psTreatmentC1" to rearrange the content to match a third design. Figure 5-5 shows the result.

Figure 5-5. *Treatment C1*

Listing 5-7 shows the CSS for treatment C1.

Listing 5-7. *CSS for Treatment C1*

```
/* Treatment C1 */
.psTreatmentC1
{
        width: 385px;
}
```

```css
.psTreatmentC1 .psImage
{
        width: 386px;
        height: 287px;
        display: block;
        margin-bottom: 20px;
}

.psTreatmentC1 .psPriceWrap
{
        text-align: left;
        margin-left: 110px;
}

.psTreatmentC1 .psTitle
{
        text-align: center;
        font-size: 27px;
}
```

We'll finish our example with the one of the simplest designs. Figure 5-6 shows that result.

A Great Thing to Behold

Sartorial williamsburg small batch
helvetica mixtape wayfarers. Art party
biodiesel before they sold out authentic.

Figure 5-6. Treatment D1

Listing 5-8 shows the CSS for treatment D1.

Listing 5-8. CSS for Treatment D1

```css
/* Treatment D1 */
.psTreatmentD1
{
  width: 261px;
  padding-left: 224px;
  min-height: 116px;
}

.psTreatmentD1 .psImage
{
  width: 184px;
  height: 114px;
  position: absolute;
  top: 20px;
  left: 20px;
}
```

```
.psTreatmentD1 .spDescriptionWrap p
{
  margin-bottom: 0;
}

.psTreatmentD1 .psPriceWrap, .psTreatmentD1 .psCTA, .psTreatmentD1 .descBulletsUL
{
  display:none;
  /* If we're using our server-side logic, we wouldn't need this as these extraneous HTML
elements wouldn't be on the page. */
}
```

Some Final Observations on Web Reuse

Think Building Blocks

We love all those toys that enable making something from a bunch of similar parts. We also think that's a great metaphor for building web components that you can reuse across your site. If your components are a collection of toy bricks, building your site amounts to picking which bricks to snap together. When a brick is the same shape but a different color, that's similar to a web component with one or more of its features turned on or off.

Thinking in terms of building blocks and creating reusable web components should speed up development, enable passing more tasks to junior developers, and lead to reduced time to change pages as business needs change. Ideally, once you have figured out all the components (and variations of those components) that your site needs, adding new pages and changing existing pages should be, well, a snap.

Everything Is Contained

Containers have a lot of names. In our own work, we talk a lot about "stacks" of various sorts. As we demonstrated earlier in this chapter, an article stack is a container holding a collection of elements that implement an article for visitors to read. Similarly, we also showed a product stack (and some of its variations). To us, even a button is a stack, because buttons often have multiple elements (such as a div element to define a block of space for the button, an anchor element if the button is a link, an image element for an image button, and so on). However, "stack" is really just another name for a container.

We want to end our discussion of reusable web components with a reminder that, on a web page, just about everything is in some kind of container and that just about everything is contained by some other container. Whatever you may call it (stack or widget or whatever), each component is really a container that both contains other containers and is itself contained by something. We find that developing and maintaining feature-rich web pages can be made much more manageable by remembering that it's all just boxes within boxes within boxes.

Summary

In this chapter, we covered the idea of creating a set of components that cover all of a business's web site needs and then parts of that collection to make each page. We strongly recommend that all major web sites use a similar technique, because it provides the following benefits:

- It ensures consistent branding across a large, complex site. To many companies, their brand is their most precious asset, and consistent treatment for the branding assets (logos, slogans, etc.) is an essential part of web site development and maintenance.

- It easily creates a consistent experience across the whole site. In fact, you have to do extra work to get outside of the look and feel provided by your standard components.

- It makes developing new web pages and maintaining existing web pages both much easier and faster.

- It allows day-to-day web development tasks to be handed off to less experienced developers, who can just put together standard components and be done.

- It frees senior developers to solve tough problems, create custom solutions, and create additional sitewide components as the business identifies the need for them.

We find this technique to be very powerful. We expect to see it get wide adoption as developers who create and maintain large and complex web sites learn about it.

PART 3

■ ■ ■

Building a Web Site

In this section, we apply all of the performance advice given in Chapters 2 through 5 to an actual web site (`http://clikz.us`). Because e-commerce sites generally require more complex layout than blogs or news listings, we use an e-commerce site as our example. Also, when we conceived of the book, we were working for a very large e-commerce company, and that was the problem we had in mind.

This section consists of two subsections. The first, Chapters 6 through 9, deals with elements that appear on every page: the HTML boilerplate, the navigation elements, the masthead, and the footer.

First, we show how we create a page template. We use `http://www.html5boilerplate.com` to get a base page that includes a number of useful options. Then we work through conditional statements to get things to work properly on the various versions of Internet Explorer. We also tackle other details, such as dealing with compatibility mode, loading jQuery, and adding Google Analytics. Finally, we set up the site's grid, which we use to control the placement of the various parts of our pages.

Then we discuss why a site should support different kinds of navigation for visitors with different agendas. Then we show how to create two different kinds of navigation. We start with a menu, for those visitors who like to browse for what they want. Then we add a search box to the menu, for those who prefer searching to browsing. We also address how to make our navigation work on browsers that don't support CSS3 and even browsers that don't support JavaScript.

Next comes creating a masthead for the top of every page. Before taking that plunge, we deal with an issue we see a lot: country selector. Although our own site doesn't use a country selector, we show how to make a country selector perform as well as possible. We use a list of absolutely positioned elements to create our masthead and discuss how to use CSS clipping to work with parts of an image. We conclude with our fundamental advice about mastheads: Keep them simple.

Then we deal with how we make the footer for our site. Reusing the content we had in our menu (Chapter 7), we turn it into a site map that rests at the bottom of the page. Then we add the legal block. Along the way, we discuss why SVG can be a good alternative to other image formats. Then we demonstrate how to create an image with SVG (which we use in the remainder of the book) and how to interact with that SVG image through JavaScript.

The second subsection deals with building controls that we reuse all through our sample site. We introduce the idea of a "fractal" design pattern—one in which complex controls consists of simple controls. Each control is really a PHP function with a stylesheet, and each requires a certain structure to the HTML that goes with it. Working through each control, we add details that you may find useful, both when using controls and when doing other web development.

One of the book's key concepts concerns the fractal (or nested) control. We first discuss the pattern's general characteristics. While discussing the pattern, we show the label control—our first and simplest control. Then comes a case study based on work we've done before (it was while doing that job that we met, and that work gave us the idea of writing a book about it). We also discuss when to segregate CSS from JavaScript and when to combine them (and how to do so).

We next discuss why we developed the link control and then show how we did it. We detail the functions and styles that constitute the control. (We added a JavaScript component to provide failover capacity for browsers that can't display tooltips via CSS.)

Moving on, we discuss why and how to create a box that contains links. We think sideboxes are useful for providing supplemental information about a product, information that would be out of place on the main part of the page. The links that make up the sidebox control's content are actually link controls. Remember the fractal notion of nested controls? The sidebox control's links offer one example.

Next, we explain our button control in detail and include seven different treatments for it. As we discussed when detailing our web reuse pattern, we practice what we preach by reusing the HTML from one treatment to the next. We get the seven different treatments by varying the styles.

Then we detail the price control, one of our most complex controls. For one thing, it's really two controls: a price control and a shipping control. For another, the price control is meant to be repeated, to create what we call a "price stack." While describing the price and shipping controls, we address an often overlooked problem: how to get a line of dots—a dot leader—to go from the end of the item to the beginning of the price.

Then we show how we create a product listing. Again, the idea is to create a complex component of a page by calling a fairly simple function. More so than any other control, the product control uses the controls-within-controls paradigm. A product control contains price, shipping, link, and button controls. Also, the product control is the first control to make use of a data object, which we construct as a JSON object.

Next, we cover controls that create tables. We provide two treatments: a table with a header row, and a table with the header content down the left side (a header column, as it were). We also create tables both without using table, tr, and td elements and with those elements. Most browsers can properly display a table that doesn't use traditional table elements. For those browsers that can't handle modern table rendering, though, we provide the traditional elements.

Then we move on to how we create a set of tabs. We again offer two treatments, horizontal (light-colored) and vertical (dark-colored). To overcome some pet peeves with the tabs we've found on many web sites, we made our tabs such that each can be a unique address. That way, users can link to an individual tab and come back to it via the browser history. We also made sure our tab content centers correctly, even when one tab has a one-line label and another has a multiline label. Finally, we added a bit of visual interest by animating the transition from one tab to another.

We close the book by describing two controls that let us make forms more easily. We define a fieldset control and an input control. As the names imply, the fieldset control creates a fieldset element and its children (both input elements and other content). The input control creates a single input element that supports all the possible types (check box, radio, etc.). As an example of our fractal paradigm, the fieldset control uses the input control. Along the way, we show how to create interesting visual effects with the :before and :after pseudo selectors. Finally, we show a technique that applies to all of our controls: making shortcut controls.

CHAPTER 6

■ ■ ■

Page Template

Throughout Section II of this book, we're going to focus on creating a sample site to demonstrate the principles we discussed in Section I. Reading about how something works only gets most people started on true understanding. Seeing it in action is a big step toward mastery. (Of course, to fully learn how to do something, you have to do it yourself, but we're sure you will do so.) To give some context to the conversation, let's look at the site before we start on how it's built. Figure 6-1 shows the sample site we're building, which you can find at http://clikz.us

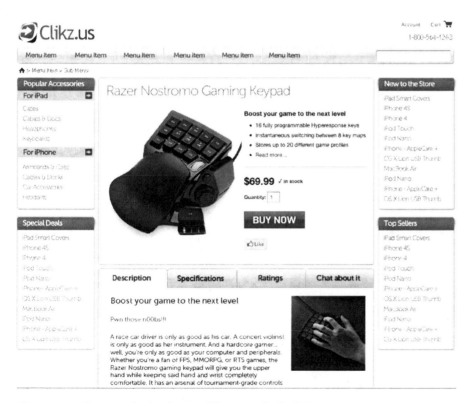

Figure 6-1. *The sample site (http://clikz.us) we're building*

We're going to start building our sample web site by first creating a page template. In the .NET world, such a template is often called a Master Page. We've also seen it called a Master Layout. Whatever it's called, the page template is the framework in which we'll build our web site.

For our sample site, we're going to both create some elements that set various options and specify a flexible grid. Between them, those items form the base of all the pages on the site.

Setting the Boilerplate Options

To get started, we're going to lean heavily on the tool available at http://www.html5boilerplate.com to generate a nice HTML5 starting point. The HTML5 Boilerplate site offers a lot of configuration detail that we won't be covering in this chapter, including web configuration, build scripts, and many others. Since we're focusing on HTML and CSS in this book, we've left off those features on our sample site. We strongly recommend checking out the HTML5 Boilerplate site in detail for items you might find useful. We'd also like to thank Paul Irish, Divya Manian, Shichaun, Mathias Bynens, and Nicolas Gallagher (to name just a few) for putting together this useful tool. They're doing great work that benefits all web developers.

Before we pick apart the code, you should probably see a complete boilerplate page. Listing 6-1 shows such a listing.

Listing 6-1. A Complete Page Template

```html
<!doctype html>
<!--[if lt IE 7 ]> <html class="ie6"> <![endif]-->

<!--[if IE 7 ]>    <html class="ie7"> <![endif]-->

<!--[if IE 8 ]>    <html class="ie8"> <![endif]-->

<!--[if IE 9 ]>    <html class="ie9"> <![endif]-->

<!--[if (gt IE 9)|!(IE)]><!--> <html class=""> <!--<![endif]-->
<head>
  <meta charset="utf-8">

<meta http-equiv="X-UA-Compatible" content="IE=edge,chrome=1">

  <title></title>
  <meta name="description" content="">

  <!-- Mobile viewport optimized: h5bp.com/viewport -->
  <meta name="viewport" content="width=device-width">

  <!-- Place favicon.ico and apple-touch-icon.png in the root directory: mathiasbynens.be/notes/
touch-icons -->

  <link rel="stylesheet" href="css/style.css">

  <!-- More ideas for your <head> here: h5bp.com/d/head-Tips -->

  <!-- All JavaScript at the bottom, except this Modernizr build.
       Modernizr enables HTML5 elements & feature detects for optimal performance.
```

```
      Create your own custom Modernizr build: www.modernizr.com/download/ -->
   <script src="js/libs/modernizr-2.5.3.min.js"></script>
</head>
<body>
   <!--[if lt IE 7]><p class=chromeframe>Your browser is <em>ancient!</em> <a href="http://
browsehappy.com/">Upgrade to a different browser</a> or <a href="http://www.google.com/chromefra
me/?redirect=true">install Google Chrome Frame</a> to experience this site.</p><![endif]-->
   <header>

   </header>
   <div role="main">

   </div>
   <footer>

   </footer>


   <!-- JavaScript at the bottom for fast page loading -->

   <!-- Grab Google CDN's jQuery, with a protocol relative URL; fall back to local if offline -->
   <script src="//ajax.googleapis.com/ajax/libs/jquery/1.7.1/jquery.min.js"></script>
   <script>window.jQuery || document.write('<script src="js/libs/jquery-1.7.1.min.js"><\/
script>')</script>

   <!-- scripts concatenated and minified via build script -->
   <script src="js/plugins.js"></script>
   <script src="js/script.js"></script>
   <!-- end scripts -->

   <!-- Asynchronous Google Analytics snippet. Change UA-XXXXX-X to be your site's ID.
        mathiasbynens.be/notes/async-analytics-snippet -->
   <script>
     var _gaq=[['_setAccount','UA-XXXXX-X'],['_trackPageview']];
     (function(d,t){var g=d.createElement(t),s=d.getElementsByTagName(t)[0];
     g.src=('https:'==location.protocol?'//ssl':'//www')+'.google-analytics.com/ga.js';
     s.parentNode.insertBefore(g,s)}(document,'script'));
   </script>
</body>
</html>
```

Conditional Statements Around the HTML Element

Often (usually, we suspect), you need to identify which browser an individual visitor to your site is using, so that you can present the best possible experience to that visitor. Wrapping the HTML element in conditional statements lets you do so, though only for Internet Explorer.

■ **Note** Our apparent focus on Internet Explorer in this chapter is really just a side effect of the fact that Internet Explorer forces web developers to do extra work to get things to work on IE and the fact that IE is the only browser (at least currently) that supports conditional statements. Given that much of the world still uses IE, we think the benefit is worth the time. You've probably run into the same issue yourself.

Listing 6-2 shows how to do so.

Listing 6-2. Conditional Statement to Identify the Browser

```
<!--[if lt IE 7 ]> <html class="ie6" lang="en"> <![endif]-->

<!--[if IE 7 ]>    <html class="ie7" lang="en">  <![endif]-->

<!--[if IE 8 ]>    <html class="ie8" lang="en">  <![endif]-->

<!--[if IE 9 ]>    <html class="ie9" lang="en">  <![endif]-->

<!--[if (gt IE 9)|!(IE)]><!--> <html  lang="en">  <!--<![endif]-->
```

At first glance this may look confusing. Also, it seems like a lot of code just to render an HTML element. However, to the site's developer and ultimately to the site's visitors, it will be invaluable.

First, let's consider the conditional statement itself. The following line shows an example:

```
<!--[if IE 7]>  Render this html<![endif]-->
```

The syntax is fairly obvious but bears explanation in order to clarify a few details. First, it's a comment. That's handy because browsers that don't recognize conditional statements (any browser except Internet Explorer) ignore the statement (so there's no page load delay for visitors who use other browsers). Second, it starts with `<!--[if condition]>` and ends with `<![endif]-->`. Finally, the bit in the middle is the code that gets run if the browser recognizes the conditional statement and if that browser can resolve the statement as being true.

In the example shown in Listing 6-2, if the visitor's browser is Internet Explorer 7, the code in the middle gets run. In the example shown in Listing 6-2, there's no operator. However, operators (such as "less than" and "greater than") can be present. The default operator is "equals," but there's no syntax for it. If you need "equals," leave out the operator. Let's look at some of the more commonly used operators. Table 6-1 shows the basic operators.

Table 6-1. Conditional Operators for Internet Explorer

Sample Operator Line	Effect
`<!--[if lt IE 7]>`	If the visitor uses a version of Internet Explorer earlier than IE7, this operator catches that fact and runs the corresponding code.
`<!--[if lte IE 7]>`	As you would expect, visitors using versions of Internet Explorer earlier than or equal to IE7 get the experience defined by the subsequent code.
`<!--[if gt IE 7]>`	If the visitor uses a version of Internet Explorer later than IE7, this operator catches that fact and runs the corresponding code.
`<!--[if gte IE 7]>`	If a visitor uses a version of Internet Explorer greater than or equal to IE7, they get the experience defined by the subsequent code.

Table 6-1. Conditional Operators for Internet Explorer

Sample Operator Line	Effect
`<!--[if IE 9]>`	If the visitor uses IE 9 and not some other version, they get the experience defined by the subsequent code. Notice that there's no operator. The default operator is "equals."

As Listing 6-2 shows, we're wrapping many versions of our HTML element in these conditional statements, but the browser will process only one version: the version that the browser can evaluate as being true (for Internet Explorer). For example, if our visitor's browser is IE7, the HTML element is defined as shown in the following line:

```
<html class="ie7" lang="en">
```

Now let's closely examine the last line of our conditional statements, shown again (we hate thumbing through pages) in the following line:

```
<!--[if (gt IE 9)|!(IE)]><!--> <html  lang="en">  <!--<![endif]-->
```

The additional comments ensure that, if the visitor uses a browser other than Internet Explorer, the browser can find the starting tag of an HTML element. Also, if the visitor uses Internet Explorer, this line matches versions greater than 9. IE10 is in beta, so it's possible.

The last part of the condition is `|!(IE)`. That translates to "or not Internet Explorer." The pipe character (`|`) means "or," and the exclamation point (`!`) means "not." We don't strictly need that syntax, since any browser other than Internet Explorer wouldn't recognize it. However, we include it to communicate with the developers (including ourselves) who may have to maintain the page at a future date and in case other browsers do start recognizing conditional statements.

We hope that IE10 will be standards-compliant and that we won't need to catch it with a condition and write special rules for it. However if do need to write special rules for IE10, we could add another line to our set of conditional statements. Listing 6-3 shows what the last two conditions would be in that case.

Listing 6-3. Accounting for IE10

```
<!--[if IE 10 ]>    <html class="ie10" lang="en">  <![endif]-->
<!--[if (gt IE 10)|!(IE)]><!--> <html  lang="en">  <!--<![endif]-->
```

Whether we check for IE10 or stop at IE9, the starting tag of the element presented to any browser that doesn't fit any of the conditions is shown in the following line:

```
<html  lang="en">
```

Now that we've shown how the syntax works, we can get down to why this technique is valuable. As you probably noticed, the conditional statements (except for the last one) add a class to the HTML element. This class corresponds to the version of Internet Explorer the visitor is using. By itself, adding a class doesn't do anything. However, it provides an awesome hook for targeting browser-specific CSS. For example, if we needed to adjust some padding for IE7, we could write the CSS shown in Listing 6-4.

Listing 6-4. Defining Padding for All Browsers and for IE7

```
.paddingDefinition
{
  padding: 10px  /* All Browsers */
}
```

```
.ie7 .paddingDefinition
{
    padding: 12px; /* Only IE7 */
}
```

Instead of writing a bunch of CSS hacks or loading additional browser-specific style sheets (which would mean more HTTP requests and worse performance), we can simply define our browser-specific code next to the existing code, making it much easier to find and to understand. Also, by adding an additional selector we've increased specificity so that our IE7 rule has more weight than the existing class—but only if the browser is IE7. Again this goes back to browsers' ignoring CSS selectors that don't make sense. So if the class "ie7" isn't added to the HTML tag by our conditional statements, the second rule (".ie7 .someClass") never gets applied.

We love that CSS lets us write rules for browsers to ignore. It sounds odd, but it sure works. If you want to find out more about this powerful technique, visit http://paulirish.com/2008/conditional-stylesheets-vs-css-hacks-answer-neither/.

Setting the Character set

As we discussed in Chapter 3, you should always set the charset (short for "character set") metatag as the first item in the head section of your HTML, because not doing so can lead to a long pause before a browser starts to present information to your visitors. The following line shows the syntax for setting the character set to UTF-8:

```
<meta charset="utf-8">
```

Not doing so can have serious consequences, for both performance and security. If the browser isn't sure what character set to use, it tries to analyze or "sniff" the type by using different algorithms (which vary by browser). This sniffing can delay page loading and offer a path for attackers to fool the browser into using the UTF-7 character set, which has significant vulnerabilities. To paraphrase an old TV commercial: UTF-8—don't leave home without it.

Controlling IE's Compatibility Mode

Starting with IE8, Microsoft introduced "Compatibility Mode" and a way for any web page to turn it on and off. When Compatibility Mode is on, the browser reverts to previous IE browser rules if it detects something it doesn't understand.

■ **Tip** Microsoft keeps a "Compatibility View List," which is a list of sites that the people at Microsoft think need to be rendered with the IE7 engine. To see if your site is on that list, visit the following site: http://ie9cvlist.ie.microsoft.com/ie9CompatViewList.xml.

If you want to test your site in Compatibility Mode, you can manually force a page to be displayed in Compatibility mode from the developer tools available in Internet Explorer (press **F12** or look in the **Tools** menu). You can also use Compatibility Mode to test cross-browser code. However, don't rely on this technique alone, as it's not 100 percent reliable; there's still no substitute for viewing and testing pages in various browsers. Figure 6-2 shows where you can find the Browser Mode and Document Mode settings in Internet Explorer. From those lists, you can choose "Compatibility Mode."

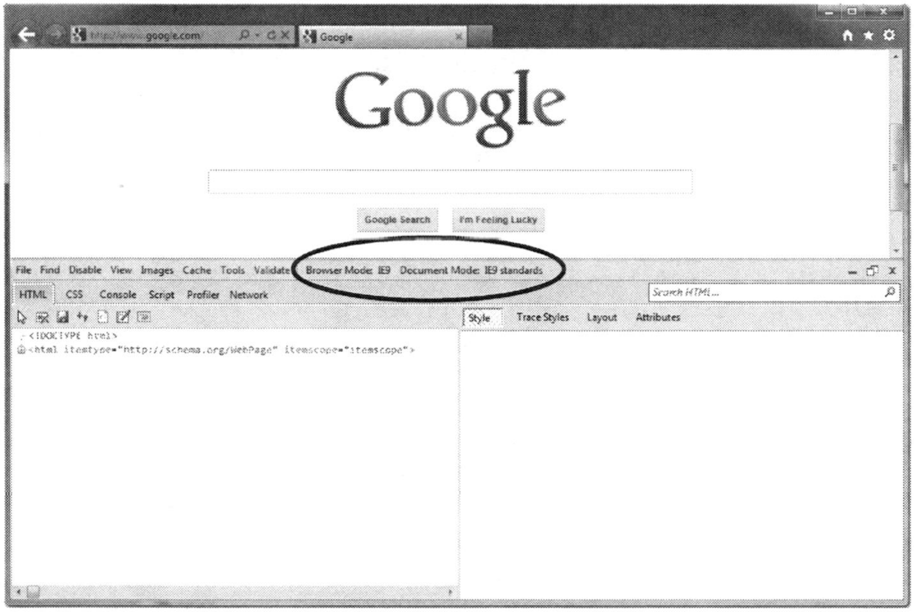

Figure 6-2. Internet Explorer's developer tools

For more information about Compatibility Mode, visit http://msdn.microsoft.com/en-us/library/dd567845(v=vs.85).aspx.

As a rule, we prefer to turn off Compatibility Mode. To do so, we use the metaelement shown in the following line:

```
<meta http-equiv="X-UA-Compatible" content="IE=edge,chrome=1">
```

■ **Caution**   The preceding metaelement can cause validation problems. It's often better to add a line to your .htaccess (or equivalent) file to set Compatibility Mode.

The http-equiv="X-UA-Compatible" attribute tells Internet Explorer (IE8 and up) that this element is going to set Compatibility Mode. The content attribute specifies which display rules (IE8, IE9, etc.) to use if the visitor uses Internet Explorer (again, only IE8 and up).

The first setting in the content attribute, IE=edge, tells the visiting IE browser not to use Compatibility Mode but instead to use the latest version available. For example, if your visitor's browser is IE9, the browser should use IE9 rules to render the page.

The second part of this metatag, chrome=1, is to tell IE that it can use the Google Chrome Frame (GCF) if the user has the plug-in installed. If you're not familiar with the GCF, it's a great free Google plug-in that lets IE browsers render HTML5 code even in IE6. It basically creates a frame in IE that uses the Chrome engine. We love it. Unfortunately, there's no way to ensure that all visitors using IE have GCF installed (but see the next section for some help in that direction). You can find out more about the GCF at the following site: http://www.chromium.org/developers/how-tos/chrome-frame-getting-started.

Prompting for Installation of Google Chrome Frame

As we noted in the previous section, you can't guarantee that visitors using older versions of Internet Explorer have installed the Google Chrome Frame (GCF). However, you can prompt them to install it. If you enable this setting on the HTML5 Boilerplate site, you get a conditional element that prompts visitors using older versions of Internet Explorer to install the GCF, as shown in Listing 6-5.

Listing 6-5: Prompting visitors to Install GCF

```
<!--[if lt IE 7]><p class=chromeframe>Your browser is <em>ancient!</em> <a href="http://
browsehappy.com/">Upgrade to a different browser</a> or <a href="http://www.google.com/chromefra
me/?redirect=true">install Google Chrome Frame</a> to experience this site.</p><![endif]-->
```

Of course, you can alter the text with a message appropriate to your site. But in a nutshell this conditional statement fires with IE browsers before IE7 and offers a way to install the Google Chrome Frame. That way, more of your visitors can have an HTML5 experience, which is very likely to be better than an IE6 experience.

Controlling the Viewport on iPhones

MobileSafari (the browser that comes on iPhones) detects the width of a page and zooms to fit the page in the screen of the phone. Most pages were designed to be viewed on desktop browsers (though that's rapidly changing as more and more web designers adopt a mobile-first approach to their work). Consequently, the page is often unreadable without zooming because the text is so small. You can prevent MobileSafari from zooming out and instead show the content at 100 percent and thus make it much more legible by using the meta element shown in the following line:

```
<meta name="viewport" content="width=device-width">
```

Loading jQuery

If your site uses jQuery (we love jQuery, by the way), you can add it to your pages with the following script elements.

Listing 6-6. Adding jQuery to Your Page Template

```
<script src="//ajax.googleapis.com/ajax/libs/jquery/1.7.1/jquery.min.js"></script>
<script>window.jQuery || document.write('<script src="js/libs/jquery-1.7.1.min.js"><\/
script>')</script>
```

The first script element tries to download version 1.7.1 of jQuery from the Google CDN. The second script element specifies a local directory as the source of the script file.

Using the Google CDN has a couple of great benefits. First, you get the benefits of a CDN. As we discussed in Chapter 3, a CDN can really improve performance by locating assets geographically closer to your user. The second and more interesting aspect is that since loading jQuery from the Google CDN is pretty popular, chances are decent that visitors to your site have already visited a site using the jQuery library for the Google CDN. In that case, it's already in the cache, and no download is needed. If visitors come with a primed cache of this jQuery library, they don't have to download it again. We save bandwidth and a pesky HTTP request. Talk about a performance booster.

But what if Google goes down (unlikely, but you never know), or (more likely) what if I'm working without an Internet connection and I want to work on the code. The second script element says, "If I can't get jQuery from the CDN, use the files located in my relative directory." In this default case, it looks for jQuery in root/js/libs/. You can set that directory to wherever you store the jQuery library. Finally, you can also customize the versions of jQuery that you want to use.

Honestly, if you're going to use jQuery, you'll be hard pressed to find a better way to load it.

▦ **Tip** Modernizr's load feature works in much the same way (good ideas get around), so that's another way to load jQuery. We discussed Modernizr in more detail in Chapter 2.

Adding Google Analytics

The script element shown in Listing 6-7 enables Google Analytics for your page.

Listing 6-7. Adding Google Analytics

```
<script>
  var _gaq=[['_setAccount','UA-XXXXX-X'],['_trackPageview']];
  (function(d,t){var g=d.createElement(t),s=d.getElementsByTagName(t)[0];
  g.src=('https:'==location.protocol?'//ssl':'//www')+'.google-analytics.com/ga.js';
  s.parentNode.insertBefore(g,s)}(document,'script'));
</script>
```

Naturally, you should replace UA-XXXXX-X with your site's Google Analytics account ID.

More Options

We've selected the options that we generally use and that we intend to use for the sample web site that we're building as part of writing this book. However, the HTML5 Boilerplate site has many more options that you might want to use in your own sites, depending on exactly what you need or want to do. For much more detail, see the HTML5 Boilerplate web site, http://www.html5boilerplate.com.

Setting up the Site's Grid

As we mentioned in Chapter 4, one common part of a responsive design is a flexible grid. For our sample site, we've chosen the 1140 CSS Grid, by Andy Taylor. Andy has created a 12column grid that fits into a 1280-pixel-wide monitor. Being flexible, it also looks good at lower resolutions, all the way down to phones and other mobile devices. You can find the 1140 CSS Grid at http://cssgrid.net and download it from http://download.cssgrid.net/1140_CssGrid_2.zip.

When you uncompress the zip file, you should get a directory structure similar to that shown in Figure 6-3.

Figure 6-3. Contents of 1140_CssGrid_2.zip

This book doesn't deal with JavaScript, so we'll focus on the HTML and CSS parts of the 1140 CSS Grid. Also, the 1140 grid doesn't need JavaScript when visitors use browsers that recognize media queries; however, it includes Google's script for handling media queries on older browsers (called css3-mediaqueries.js). The file index.html is interesting, because it shows many possible arrangements of the columns. There are other possible arrangements, but the permutations shown in the sample index.html file cover most use cases. The css/1140.css file does the heavy lifting of creating the grid. The css/styles.css file provides hooks for adding your own styles at various resolutions. The css/ie.css file provides workarounds for versions of Internet Explorer prior to IE9. You should write a conditional statement to load css/ie.css when visitors who use older versions of Internet Explorer visit your site. The following line shows an example of such a statement:

```
<!--[if lte IE 9]><link rel="stylesheet" href="css/ie.css" type="text/css" media="screen"
/><![endif]-->
```

Sometimes, by the way, it's worthwhile to skip the condition and merge the various style sheets into a single style sheet. It seems counterintuitive that a single large style sheet can perform better than conditionally loading a specific style sheet. However, we recently did some testing of merged style sheets and found better page-load times. It really is true that the best thing one can do for page-load times is reduce HTTP requests. Each situation is unique, though, so test your own alternative solutions to discover what's best for your site.

Let's start with some of this grid's basic ideas. Essentially, you assign class names to denote how many columns (out of twelve) you'd like your particular element to occupy (i.e., onecol, twocol, etc). The 1140 CSS Grid is named after its maximum width of 1140 pixels. This is as big as your site can get with this grid. This may seem a bit wide to many who are used to using 960 pixels as standard size (to accommodate smaller screen resolutions). However, thanks to flexible grids, no one is tied to a static size any longer. If a visitor has a screen resolution of 1024 x 768, the grid resizes all of its columns so that 12 columns still fit in the width of that screen. That's pretty liberating. Of course, you still need to test your site at different resolutions to make sure you're comfortable with the layout changes. Once you go below tablet size, you probably want to make some more drastic decisions with regard to your layout. Until then, though, the smaller columns work pretty well.

Once you've got the grid installed and figured out, you can make some basic page structure decisions such as where to put the header, body, footer, and so on. The great thing is that these elements will all resize properly without any further work. For our sample e-commerce site, we've chosen the basic layout shown in Figure 6-4.

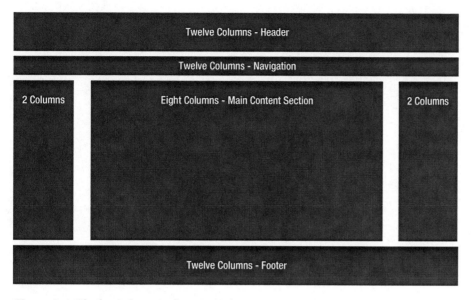

Figure 6-4. The basic layout of our sample e-commerce site

To achieve this layout intention, we have to wrap column elements in a couple of parent elements. Listing 6-8 shows this relationship.

Listing 6-8. Relationship of Parent Elements to the Grid

```
<div class="container">
  <div class = "row">
    <div class="twelvecol"></div>
  </div>
</div>
```

The div element with the class of container spans the entire width of your visitor's browser. The div element with a class of row will be the outer width of your site. If your visitor has a browser width of 1200 pixels or more, the grid's width is 1140 pixels (the maximum set by the 1140 grid). As visitors using smaller resolutions arrive at your site, its width shrinks as resolutions go below 1140. The div element with the class of twelvecol holds the content of your site. Because we've used the maximum number of columns, this div element's width will be 100 percent of the width of the row div. This arrangement may remind you of an HTML table structure, which it resembles not only structurally but also functionally, because the column widths flex according to the available width. The container div corresponds to the table element, the row div corresponds to the tr element, and the twelvecol div corresponds to the td element.

Getting back to our sample e-commerce site, Listing 6-9 shows the HTML elements that form the site's framework.

Listing 6-9. Our Sample e-Commerce Site's Base Structure

```
<header class="container">
  <section class="row">
    <nav class="twelvecol">
      This is the Main Header Section
    </nav>
  </section>
</header>

<nav class="container">
  <section class="row">
    <div class="twelvecol">
      This is the Main Navigation Section
    </div>
  </section>
</nav>

<section class="container">
  <div class="row">
    <div class="twocol">
      Left Column
    </div>
    <div class="eightcol">
      Content Area
    </div>
    <div class="twocol last">
      Right Column
    </div>
  </div>
</section>

<footer class="container mainFooter">
  <section class="row">
    <nav class="twelvecol">
      This is the Main Footer Section
    </nav>
  </section>
</footer>
```

As you can see, we set our container, row, and column classes on elements other than divs. To retain a clean intention, it's best to set these classes on block level elements. You can also see that we've added a class of last to the right column div. You need to do this to the last column of a multicolumn layout. Its sole function is to take away the right margin so that content doesn't wrap unexpectedly.

We now have the basic structure for our responsive e-commerce site. We'll further tweak the layout for tablets and mobile devices after we've completed filling out our new structure with our controls and content.

Summary

In this chapter, we introduced the idea of using a template page as the foundation of all (or at least most of) the pages on a site. To make such a page, we introduced the excellent tool made available by the good people behind `http://html5boilerplate.com`.

We also covered all the various settings created for us by the html5boilerplate.com tool, including

- Conditional statements in Internet Explorer.
- Setting the character set.
- Controlling IE's compatibility mode.
- Prompting for installation of Google Chrome frame.
- Controlling the viewport on iPhones.
- Loading jQuery.
- Adding Google Analytics.

Last but not least, we described the grid system we'll use for the entire site. The 1140 CSS grid does everything we need in a flexible grid, even gracefully handling mobile devices.

We won't address most of this information (except for possibly a passing reference here and there) throughout the rest of the book. However, when you examine the code behind our sample site, you'll see these features on every page.

CHAPTER 7

■ ■ ■

Navigation

Unless you're making just a splash page, navigation is an essential aspect of your site. So you should really think about your strategy when it comes to this crucial element of your site's success. Besides having a good taxonomy, you need to have a clear way for visitors to find and explore the different offerings available on your site. You can sometimes be tempted to throw a lot of pizzazz and weight into your interface, especially if you start with the design first. However, content is king. Consequently, as a rule, your navigation should never compete for attention with your content. That being said, your navigation should be easy to see and, more importantly, easy to use.

To make a navigation scheme really easy to use, you should support different kinds of visitor behavior. Different people like to navigate sites in different ways, and you should support all the common ways of navigating a site, lest you drive away users who can't navigate as they wish. A great book on usability, *Don't Make Me Think*,[1] has an analogy: think of your site as a department store. Some shoppers look at department signs and then go through the aisles until they find the item they want. Some seek out a store employee to ask where that item is. The first shoppers are the visitors who use menus to find the content they want. The shoppers who ask clerks are those who would use a site search. You should provide mechanisms for both groups.

To extend the analogy a bit, department stores put some items from the aisles on the end caps so that they can show the items to visitors as they stroll by. You should consider offering a similar form of navigation, through a design element such as side navigation, which includes items that are also available in the main navigation (usually a drop-down menu). We call that kind of navigation "tertiary navigation," because it is the third of our navigation schemes, with the menu and search being the first two.

Before plunging into the code behind the menu, it make sense to show an image of the menu we create in the rest of this chapter. Figure 7-1 shows most of the menu (it's wider than the width of the page, but the figure shows most of it).

Computer Hardware   Electronics   Gaming   Accessories   Software

Figure 7-1. Menu in a ready state

While we're at it, let's look at some of the menu's expanded forms. Figure 7-2 shows an expanded view of the Gaming submenu.

---

1   Steve Krug, *Don't make me think! A common sense approach to Web usability* (New Riders Press, second edition, 2005)

Figure 7-2. Menu with Gaming responding to a mouse hover

Menu Structure

When creating a menu structure, you want the HTML that defines the menu's content to

- Be meaningful.
- Be readable.
- Be easy for screen readers to follow (or ignore).
- Be a good fit for progressive design goals.

When we say that you want meaningful HTML for the menu, we mean that you want to be able to look at its source and see the relationships between the various elements (containers and content). When we say that you want readable HTML, we mean that you don't want it to be a pain to follow because it's jumbled up or uses hard-to-understand class names. When we say you want a menu structure that's easy for screen readers to follow, we mean that you want a menu structure that won't waste undue amounts of time for visually impaired visitors (this will be covered in more detail later in the chapter). Finally, when we say you want HTML that meets progressive design goals, we mean that you want content that won't hinder you from providing the best possible display for each of your target browsers.

We can choose from a large number of possible representations of the menu structure, because HTML provides considerable flexibility for expressing this kind of content. To meet those goals, nested unordered lists make the most sense. Since the list-within-list approach is a natural mapping of a menu's content, it readily meets the goals of being meaningful and readable. When we listen to screen readers go through a menu, the list-within-list structure offers the most direct aural representation of a menu. Finally, we know we can make a list-within-list structure work for progressive enhancement goals, as we demonstrate in the rest of the chapter.

Finally, the relatively natural structure of the nested-list approach should be as future-proof as anything can be. The number of web-enabled devices continues to grow by leaps and bounds, so there is no way to know when your site will show up on someone's refrigerator (honestly, don't be surprised).

Listing 7-1 shows the basic menu structure.

▓ **Note** nm in the class names that follow stands for navMain. Similarly, L2 indicates a component of a second-level list. We're fiends for saving bytes and also lazy typists.

Listing 7-1. Basic Menu Structure

```
<ul class="navMainUL">
  <li class="nmLI"><a href="javascript:;" class="nmA">Level 1 Menu Item</a>
    <ul class="nmUL-L2">
      <li class="nmLI-L2"><a href="javascript:;" class="nmA-L2">Level 2 Menu Item</a></li>
      <li class="nmLI-L2"><a href="javascript:;" class="nmA-L2">Level 2 Menu Item</a></li>
      <li class="nmLI-L2"><a href="javascript:;" class="nmA-L2">Level 2 Menu Item</a></li>
    </ul>
  </li>
  <li class="nmLI"><a href="javascript:;" class="nmA">Level 1 Menu Item</a></li>
  <li class="nmLI"><a href="javascript:;" class="nmA">Level 1 Menu Item</a></li>
  <li class="nmLI"><a href="javascript:;" class="nmA">Level 1 Menu Item</a></li>
  <li class="nmLI"><a href="javascript:;" class="nmA">Level 1 Menu Item</a></li>
</ul>
```

We use a very basic structure that you'll find in many navigation schemes (following convention is good when convention works well). With no styling or scripting, a browser renders this structure as shown in Figure 7-3.

- Level 1 Menu Item
  - Level 2 Menu Item
  - Level 2 Menu Item
  - Level 2 Menu Item
- Level 1 Menu Item
- Level 1 Menu Item
- Level 1 Menu Item
- Level 1 Menu Item

Figure 7-3. Unordered list before styling

You can see that the menu structure is readable and expresses the correct nesting. In this case, the Level 2 Menu Items are children of a parent Level 1 Menu Item. We can now add styling and functionality to bring out your intent. Before getting to styling, though, let's look at the HTML that provides the actual menu.

As you read the following listing, you are likely to notice the extra div element surrounding the tier 2 navigation. Its class name is nmSlideout zeroHeight. The extra markup enables the slideout trickery (which we'll cover with the styling of the menu elements). Next, you'll probably noticed that we added a search box in the last LI element (with a class of nmLI searchWrap) in the tier 1 menu.

Let's take a moment to discuss what might be a sticking point for some standards-based developers: the expressive use of class names throughout this example (and all of our HTML code). We've adopted this approach because it has served us well, as we'll now explain.

On the one side, you might say that giving class names to nested elements can be done with less markup by using CSS nesting. For example, instead of having an li element with a class of nmLI, you could instead get at that li element by declaring its parent and drilling in as follows: .nmUL li. That would indeed get the first-level li elements, the second-level li elements, and any li elements thereafter. While a selector such as .nmUL li li could be used to target those further nested li elements, doing so gets more convoluted (and harder to read is hard to maintain—a future drag on development is definitely not wanted).

As important as avoiding convoluted code is, it is not the best reason to use more code to give these elements their own class. Rendering performance is the bigger reason. Using the descendant approach of selecting elements yields less than optimal performance. Here's why: the CSS selector engine works from right to left. In the case of the .nmUL li selector, the browser first gathers all of the li elements into a collection and then tries to find li elements whose ancestors have a class of .nmUL. That's a lot of crawling up the DOM tree to find out if each li element has a .nmUL ancestor somewhere up the tree. Far better performance can be had by using selectors with identifiers. The best performance (but not much better than identifiers) comes from using ID attributes as selectors. It's worth taking the tiny hit on performance from using identifiers rather than ID attributes, because the identifiers can be used many times over. However, don't accept the much larger performance hit of going up and down the DOM many times because of descendant selectors.

Another great reason not to use descendant selectors is that that approach ties your CSS to the structure of your HTML. So if you ever change the structure to ul li span span, for example, you now have broken CSS—and a glaring black eye in the middle of your navigation. Also, you lose the ability to reuse classes you've defined for other elements that might have similar styling but different structure.

Finally, it's just plain easier for a developer to work with explicitly named elements. Considering that the cost of all of these benefits is probably going to be less than that of a couple of thousand additional instances of class names, you gain a lot for a low cost.

Listing 7-2 shows the actual code we're going to use for the navigation.

Listing 7-2. Navigation HTML

```html
<ul class="navMainUL nmDropDown clearfix" role="navigation">
  <li class="visuallyhidden">
    <h3 class="assistive-text">Main menu</h3>
    <div class="skip-link">
        <a class="assistive-text" href="#content" title="Skip to primary content">Skip to
primary content</a>
    </div>
  </li>
  <li class="nmLI first">
    <a href="javascript:;" class="nmA">Computer Hardware
    </a>
    <div class="nmSlideout zeroHeight">
      <ul class="nmUL-L2 ">
        <li class="nmLI-L2">
          <a href="" class="nmA-L2">Computer Cases</a>
        </li>
        <li class="nmLI-L2">
          <a href="" class="nmA-L2">Hard Drives</a>
        </li>
        <li class="nmLI-L2">
          <a href="" class="nmA-L2">Monitors</a>
        </li>
        <li class="nmLI-L2 nmLast">
          <a href="" class="nmA-L2">Printers &amp; Scanners</a>
```

```
      </li>
    </ul>
  </div>
</li>
<li class="nmLI">
  <a href="javascript:;" class="nmA">Electronics</a>
  <div class="nmSlideout zeroHeight">
    <ul class="nmUL-L2 ">
      <li class="nmLI-L2">
        <a href="" class="nmA-L2">Television</a>
      </li>
      <li class="nmLI-L2">
        <a href="" class="nmA-L2">Home Video</a>
      </li>
      <li class="nmLI-L2 nmLast">
        <a href="" class="nmA-L2">Home Theater Solutions</a>
      </li>
      <li class="nmLI-L2 nmLast">
        <a href="" class="nmA-L2">Headphones &amp; Accessories</a>
      </li>
      <li class="nmLI-L2 nmLast">
        <a href="" class="nmA-L2">Tablets &amp; Accessories</a>
      </li>
    </ul>
  </div>
</li>
<li class="nmLI">
  <a href="javascript:;" class="nmA">Gaming</a>
  <div class="nmSlideout zeroHeight">
    <ul class="nmUL-L2 ">
      <li class="nmLI-L2">
        <a href="" class="nmA-L2">Xbox 360</a>
      </li>
      <li class="nmLI-L2">
        <a href="" class="nmA-L2">Playstation 3</a>
      </li>
      <li class="nmLI-L2 nmLast">
        <a href="" class="nmA-L2">PC Games &amp; Accessories</a>
      </li>
      <li class="nmLI-L2">
        <a href="" class="nmA-L2">Nintendo</a>
      </li>
      <li class="nmLI-L2">
        <a href="" class="nmA-L2">Mac Games</a>
      </li>
    </ul>
  </div>
</li>
<li class="nmLI">
  <a href="javascript:;" class="nmA">Accessories</a>
  <div class="nmSlideout zeroHeight">
```

```
        <ul class="nmUL-L2 ">
          <li class="nmLI-L2">
            <a href="" class="nmA-L2">Cables</a>
          </li>
          <li class="nmLI-L2">
            <a href="" class="nmA-L2">Desktop Computer Accessories</a>
          </li>
          <li class="nmLI-L2">
            <a href="" class="nmA-L2">Display Accessories</a>
          </li>
          <li class="nmLI-L2">
            <a href="" class="nmA-L2">Network Accessories</a>
          </li>
          <li class="nmLI-L2">
            <a href="" class="nmA-L2">Gaming Accessories</a>
          </li>
        </ul>
      </div>
    </li>
    <li class="nmLI last">
      <a href="javascript:;" class="nmA">Software</a>
      <div class="nmSlideout zeroHeight">
        <ul class="nmUL-L2 ">
          <li class="nmLI-L2">
            <a href="" class="nmA-L2">Books</a>
          </li>
          <li class="nmLI-L2">
            <a href="" class="nmA-L2">Graphic &amp; Design</a>
          </li>
          <li class="nmLI-L2">
            <a href="" class="nmA-L2">Mac Games</a>
          </li>
          <li class="nmLI-L2">
            <a href="" class="nmA-L2">Mac Software</a>
          </li>
          <li class="nmLI-L2">
            <a href="" class="nmA-L2">Server Software</a>
          </li>
        </ul>
      </div>
    </li>
    <li class="nmLI searchWrap">
      <input type="search" id="searchInput" class="searchInput" placeholder="Site Search" />
      <button class="searchBtn siteGrad">Search</button>
    </li>
</ul>
```

When the rendering engine finishes with the CSS, it'll look like Figure 7-4.

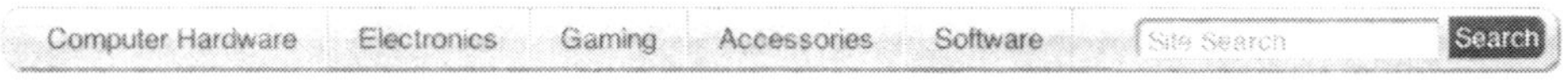

Computer Hardware   Electronics   Gaming   Accessories   Software   Site Search   Search

Figure 7-4. Tier 1 Styling

■ **Note**   Before talking about the rest of the menu, we want to point out the invisible menu item, identified by `class="visuallyhidden"`. That menu item, along with the link within it, lets visitors who use screen readers skip the menu. If you've ever suffered through listening to a menu, you can understand why this option is friendly to visually impaired visitors. Since it's very important to accommodate all users, be careful to include this kind of convenience for people whose visual abilities differ from those of the average visitor.

Styling the Menu

Now that we've detailed the structure of the menu and its selectors, let's move on to turning that nested list into a menu. We'll start by styling the parent ul element. Figure 7-5 shows the desired design treatment.

Figure 7-5. UL styling viewed in a modern browser

We're not using images for this treatment; in other words, the menu is defined entirely through code. We're heavily leveraging CSS3 to get a lot of extra visual impact, so you might reasonably wonder, "What about IE8?" Well, that brings up another point, and it's a big one. Not all browsers need to show the exact same presentation. In fact, it's a mistake to try to get all browsers to show exactly the same presentation. As we stated before, we worked at one of the top-five e-commerce sites. And got everyone in our organization on board with having a degraded state for IE6 through IE8. What this means is that if you're viewing our site with IE6 through IE8, you're still going to see a great site. It just won't have rounded corners and drop-shadows.

Dropping the insistence that every browser get the same treatment buys greatly increased speed of development, leaner and simpler code, responsive design options, and faster page loads (since there aren't any extra HTTP requests). That's a lot of gain for square corners and shadowless boxes on the older browsers that, as our statistics show, not many of our visitors use.

Of course, it's up to you and your employer or customer to decide if this is an option for you, and you can still make all of these menus however you like. Still, we strongly recommend evangelizing the concept of a degraded state for older browsers. It's really a win for everybody. Since people who use older browsers don't often see cutting-edge designs, they are not likely to notice that they're not getting it at your site, and you gain all the benefits of a much cleaner code base. Of course, that's not a license to give visitors with older browsers a poor experience; they should still get the best experience their browser can readily accommodate. As our technical reviewer (hi, Jeff) noted, it's a lot like watching a color TV program on a black-and-white TV; there's definitely something missing, but it's what that viewer gets. All the TV crew can do is try to ensure that the picture at least shows up on a black-and-white TV. Finally, with rounded corners losing their cachet in the design world, we're all chasing a diminishing return for no good reason.

Figure 7-6 shows what IE8 visitors actually see. It still provides the correct information and functionality and doesn't look bad, especially for visitors who seldom see rounded corners anyway. (Jay says it looks cleaner, in fact, but he was never a devotee of rounded corners.)

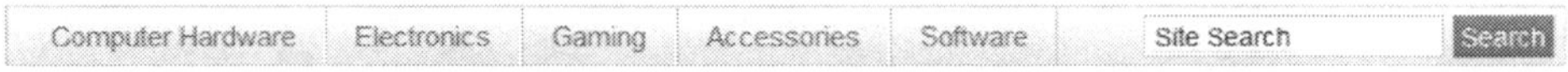

Figure 7-6. Tier 1 styling as viewed on older browsers

Let's get back to styling this menu. Listing 7-3 shows the CSS for the parent ul element:

Listing 7-3. CSS for the Parent UL

```
.navMainUL {
  display: block;
  min-height: 31px;
  padding: 0 5px 0 8px;
  border: 1px solid #cdbec4;
  width: 100%;
  margin-right: 5px;
  -webkit-box-sizing: border-box;
  -moz-box-sizing: border-box;
  box-sizing: border-box;
  -webkit-box-shadow: 2px 2px 2px #999999;
  -moz-box-shadow: 2px 2px 2px #999999;
  box-shadow: 2px 2px 2px #999999;
  -webkit-border-radius: 10px;
  -moz-border-radius: 10px;
  border-radius: 10px;
  -moz-background-clip: padding;
  -webkit-background-clip: padding-box;
  background-clip: padding-box;
  z-index: 20;
  position: relative;
  -moz-background-clip: padding;
  -webkit-background-clip: padding-box;
  background-clip: padding-box;
  /* Background */

  background: #fefefe;
  background: url(data:image/svg+xml;base64,PD94bWwgdmVyc2lvbj0iMS4wIiA/Pgo8c3ZnIHhtbG5zPSJodHRw
```

Oi8vd3d3LnczLm9yZy8yMDAwL3N2ZyIgd2lkdGg9IjEwMCUiIGhlaWdodD0iMTAwJSIgdmlld0JveD0iMCAwIDEgMSIgcHJl
c2VydmVBc3BlY3RSYXRpbz0ibm9uZSI+CiAgPGxpbmVhckdyYWRpZW50IGlkPSJncmFkLXVjZ2ctZ2VuZXJhdGVkIiBncmFk
aWVudFVuaXRzPSJ1c2VyU3BhY2VPblVzZSIgeDE9IjAlIiB5MToiMCUiIHgyPSIwJSIgeTI9IjEwMCUiPgogICAgPHN0b3Ag
b2Zmc2V0PSIwJSIgc3RvcC1jb2xvcj0iI2ZlZmVmZSIgc3RvcC1vcGFjaXR5PSIxIi8+CiAgICA8c3RvcCBvZmZzZXQ9IjEz
JSIgc3RvcC1jb2xvcj0iI2ZiZjlmYSIgc3RvcC1vcGFjaXR5PSIxIi8+CiAgICA8c3RvcCBvZmZzZXQ9IjQzJSIgc3RvcC1j
b2xvcj0iI2VjZTVlOCIgc3RvcC1jb2xvcGFjaXR5PSIxIi8+CiAgICA8c3RvcCBvZmZzZXQ9IjUyJSIgc3RvcC1jb2xvcj0iI2Rh
ZDNkNiIgc3RvcC1jb2xvcGFjaXR5PSIxIi8+CiAgICA8c3RvcCBvZmZzZXQ9IjU4JSIgc3RvcC1jb2xvcj0iI2RhZGNkNyIgc3Rv
cC1vcGFjaXR5PSIxIi8+CiAgICA8c3RvcCBvZmZzZXQ9IjEwMCUiIHN0b3AtY29sb3I9IiNlOGU4ZTgiIHN0b3Atb3BhY2l0
eToiMSIvPgogIDwvbGluZWFyR3JhZGllbnQ+CiAgPHJlY3QgeDoiMCIgeToiMCIgd2lkdGg9IjEiIGhlaWdodD0iMSIgZmls

```
bDOidXJsKCNncmFkLXVjZ2ctZ2VuZXJhdGVkKSIgLz4KPC9zdmc+);
  background: -moz-linear-gradient(top, #fefefe 0%, #fbf9fa 13%, #ece5e8 48%, #dad3d6 52%,
#dad3d7 58%, #e8e8e8 100%);
  background: -webkit-gradient(linear, left top, left bottom, color-stop(0%, #fefefe),
color-stop(13%, #fbf9fa), color-stop(48%, #ece5e8), color-stop(52%, #dad3d6), color-stop(58%,
#dad3d7), color-stop(100%, #e8e8e8));
  background: -webkit-linear-gradient(top, #fefefe 0%, #fbf9fa 13%, #ece5e8 48%, #dad3d6 52%,
#dad3d7 58%, #e8e8e8 100%);
  background: -o-linear-gradient(top, #fefefe 0%, #fbf9fa 13%, #ece5e8 48%, #dad3d6 52%, #dad3d7
58%, #e8e8e8 100%);
  background: -ms-linear-gradient(top, #fefefe 0%, #fbf9fa 13%, #ece5e8 48%, #dad3d6 52%,
#dad3d7 58%, #e8e8e8 100%);
  background: linear-gradient(top, #fefefe 0%, #fbf9fa 13%, #ece5e8 48%, #dad3d6 52%, #dad3d7
58%, #e8e8e8 100%);
  filter: progid:dximagetransform.microsoft.gradient(startColorstr='#fefefe',
endColorstr='#e8e8e8', GradientType=0);
}
```

There's a lot of CSS here, but most of it is the different vendor prefixes (i.e., –moz, -webkit, etc.). There's no need to explain all of the CSS, because it's pretty basic. However, it would help to go over some of the CSS3 goodness that's going on. Specifically, we should explain that funky background base64 image about which you might be scratching your head.

■ **Note** Microsoft filters can lead to very poor performance. If you can do without them, skip them. We included them here to support Internet Explorer and to provide a complete example.

Box sizing

Box sizing has been a bone of contention since the early days of browsers (and the problem goes back much further, to the earliest days of page-layout software). The fundamental issue is what to do with the padding, the margins, and the border.

Suppose you specify a div element with a width of 100 pixels, 20 pixels of padding, and 20 pixels of margin. (For simplicity's sake, let's set the border to 0.) How wide will the resulting element actually be? Well, it depends on who implemented the box sizing. (If anything drives developers nuts, it's the phrase "it depends," which always means they have to code for multiple conditions.) Some folks at Microsoft thought that the box should be 140 pixels wide: 20 for the left margin, 100 for the box itself, and 20 for the right margin. In that case, the padding is inside the box, so the content area is 60 pixels wide. The specification and most of the folks implementing it say the box should be 180 pixels wide. In that implementation both the margins and the padding are outside the box, leaving a content area 100 pixels wide.

Which one seems right is largely a matter of taste, and many folks have taken a whack at justifying one method or another. Strictly speaking, Microsoft's implementation was a bug. However, their implementation made sense to a lot of people, including Michael. So the whole issue has raised a bit of a controversy.

To make matters more interesting (in the sense of a certain well-known curse, that is), different versions of Internet Explorer implement box sizing in different ways. Prior to version 6, Internet Explorer reduced the content area by the value of the padding. Starting with version 6, Internet Explorer would honor the specification (putting padding outside the content area) in its standards-compliant mode but not in its quirks mode. Since Internet Explorer goes into standards-compliant mode when a valid document type is present, specifying a valid document type turns out to be the way to control this behavior. For an added wrinkle, Internet Explorer for the Mac never reduced the content area.

▓ **Author's Note**   Michael says, "Personally, and as much as it pains me to say this, I actually agreed with the way the IE version of the box model worked. To me it made more sense when you tried to use real-world analogies. If I had a shipping box and added padding to it, the box itself didn't get bigger. The space inside got smaller."

Jay prefers sticking to standards like glue, but he let Mike do it Mike's way this time, because Jay agrees that the content area changing its width would be bad.

We do agree that the box-sizing property can be handy if you're doing mobile web development or can otherwise rely on visitors having CSS3-capable browsers.

We elected to use a box-sizing property so that we can set a width of 100 percent and still set padding in pixel units. That's handy because we don't want the padding to flex or "self-adjust" because of resizing across different display devices.

Listing 7-4. *Setting the Box-Sizing Model*

```
box-sizing: border-box;
```

Standard CSS3 candy

Of course, we've used rounded corners and drop shadows. We won't go into detail, because the code reads pretty well on its own. Also, chances are good that you've heard enough about these particular features.

The gradient

If you're saying that this is a verbose piece of CSS to describe the background of the ul element, we agree with you. The good news is we didn't have to write all that, and neither do you. The fine folks at ColorZilla, who brought you the color picker plug-in for Firefox, have also made quite possibly one of the coolest CSS web apps we've seen. It's called, appropriately, Ultimate CSS Gradient Generator. You can find it at http://www.colorzilla.com/gradient-editor/.

In essence, it's a very powerful ("ultimate" comes pretty close) gradient generator that outputs a fairly bulletproof piece of code to make sure your gradient either displays well or falls back progressively. All for the low, low price of free! Let's check out the gradient in their interface, as shown in Figure 7-7.

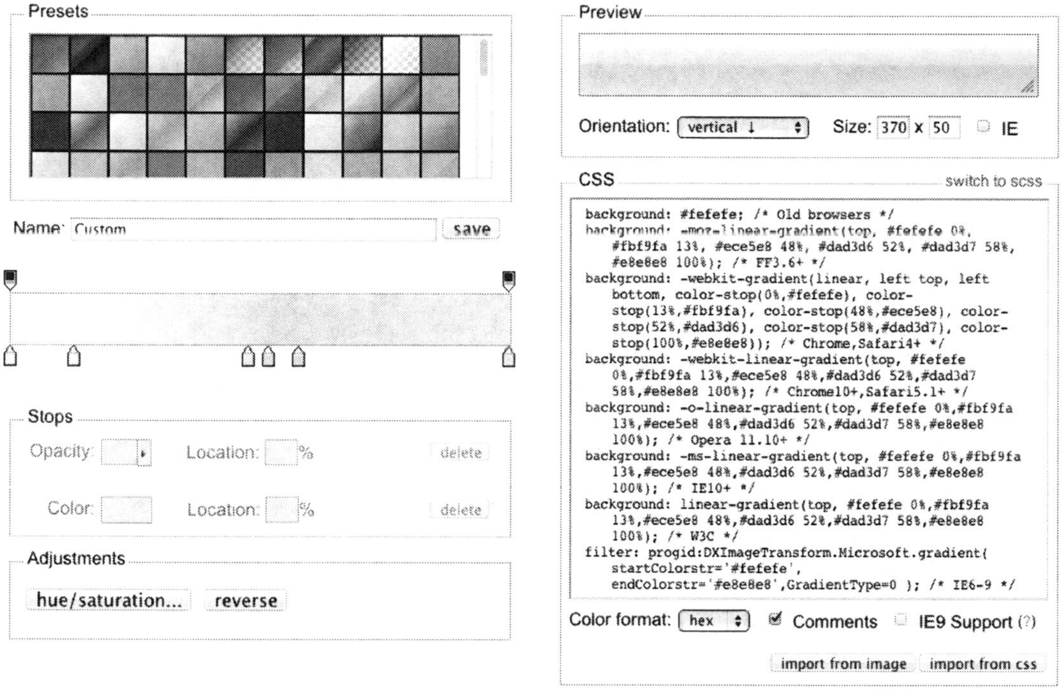

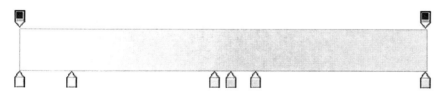

Figure 7-7. *The Ultimate CSS Gradient Generator*

Notice in the Presets pane that you can choose from a lot of different starting points. You can also just dive in, ignore the presets, and brew up your own gradient from scratch.

Below the Presets pane is where the magic happens. You can save your gradient by entering a name and hitting Save. This comes in handy if you need to tweak your creation later. The actual inputs for your gradient are below the Save feature.

Figure 7-8. *Gradient picker*

On the top of Figure 7-8, the two black boxes constitute the opacity chooser. For this example, we'll be using 100 percent opacity (that's why the handles are solid black), but you have the option to make some really interesting combinations with the opacity. We encourage you to experiment. The row of boxes on the bottom is where the colors are defined and where the "stops" are. Stops, defined in percentages, basically tell the tool where the colors may change. Then the tool takes care of working out the colors that map between the stops to make a smooth gradient. You can change the colors by double-clicking on the squares and make more stops by clicking in an adjacent area to the left or right. You can also change colors by clicking one of the color boxes and then clicking in the Color box in the Stops pane below it. It's helpful to have to alternative ways to choose colors because it's easy to accidentally move the color boxes when you double-click.

Figure 7-9 shows the colors we selected.

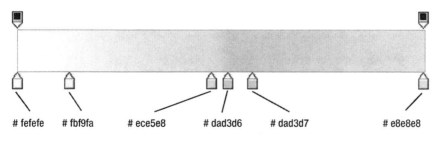

Figure 7-9. *Gradient colors*

In the Adjustments pane below the Stops pane you'll have some additional options to make sweeping hue/saturation changes and also reverse your color order.

Directly to the right of the Presets pane is the Preview pane, which is where you'll see your gradient take shape. Under the preview bar are options for orientation: vertical, horizontal, diagonal, and radial. The size option is just the size of the preview; it doesn't affect the outputted CSS. Next to that is the IE check box, which will let you see your gradient expressed with two colors (this is the fallback part mentioned earlier). Again, this check box doesn't affect the code; it's just another way of previewing.

The CSS pane contains the output. There are several options, including what format you want for your colors (hex, rgba, hsl, etc.). You have the option to leave comments in the code (we usually save the bytes here and turn those off). You can also use the IE9 Support check box. IE9 has come a long way from earlier versions in supporting HTML5 and related technologies. However, some gaps remain, and gradients (at least complex gradients, such as this example) is one of them. You can still use a gradient (by specifying `filter: progid:DXImageTransform.Microsoft.gradient`), but it supports only two colors. One of the great abilities of this tool is that it creates a base64-encoded SVG that matches the gradient being defined. How cool is that? To make that work, though, you need to disable the filter option for IE9. The tool offers code for that purpose, as shown in Listing 7-5.

Listing 7-5. *Turning Off the Filter for IE9*

```
<!--[if gte IE 9]>
<style type="text/css">    .gradient {        filter: none;    }  </style> <![endif]-->
```

Here's our old friend, the conditional statement. If the browser is IE9, this statement disables the filter. From there, you need only add the `gradient` class to the applicable elements, as shown earlier in Listing 7-3.

In addition to a long list of browser prefixes, it also gives support for different versions of those browsers. And if all else fails, it defines a flat background color that matches the first color in the slider.

Next, we have the `li` elements within the `ul` element; they form the containers for the tier 1 and tier 2 navigation elements. Figure 7-10 reminds you what it looks like.

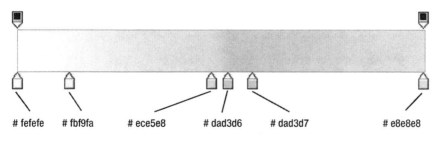

Figure 7-10. *Main menu in a modern browser*

Listing 7-6 shows an li element that defines a menu item

Listing 7-6. An li Element to Define a Menu Item

```
<li class="nmLI">
  <a href="javascript:;" class="nmA">Computer Hardware </a>
  <div class="nmSlideout zeroHeight"></div>
</li>
```

Listing 7-7 shows the CSS that styles a menu item.

Listing 7-7. The CSS That Styles a Menu Item

```
.nmLI {
  border-right: 1px solid white;
  border-left: 1px solid #ccc;
  list-style: none;
  text-align: center;
  position: relative;
  background: rgba(0, 0, 0, 0);
  display: block;
  float: left;
  padding: 0px;
  min-height: 31px;
}
.nmLI.first {
  border-left: none;
}
.nmLI.last {
  border-right-color: #ccc;
  border-left-color: #ccc;
}
.nmLI:hover {
  background: #a29da0;
}
.nmLI:hover:before {
  content: "";
```

```
  background: url(data:image/gif;base64,iVBORw0KGgoAAAANSUhEUgAAAAQAAAAjCAMAAACEhlvCAAAAGXRFWHRT
b2Z0d2FyZQBBZG9iZSBJbWFnZVJlYWR5ccllPAAAA+dpVFh0WE1MOmNvbS5hZG9iZS54bXAAAAAAADw/eHBhY2tldCBiZWdp
bj0i77u/IiBpZD0iVzVNME1wQ2VoaUh6cmVTek5UY3prYZlkIj8+IDx4OnhtcG1ldGEgeG1sbnM6eD0iYWRvYmU6bnM6bWV0
YS8iIHg6eG1wdGs9IkFkb2JlIFhNUCBDb3JlIDUuMC1jMjYwIDYxLjEzNDc3NywgMjAxMC8wMi8xMi0xNzozMjowMCAgICAg
ICAgIj4gPHJkZjpSREYgeG1sbnM6cmRmPSJodHRwOi8vd3d3LnczLm9yZy8xOTk5LzAyLzIyLXJkZi1zeW50YXgtbnMjIj4g
PHJkZjpEZXNjcmlwdGlvbiByZGY6YWJvdXQ9IiIgeG1sbnM6eG1wPSJodHRwOi8vbnMuYWRvYmUuY29tL3hhcC8xLjAvIiB4
bWxuczpkYz0iaHR0cDovL3B1cmwub3JnL2RjL2VsZW1lbnRzLzEuMS8iIHhtbG5zOnhtcE1NPSJodHRwOi8vbnMuYWRvYmUu
Y29tL3hhcC8xLjAvbW0vIiB4bWxuczpzdFJlZj0iaHR0cDovL25zLmFkb2JlLmNvbS94YXAvMS4wL3NUeXBlL1Jlc291cmNl
UmVmIyIgeG1wOkNyZWF0b3JUb29sPSJBZG9iZSBQaG90b3Nob3AgQ1M1IE1hY2ludG9zaCIgeG1wOkNyZWF0ZURhdGU9IjIw
MTItMDUtMDFUMDA6NDk6MTgtMDU6MDAiIHhtcDpNb2RpZnlEYXRlPSIyMDEyLTA1LTAxVDA20jI20jA3LTA1OjAwIiB4bXA6
TWV0YWRhdGFEYXRlPSIyMDEyLTA1LTAxVDA20jI20jA3LTA1OjAwIiBkYzpmb3JtYXQ9ImltYWdlL3BuZyIgeG1wTU06SW5z
dGFuY2VJRD0ieG1wLmlpZDpGODBFRRTIORDhCNzcxMUUxQjc2RUI3REExQzg1RUEyMSIgeG1wTU06RG9jdW1lbnRJRD0ieG1w
LmRpZDpGODBFRRTIORThCNzcxMUUxQjc2RUI3REExQzg1RUEyMSI+IDx4bXBNTTpEZXJpdmVkRnJvbSBzdFJlZjppbnN0YW5j
ZUlEPSJ4bXAuaWlkOkY4MEVFRFmjRCOEI3NzExRTFCNzZFQjdEQTFDODVFQTIxIiBzdFJlZjpkb2N1bWVudElEPSJ4bXAuZGlk
OkY4MEVFRmjRDOEI3NzExRTFCNzZFQjdEQTFDODVFQTIxIi8+IDwvcmRmOkRlc2NyaXB0aW9uPiA8L3JkZjpSREY+IDwveDp4
```

bXBtZXRhPiA8P3hwYWNrZXQgZW5kPSJyIj8+tVKbSQAAABhQTFRFmJSXb2ttgX1/j4uNk4+ShYGDcm5wnpmckwoARwAAABdJ
REFUeNpiYGRiZmBgY2VhHxIEQIABAPz1AvMeVbYrAAAAAElFTkSuQmCC);

```
    display: block;
    position: absolute;
    width: 4px;
    height: 33px;
    left: 0;
    top: 0;
}
```

The only tricky item here is the last ruleset, .nmLI:hover:before, which we'll get to next. Before we proceed, we thought you should see how the menu looks. Of course, you can also go to our sample web site (http://clikz.us) to see it in action. Figure 7-11 shows the Gaming submenu.

Figure 7-11. *The Gaming submenu*

:before and :after Pseudo-classes

Remember the :before pseudo-class? To save you the trouble of finding it, Listing 7-8 repeats that class.

Listing 7-8. *The :before Pseudo-class*

```
.nmLI:hover:before {
    content: "";
    background: url(data:image/gif;base64,iVBORw0KGgoAAAANSUhEUgAAAAQAAAAjCAMAAACEhlvCAAAAGXRFWHRT
```
b2Z0d2FyZQBBZG9iZSBJbWFnZVJlYWR5ccllPAAAA+dpVFh0WE1MOmNvbS5hZG9iZS54bXAAAAAAADw/eHBhY2tldCBiZWdp
bj0i77u/IiBpZD0iVzVNME1wQ2VoaUh6cmVTek5UY3prYzlkIj8+IDx4OnhtcG1ldGEgeG1sbnM6eD0iYWRvYmU6bnM6bWV0Y
YS8iIHg6eG1wdGs9IkFkb2JlIFhNUCBDb3JlIDUuMC1jMDYwIDYxLjEzNDc3NywgMjAxMC8wMi8xMi0xNzozMjowMCAgICAg
ICAgIj4gPHJkZjpSREYgeG1sbnM6cmRmPSJodHRwOi8vd3d3LnczLm9yZy8xOTk5LzAyLzIyLXJkZi1zeW50YXgtbnMjIj4g
PHJkZjpEZXNjcmlwdGlvbiByZGY6YWJvdXQ9IiIgeG1sbnM6eG1wPSJodHRwOi8vbnMuYWRvYmUuY29tL3hhcC8xLjAvIiB4
bWxuczp4cYz0iaHR0cDovL3B1cmwub3JnL2RjL2VsZW1lbnRzLzEuMS8iIHhtbG5zOnhtcE1NPSJodHRwOi8vbnMuYWRvYmUu
Y29tL3hhcC8xLjAvbW0vIiB4bWxuczpzdFJlZj0iaHR0cDovL25zLmFkb2JlLmNvbS94YXAvMS4wL3NUeXBlL1Jlc291cmNl
UmVmIyIgeG1wOkNyZWF0b3JUb29sPSJBZG9iZSBQaG90b3Nob3AgQ1M1IE1hY2ludG9zaCIgeG1wOkNyZWF0ZURhdGU9IjIw

MTItMDUtMDFUMDA6NDk6MTgtMDU6MDAiIHhtcDpNb2RpZnlEYXRlPSIyMDEyLTA1LTAxVDA2OjI2OjA3LTA1OjAwIiB4bXA6
TWV0YWRhdGFEYXRlPSIyMDEyLTA1LTAxVDA2OjI2OjA3LTA1OjAwIiBkYzpmb3JtYXQ9ImltYWdlL3BuZyIgeG1wTU06SW5z
dGFuY2VJRD0ieG1wLmlpZDpGODBFRTIORDhCNzcxMUUxQjc2RUI3REExQzg1RUEyMSIgeG1wTU06RG9jdW1lbnRJRD0ieG1w
LmRpZDpGODBFRTIORThCNzcxMUUxQjc2RUI3REExQzg1RUEyMSI+IDx4bXBNTTpEZXJpdmVkRnJvbSBzdEJlZjppbnN0YW5j
ZUlEPSJ4bXAuaWlkOkY4MEVFMjRCOEI3NzExRTFCNzZFQjdEQTFDODVFQTIxIiBzdEJlZjpkb2N1bWVudElEPSJ4bXAuZGlk
OkY4MEVFMjRDOEI3NzExRTFCNzZFQjdEQTFDODVFQTIxIi8+IDwvcmRmOkRlc2NyaXBOaW9uPiA8L3JkZjpSREY+IDwveDp4
bXBtZXRhPiA8P3hwYWNrZXQgZW5kPSJyIj8+tVKbSQAAABhQTFRFMjSXb2ttgX1/j4uNk4+ShYGDcm5wnpmckwoARwAAABdJ
REFUeNpiYGRiZmBgY2VhHxIEQIABPz1AvMeVbYrAAAAAElFTkSuQmCC);

```
    display: block;
    position: absolute;
    width: 4px;
    height: 33px;
    left: 0;
    top: 0;
}
```

That code may look strange because of the :before pseudo-class in the selector and because of the block of funky-looking code. Let's talk about :before and :after pseudo-classes first. The idea might seem a little strange at first, but once you get used to these pseudo-classes, they can be game changers.

First, let's consider browser support. The following browsers support the :before and :after pseudo-classes:

- Firefox 3.5+ (versions before 3.5 have partial support)
- Safari 1.3+
- Chrome: all versions
- Opera: 6+
- IE: 9+ (partial support for IE8)

Consequently, don't use these pseudo-classes for mission-critical code, but they're great for progressive enhancement. In fact, we don't usually use these pseudo-classes due to the limited browser support.

Both the :before and :after pseudo-classes create another element in the DOM that you can style. In addition, you can also add text. You can use it for adding dollar signs or funky quotation marks or any of a thousand other things. In this case, let's go for a little presentation flair. In the menu, when a visitor's mouse hovers on the tier 1 li elements, let's show the drop-down menu and change the li elements' background. To give an appearance of depth, let's add a small shadow to the left of the li element, making it appear slightly sunken. If it doesn't appear on older browsers, that's OK, since it's just eye candy.

That's a fine example of progressive enhancement. We have created an experience that works for all visitors, with visitors using more capable browsers getting an experience that matches their browsers' capabilities and that's consequently just a bit nicer.

Using Base64 Encoding

Now let's talk about the background image and the funky code. We wanted to show how to embed the actual code for an image in the CSS rather than supply a path to it. The technique that generates the seemingly random block of characters is called base64 encoding. It's a way to store an image as a block of characters. (If you open an image file, you'll see it's also just a block of characters of one sort or another, depending on the image; base64 encoding creates a similar construct within your code.)

Using base64 encoding can be tricky, because you have to be cognizant of caching. If you add a base64-encoded image to your HTML, that image won't be cached. As a result, if that image is needed again, it has to be added to the next page where it needs to appear. That's a pain. Instead, put base64-encoded images in your CSS, because the CSS gets cached.

Even though you can put them in CSS and get them from the cache later, it's usually easier to deal with referenced images, because they're easier to maintain and don't clutter up your code. In this case, though, a little more performance can be squeezed out of the site by not having an HTTP request get this image. Mostly, though, let's put it here for demonstration purposes.

Another limitation is that IE7 and earlier versions don't support base64 encoding. In this example, because we know IE7 won't support the :before pseudo-class, we don't have to worry about it. In sites where we've used this technique and had to factor IE7 use, we had server-side controllers encode the image on the fly or replace the base64 encoding with a path if the visitor's browser couldn't handle it (we discussed the basic idea of using feature detection in Chapter 2). Using base64 encoding for browsers that support it is another example of detecting the capabilities of visitors' browsers and coding for them.

Listing 7-9 shows the anchor tags in the tier 1 li elements.

Listing 7-9. *Tier 1 Anchor Styles*

```
.nmA {
  display: block;
  line-height: 110%;
  font-size: 15px;
  color: #606060;
  text-decoration: none;
  background-color: rgba(0, 0, 0, 0);
padding: 7px 15px 3px;
}
.nmA:visited {
  color: #606060;
}
.nmA:hover {
  color: #606060;
  text-decoration: none;
}
 nmLI:hover .nmA {
  text-shadow: 1px 1px 1px rgba(0, 0, 0, 0.4);
}
```

The only thing of note here is the last ruleset: .nmLI:hover .nmA{}.

We're specifying that, while the .nmLI is being hovered over, the anchor inside the li element (identified by the .nmA identifier) should have a different style. In this case, we specify putting a drop shadow on the text so that it matches the other links inside the drop-down section. We'll use the same technique to activate the drop-down menu if JavaScript is disabled. More on that shortly.

Now let's look at the drop-down; first, we'll need the actual drop-down container. That's the div with a class of nmSlideout zeroHeight sitting next to our tier 1 anchor tags. Listing 7-10 shows the CSS.

Listing 7-10. *CSS for a Drop-Down Container*

```
.nmSlideout {
  overflow: hidden;
  min-width: 100%;
```

```
  -webkit-transition: all 0.25s ease-in-out;
  -moz-transition: all 0.25s ease-in-out;
  -ms-transition: all 0.25s ease-in-out;
  -o-transition: all 0.25s ease-in-out;
  transition: all 0.25s ease-in-out;

  position: absolute;
  z-index: 11;
  -webkit-border-top-right-radius: 0;
  -webkit-border-bottom-right-radius: 5px;
  -webkit-border-bottom-left-radius: 5px;
  -webkit-border-top-left-radius: 0;
  -moz-border-radius-topright: 0;
  -moz-border-radius-bottomright: 5px;
  -moz-border-radius-bottomleft: 5px;
  -moz-border-radius-topleft: 0;
  border-top-right-radius: 0;
  border-bottom-right-radius: 5px;
  border-bottom-left-radius: 5px;
  border-top-left-radius: 0;
  -moz-background-clip: padding;
  -webkit-background-clip: padding-box;
  background-clip: padding-box;
  background-color: #a29da0;
  background: -webkit-gradient(linear, left top, left bottom, from(#a29da0), to(#898587));
  background: -webkit-linear-gradient(top, #a29da0, #898587);
  background: -moz-linear-gradient(top, #a29da0, #898587);
  background: -ms-linear-gradient(top, #a29da0, #898587);
  background: -o-linear-gradient(top, #a29da0, #898587);
  -webkit-box-shadow: 3px 3px 3px rgba(0, 0, 0, 0.4);
  -moz-box-shadow: 3px 3px 3px rgba(0, 0, 0, 0.4);
  box-shadow: 3px 3px 3px rgba(0, 0, 0, 0.4);
  top: 100%;
  min-width: 170px;
}
```

Besides a whole lot of bulletproofing with the vendor prefixes, we have some other interesting code. Most notable is the following line:

```
transition: all 0.25s ease-in-out;
```

That line provides the animation when CSS3 is available. Translated into English, it basically says, "If there's a change to certain properties, let's animate it." Listing 7-11 shows how to make it run.

Listing 7-11. *General Pattern of a CSS Transition*

```
transition: [what properties to animate; i.e., width, height, etc.] [how long should the
animation take] [what kind of easing should be used];
```

So in the example, all aspects (keyword all after the colon) are being animated. The next value specifies the animation duration, which is the time between the original state and the end state that you've set. In this case, that's a quarter of a second (0.25s). Then comes the easing specifier, which is a little more tricky. It's really a curved acceleration rate. So if you use a value of linear, it will be a constant rate of change, but if you use ease-in-out, it will accelerate more sharply at the beginning and end, while the middle slows a bit. The ease-in-out setting tends to make the animation seem more realistic; when things move in real life, they don't usually move at the same exact rate.

You might be thinking, "How do I tell it to change." Good question. There are several ways; the simplest is to use a pseudo-class, like :hover. Now you can define a different color in .nmSlideout:hover, and the animation automatically happens. That's some good magic. Alternatively, as in our example, you can use JavaScript to change a class or CSS properties and the transition will trigger from that.

Table 7-1 shows the numerous properties that can be animated.

Table 7-1. Properties That Can Be Animated

Property Name	Type
background-color	Color
background-image	only gradients
background-position	percentage, length
border-bottom-color	Color
border-bottom-width	Length
border-color	Color
border-left-color	Color
border-left-width	Length
border-right-color	Color
border-right-width	Length
border-spacing	Length
border-top-color	Color
border-top-width	Length
border-width	Length
Bottom	length, percentage
Color	Color
Crop	Rectangle
font-size	length, percentage
font-weight	Number
grid-*	Various
Height	length, percentage
Left	length, percentage
letter-spacing	Length
line-height	number, length, percentage
margin-bottom	Length
margin-left	Length
margin-right	Length
margin-top	Length
max-height	length, percentage
max-width	length, percentage

Property Name	Type
min-height	length, percentage
min-width	length, percentage
Opacity	Number
outline-color	Color
outline-offset	Integer
outline-width	Length
padding-bottom	Length
padding-left	Length
padding-right	Length
padding-top	Length
Right	length, percentage
text-indent	length, percentage
text-shadow	Shadow
Top	length, percentage
vertical-align	keywords, length, percentage
Visibility	Visibility
Width	length, percentage
word-spacing	length, percentage
z-index	Integer
Zoom	number

■ **Author's Note** Yes, it's been a long campaign, and we're still not done with describing how our menu works. Please bear with us. If it's any consolation, it was a long chapter to write (and rewrite a couple times), too.

Now let's style the links inside the drop-down. Once again, let's use an unordered list that contains anchor tags. Listing 7-12 shows the CSS for the ul and li classes.

Listing 7-12. CSS for the UL and LI Classes

```
.nmUL-L2 {
  text-align: left;
  position: absolute;
  bottom: 0;
  display: block;
  padding: 5px 10px 10px 10px;
  float: left;
}
.nmLI-L2 {
  padding: 1px 0;
}
```

That bit of styling contains no surprises. However, we're about to bump into some more transition fun in the anchor tags and with the :before pseudo-class. We're going to use those techniques to highlight a menu item, as shown in Figure 7-12.

Account   Cart 🛒
1-800-555-1212

Figure 7-12. The Gaming menu with an item highlighted

Listing 7-13 shows the code we used to define the menu-highlighting behavior.

Listing 7-13. Animating and Highlighting a Menu Item

```css
.nmA-L2 {
  color: white;
  background: rgba(0, 0, 0, 0);
  text-shadow: 1px 1px 1px rgba(0, 0, 0, 0.4);
  padding: 7px 5px 5px 18px;
  display: block;
  position: relative;
  -webkit-transition: all 0.5s ease-in-out;
  -moz-transition: all 0.5s ease-in-out;
  -ms-transition: all 0.5s ease-in-out;
  -o-transition: all 0.5s ease-in-out;
  transition: all 0.5s ease-in-out;
  -webkit-border-radius: 10px;
  -moz-border-radius: 10px;
  border-radius: 10px;
  -moz-background-clip: padding;
  -webkit-background-clip: padding-box;
  background-clip: padding-box;
  border: 1px solid rgba(0, 0, 0, 0);
}
.nmA-L2:visited {
  color: #ffffff;
}
.nmA-L2:hover {
  background: rgba(0, 0, 0, 0.3);
  text-decoration: none;
  color: white;
  border: 1px solid #c5bfc3;
}
.nmA-L2:before {
  content: "::";
  /*background: url(../images/menu-arrow.png) no-repeat;*/

  width: 15px;
  height: 16px;
  font-family: times, serif;
  display: inline-block;
```

```
  color: #828282;
  font-weight: 700;
  position: absolute;
  text-shadow: -1px 0 #f3f3f3, 0 1px #f3f3f3, 1px 0 #f3f3f3, 0 -1px #f3f3f3;
  top: 6px;
  left: 5px;
}
```

You probably noticed the transition in the .nmA-L2 ruleset. That ruleset handles the slight transition when we hover over the tier 2 links so that we see a box fade in around them. We pull that off by setting the initial background with the following line:

```
background: rgba(0, 0, 0, 0);
```

That value sets the red, green, blue, and alpha for the highlighted menu item. (We know you know that, but we had to tell you that bit so that we could tell you the next bit.) The alpha part is what we're most interested in. Setting the initial value to 0 (zero) makes it totally transparent. Then we set the hover state in .nmA-L2:hover with the following line:

```
background: rgba(0, 0, 0, 0.3);
```

That setting makes it a 30 percent opacity black box. Fun stuff.

You can also see that we've used the :before pseudo-class and that we've done something we said we don't usually do: insert text with CSS. However, we did it this time for a good reason: We can get a simple icon that performs better than one we could get with an image. To do so, we use :: (two colon characters) and then give the menu item an outline. Listing 7-14 shows the line that adds the two colon characters.

Listing 7-14. Adding Two Colons with CSS

```
nmA-L2:before {
  content: "::"; /* The insertion of colon characters
  text-shadow: -1px 0 #f3f3f3, 0 1px #f3f3f3, 1px 0 #f3f3f3, 0 -1px #f3f3f3;
}
```

▓ **Tip** As we mentioned in Chapter 1, pragmatism beats purism. Having said we never insert text via CSS, we could refuse to do it. Then we'd have to use an image to create this little icon. That would be a mistake, as it would force us to manage another asset and put a hit on performance. If breaking a rule provides a benefit, then break that rule. Of course, the trick is knowing *when* to break the rules.

Getting the outline on the text was a little tricky. Since there isn't a concept of an outline on the text, we can fool it by using a series of basically solid text shadows. Listing 7-15 shows the general pattern for defining a text shadow.

Listing 7-15. General Pattern for Defining a Text Shadow

```
Text-shadow: [horizontal offset] [vertical offset] [blur] [color];
```

Since we're not defining a blur, it's assuming a blur of 0. In this case, a blur of 0 makes it look like a solid line. Because we make sure there's a solid shadow going in each direction, the shadows overlap, and the net result is a solid line. Neat trick, isn't it?

Then all that's left is to position it absolutely, get it over to the left, and use a left padding to make sure the button text doesn't intersect with it. That's our kind of technique: easy and effective.

The Drop-Down Effect

Now that the styling's in place, that leaves animating the drop-down in a fashion that embraces the core value of progressive enhancement. You'll have to lean on JavaScript a bit here. You could actually do this whole thing in CSS3 if the height of each element was set manually with the `.nmSlideout` identifier such that each one would be as high as its contents. Were all those values set manually, the animation of the drop-down menus could be defined with the simple rule shown in Listing 7-16.

Listing 7-16. CSS3 Way to Animate a Drop-Down

```
.nmLI:hover .nmSlideout {
        height: some number px;
}
```

That would work just fine, but there'd be a lot more up-front coding to do. Much worse, if the contents ever changed, you'd have to remember to remeasure the new contents. Worst of all, if the folks who maintain the content aren't the same folks who maintain the design, you've just guaranteed a very visible error on your pages. So take the easy (and smart) way out and let JavaScript lend a hand. However, it's best to go with an approach that leans on JavaScript for very little and thus performs very well (remember that calculation always has a cost, too). Listing 7-17 shows the code.

Listing 7-17. JavaScript for Setting the Heights of the Drop-Downs

```
var nmLICol = $(".nmLI"), slideoutCol = $(".nmSlideout");
$(".nmSlideout").each(function() {
  var t = $(this), level2Nav = $(".nmUL-L2", t);
  t.css({
    "height" : level2Nav.outerHeight() + "px"
  }).attr("data-height", level2Nav.outerHeight() + "px");
})
```

This code grabs all the elements with an identifier of `.nmSlideout`; then, for each one, it finds out how tall the ul element inside it is and sets the style of the elements with an identifier of `.nmSlideout` to that height. Finally, it sets the `data-height` attribute's value to the same height in pixels(+ `"px"`). That value will be needed later, so let's set it here.

Now let's take what the `.nmSlideout` height should be to accommodate the inner contents and make it explicit. However, you still need a height into which to transition. The only problem is that it's not a height of 0 any more, because its inline style has just been set to a new height. Here's where a little trickery comes in.

You probably noticed that second class on our `.nmSlideout` element: zeroHeight. Listing 7-18 shows that class.

Listing 7-18. The .zeroHeight Class

```
.zeroHeight {
  height: 0 !important;
  -webkit-box-shadow: 0 0 0 rgba(0, 0, 0, 0) !important;
  -moz-box-shadow: 0 0 0 rgba(0, 0, 0, 0) !important;
  box-shadow: 0 0 0 rgba(0, 0, 0, 0) !important;
```

```
}
```

The most important thing in this class is that it sets the .nmSlideout element to a height of 0 (zero) with an !important declaration added so that it trumps any rule without an !important declaration. So it's back to a height of zero. To animate it, use jQuery to remove the zeroHeight class on the mouseenter event and add it on to the mouseleave event. That will make the browser honor the height previously set with JavaScript. And when it's set back, it will animate back to zero height. Listing 7-19 shows the JavaScript code for setting classes on the mouseenter and mouseleave events.

Listing 7-19. JavaScript for Changing Classes on mouseenter and mouseleave Events

```
nmLICol.each(function() {
  var t = $(this);
  t.hover(function() {
    var slideout = $(".nmSlideout", t);
    setTimeout(function() {
      slideout.removeClass("zeroHeight");
    }, 0);
  }, function() {
    var slideout = t.find(".nmSlideout");

    slideout.addClass("zeroHeight");
  })
})
```

The tier 1 li elements have been gathered into a collection and then, for each one, a hover event's been added. This jQuery .hover() takes two functions: the first is hover enter function, and the second hover leave function. (By the way, the functions are anonymous and are identified at run time by their signatures – that is, the number of arguments.) Under the hood it's adding mouseenter and mouseleave event handlers. The setTimeout function with a delay of zero was needed to get Firefox to play nice.

Now we have navigation for modern browsers, using JavaScript that should run in under 20 milliseconds on most machines and that utilizes CSS3 to handle animations. It's fast and smooth for many visitors. But what about non-CSS3 browsers? For that, we rely on Modernizr to identify whether CSS3 is available. When it's not available, rely on jQuery and its animation functionality. As we mentioned in Chapter 2, we're firm believers in using feature detection to help shape the experience provided to each visitor. Listing 7-20 shows how to detect the browser's ability to handle CSS3 and what to do when the browser can't handle CSS3.

Listing 7-20. Feature Detection and Animation for non-CSS3 Browsers

```
nmLICol.each(function() {
  var t = $(this);
  t.hover(function() {
    var slideout = $(".nmSlideout", t);
    setTimeout(function() {
      slideout.removeClass("zeroHeight")
    }, 0);
    //Add fallback if CSS3 animations are not available
    if(!Modernizr.cssanimations) {
      slideout.css("height", 0);
      slideout.stop().animate({
        "height" : slideout.attr("data-height")
```

```
      }, 400);
    }
  }, function() {
    var slideout = t.find(".nmSlideout");
    if(!Modernizr.cssanimations) {
      slideout.stop().animate({
        "height" : 0
      }, 400, function() {
        slideout.addClass("zeroHeight");
      });
    } else {
      slideout.addClass("zeroHeight");
    }
  })
})
```

Some logic has been baked in to detect whether CSS3 animations are available and, if they're not, to use jQuery's animate function. We're leaning on Modernizr to detect whether the CSS3 animation feature is available with !Modernizr.cssanimations. If the condition evaluates to false, we mimic what the CSS3 was doing by animating between a height of zero and the height the .nmSlideout would need to be to display its contents. We grab that height from the data-height attribute we set when the script was first run in Listing 7-15. In addition to setting the height to zero on the mouseleave event, we'll also need to set the zeroHeight class back. Why do that if we're already setting the height to zero? Because we need that CSS to make the default state behave as if it has a transparent border so elements don't shift when the animation happens.

You're almost done. (Thanks for bearing with us. As we wrote earlier, it's been a long chapter for us, too.) Now we have a menu that works on browsers that support CSS3 and browsers that don't support CSS3. Now for the hat trick. What if your visitor doesn't have JavaScript? No problem. Because of the way the HTML is structured, it's easy to use an established method of showing and hiding the drop-down menu on hover. Again, let's use Modernizr but by relying on its absence when the visitor has JavaScript turned off. It may sound crazy, but it's another great feature of Modernizr: It looks in the HTML tag and removes the no-js class and inserts the js class. You can now use the fact that no-js is in the HTML tag because, without JavaScript, Modernizr can't run and therefore can't remove the no-js class. It's subtle and effective—just the way we all like things. Listing 7-21 shows the .no-js classes for our menu:

***Listing 7-21.** The no-js Classes for the Menu*

```
.no-js .zeroHeight {
  height: auto ! important;
}
.no-js .nmSlideout {
  display: none;
}
.no-js .nmLI:hover .nmSlideout {
  display: block;
}
```

On .nmLI:hover, the element identified as .nmSlideout is shown. When the hover state is no longer active, the element identified as .nmSlideout is hidden.

Search Box

Last but not least, there's the search box. Given that a significant number of web users rely on Search to find things, you need to provide the capability and make it easy to find. For this site, let's style the site search box such that it ends up to the right of the navigation. Listing 7-22 shows how to do it.

Listing 7-22. Styling the Search Box

```
.searchWrap {
  text-align: right;
  border: 0;
  padding: 0 0 0 10px;
  float: right;
}
.searchWrap:hover {
  background: none;
}
.searchWrap:hover:before {
  background: none;
}
.searchInput {
  border: 1px solid #ccc;
  display: inline-block;
  position: relative;
  margin: 4px 0 0 0;
  height: 14px;
  padding: 5px 4px 2px 5px;
  width: 150px;
  -webkit-border-top-right-radius: 0;
  -webkit-border-bottom-right-radius: 0;
  -webkit-border-bottom-left-radius: 5px;
  -webkit-border-top-left-radius: 5px;
  -moz-border-radius-topright: 0;
  -moz-border-radius-bottomright: 0;
  -moz-border-radius-bottomleft: 5px;
  -moz-border-radius-topleft: 5px;
  border-top-right-radius: 0;
  border-bottom-right-radius: 0;
  border-bottom-left-radius: 5px;
  border-top-left-radius: 5px;
  -moz-background-clip: padding;
  -webkit-background-clip: padding-box;
  background-clip: padding-box;
  -webkit-box-shadow: inset 2px 2px 2px #999999;
  -moz-box-shadow: inset 2px 2px 2px #999999;
  box-shadow: inset 2px 2px 2px #999999;
}
.searchBtn {
  -webkit-border-top-right-radius: 7px;
  -webkit-border-bottom-right-radius: 7px;
  -webkit-border-bottom-left-radius: 0;
```

```
    -webkit-border-top-left-radius: 0;
    -moz-border-radius-topright: 7px;
    -moz-border-radius-bottomright: 7px;
    -moz-border-radius-bottomleft: 0;
    -moz-border-radius-topleft: 0;
    border-top-right-radius: 7px;
    border-bottom-right-radius: 7px;
    border-bottom-left-radius: 0;
    border-top-left-radius: 0;
    -moz-background-clip: padding;
    -webkit-background-clip: padding-box;
    background-clip: padding-box;
    border: 1px solid #ccc;
    top: -2px;
    position: relative;
    color: white;
    display: inline-block;
    padding: 3px;
    text-shadow: 0 0 4px rgba(0, 0, 0, 0.3);
}
.searchBtn:hover {
    background: #c62125;
}
```

As you can see, the `.searchWrap` class positions the search box, while the other `.search` classes style both the search text box and its associated button. We're sure that you've seen this kind of structure before, so we won't dwell on the topic.

Summary

While the length of a chapter isn't really important (though we do try to keep them from being more than the average person can digest over a lunch hour), it reveals that creating an effective navigation paradigm requires a fair bit of code. It doesn't take much HTML, but it does require some sophisticated CSS and (to a lesser extent) JavaScript.

In this chapter, the primary idea we'd like to leave you with is that of using progressive enhancement to ensure that your visitors get a navigation experience that is the best experience their browsers can deliver. We started at the "fully enhanced" end of the spectrum, by writing rules for visitors whose browsers support CSS3. Then we dealt with browsers that can't handle CSS3 but do have JavaScript enabled. Finally, we provided a solution for visitors whose browsers can't use JavaScript.

We strongly encourage you to apply this idea to your own navigation elements and to other aspects of the sites you develop, wherever such a technique does your visitors some good.

CHAPTER 8

■ ■ ■

Masthead

After the marathon of the last chapter, we thought you might like a break. Because we don't have a lot to say about mastheads, we decided to balance that long chapter by following it with this short chapter. Our fundamental advice about mastheads is to keep them simple. Don't try to stuff everything (or anything beyond the basics, really) into the masthead.

The term "masthead" comes from the era of sailing ships. Picture a mast loaded with a bunch of big square sails and a flag at the top (literally, at the head of the mast). The sails did all the work. The flag got all the glory, because it carried information that was very important both to the people on that ship and to people on other ships. By indicating nationality, it was a source of pride for the people on its ship and an indicator of friend or foe to everyone else.

When newspapers became commonplace, they adopted the masthead idea as a metaphor for part of their layout. Most of a newspaper's layout is taken up with its own "sails": its sheets—big areas that do the work of conveying information, both news stories and advertising. The masthead identifies the paper, just as the flag does a ship. The metaphor is a handy reminder that the masthead's job is identifying or branding the newspaper. In other words, the masthead is where to identify the brand and, in both newspapers and web sites, display other handy information.

In web design, the masthead is the place for the brand's logo, the starting place for setting the site's look and feel. In addition, the masthead often contains crucial navigation items,: "About us," "Contact us," "Cart," and often others. In the example that follows, we use content commonly found on e-commerce websites: logo, account, cart, and phone. One of the items often found on international websites is a country/language selector. Though we don't include it in the sample site, we mention a performance technique for accelerating this feature.

Building a Better Country Selector

It's common for large sites that sell in a wide variety of countries to offer a drop-down menu with every country/language selection they offer. Figure 8-1 shows a typical language selector in its closed state.

Africa ⬍

Figure 8-1. A typical language selector from a large e-commerce web site in its closed state

Figure 8-2 shows the same language selector in its open state.

Africa ⇕
Africa
Albania
Algeria
Angola
Anguilla
Antigua & Barbuda
Argentina
Armenia
Aruba
Asia Pacific
Australia
Austria
Azerbaijan

Figure 8-2. A typical language selector from a large e-commerce web site in its open state

This design element can become quite complex, sometimes offering 50 or more combinations. And while it's possible to abstract that select box to a dynamically referenced piece of code, the HTML to generate the select list has to be downloaded every time. In the case of the country selector shown in Figures 8-1 and 8-2, more than 200 lines of code were inserted into every page for every visitor. That's a lot of overhead for a feature most visitors never use and that very few visitors use more than once.

A better approach is to link to a country/language page that lists the selections available in a far more meaningful way, perhaps with flags for easy recognition. Since you've got a whole page with which to work, these flags can be larger than those typically found in drop-down country selectors. This technique saves a great deal of HTML generation and has fewer elements to render. Also, consider that visitors generally set their location and language preferences only once. Thus, it's not much of a speed bump to have them go to this page before getting on with their shopping. The savings in bandwidth (and, to a lesser extent, page-load time) can be sizable, and most visitors will never notice the difference.

Look & Feel

We're going for a pretty straightforward look and feel in our sample e-commerce site: just a container to hold the masthead and some absolutely placed elements to convey crucial information. Figure 8-3 shows the sample site's masthead.

Figure 8-3. The masthead

Listing 8-1 shows the HTML that defines the masthead.

Listing 8-1. Masthead HTML

```
<header class="headNav twelvecol">
  <img class="logo_166" src="images/sprites/clikz-sprite.png" href="/" />
  <nav>
    <ul class="acctNav">
      <li class="acctNavLI">
        <a href="" class="acctNavA">Account</a>
      </li>
      <li class="acctNavLI">
        <a href="" class="acctNavA mhCart"><span class="cartText">Cart</span> <i class="icon_
cart ir"></i></a>
      </li>
      <li class="mhContactPhone">
        1-800-555-1212
      </li>
    </ul>
  </nav>
</header>
```

The masthead HTML has no mind-blowing content; we've all probably seen similar HTML many times. However, we do want to point out one thing: the header wrapper with a class of headNav twelvecol. The twelvecol identifier refers to the flexible grid that we're using. We'll get to that later.

Listing 8-2 shows the CSS that styles the masthead.

Listing 8-2. Masthead CSS

```
.headNav {
  height: 70px;
}
.logo_166 {
  position: absolute;
  top: 12px;
  clip: rect(2px, 168px, 48px, 2px);
}
.headNav {
  position: relative;
  font-size: 12px;
}
.acctNav {
  position: absolute;
  right: 0;
  top: 15px;
}
.acctNavLI {
  float: left;
  margin-left: 20px;
}
.acctNavA, .acctNavA:visited {
  text-decoration: none;
  color: #666666;
  display: inline-block;
```

```
}
.acctNavA:hover {
  text-decoration: underline;
}
.mhCart {
  padding-right: 23px;
}
.mhCart:hover {
  text-decoration: none;
}
.mhCart:hover .cartText {
  text-decoration: underline;
}
.icon_cart {
  background: url(../images/sprites/clikz-sprite.png) no-repeat -22px -54px;
  width: 19px;
  height: 16px;
  position: absolute;
  z-index: 1;
  right: 0;
  top: 0;
}
.mhContactPhone {
  float: right;
  clear: both;
  margin-top: 5px;
}
```

We should point out one bit of trickery here: The brand logo's image element. We chose to use an image instead of a background image for one reason: printing. You can't count on browsers printing background images. In fact, you can count on browsers *not* printing background images. There are exceptions, as when a user has changed preferences in the browser, but of course we can't rely on that. So we opted instead for an image element. However, we couldn't stomach the performance hit from the extra HTTP request, so we added the logo to the sprite we're using for other elements and clipped away the rest of the sprite image to leave just the logo.

CSS Clipping

The technique we covered in Listing 8-2 is a combination of the old and the new. The clip property has support back to IE6, but the broad adoption of image sprites is somewhat new (well, not exactly new, but newer).

So let's talk about how it works. First, consider Listing 8-3.

Listing 8-3. Defining a Clipping Rectangle

```
clip: rect(2px, 168px, 48px, 2px);
```

The only shape that the clip property can take is rect(). (Remember that browsers draw only rectangles.) Inside there is the CSS classic order. (An easy way to remember the order is just to think how much *TRouBLe* it is to recall the order: Top, Right, Bottom, Left.) We use this order because it's the same order that most browsers use when rendering an area of the pages. We're describing a box, as defined from the top left corner of the image. The idea can be a little tricky to follow, so let's look at a diagram. Figure 8-4 shows our sprite.

Figure 8-4. *Our sprite*

In this case, we want just the logo portion, which is in the upper left. Figure 8-5 shows a more detailed view of the sprite with various characteristics called out.

Figure 8-5. *Sprite characteristics*

The tricky part can be visualizing the bottom and right sides. An easy way to think of them is as a sum: their margins plus the size of the image we're after. Listing 8-4 shows the details in pseudo code.

Listing 8-4. *Sprite Pseudo Code*

```
Bottom = Top (2px) + height of image (46px);
Right = Left (2px) + width of image (166px);
```

In order for this to work, we also have to set the position property to absolute. Now we have an image element working like a sprite. Pretty cool, no? Well, cool or not, it's a handy technique.

Links with Icons

With our cart link, we have a shopping cart icon. This effect can be achieved in lots of different ways, but let's stick to one that's always been pretty reliable. Listing 8-5 shows the HTML.

Listing 8-5. *HTML for the Masthead Links*

```
<a href="javascript:;" class="acctNavA mhCart">
  <span class="cartText">Cart</span>
  <i class="icon_cart ir"></i>
</a>
```

Listing 8-6 shows the CSS.

Listing 8-6. *CSS to Style the Masthead Links*

```
.mhCart {
  padding-right: 23px;
}
.mhCart:hover {
  text-decoration: none;
}
.mhCart:hover .cartText {
  text-decoration: underline;
}
.icon_cart {
  background: url(../images/sprites/clikz-sprite.png) no-repeat -22px -54px;
  width: 19px;
  height: 16px;
  position: absolute;
  z-index: 1;
  right: 0;
  top: 0;
}
```

As you can see, both the text and the image are inside the anchor tag. This makes both of them clickable.

▨ **Note**   To define the image, we've used an <i> element. That may seem strange to people who care about semantic markup, because it's the old way to render text as italic. After the early days of the Web, when the <i> element was common, the fashion moved on to <em> (emphasis) elements to fulfill the need for italic text. Nowadays, both <i> and <b> have made a comeback and are used for visual styling instead of text denoting. So while this use of an <i> element may be a bit of a departure from the intended use and may strike some readers as odd or even wrong, it's actually quite the fashion to use the <i> element to represent icons. In short, think of using <i> and <b> elements as pure styling rather than semantic markup.

You can see the CSS for the cart link in the `.icon_cart` ruleset in Listing 8-6. We'll use the padding trick that we explained earlier and give the anchor enough padding to hold the icon, with a little space between to pad the text. Now we're cooking—but there's still one problem. Since we've defined the `:hover` state of the anchor as `text-decoration: underline`, the icon also gets underlined. That's no good; we want just the text to be underlined. Here's how to solve that problem: add a span around the text with a class of spanText. Within the anchor, disable the `:hover` state inherited from the default anchor ruleset. Then use a descendant selector with a `:hover` state, as shown in Listing 8-7.

Listing 8-7. *Descendant Selectors with :hover States*

```
.mhCart:hover {
  text-decoration: none;
}
.mhCart:hover .cartText {
  text-decoration: underline;
}
```

This way, when visitors hover over elements with `.mhCart` identifiers, the `span.cartText` element gets an underline but the image doesn't.

We think the extra markup is worthwhile, because it lets us make both the text and the icon selectable. Besides, it embraces the "think inside the box" paradigm that lets us keep our concerns contained in a modular fashion.

Summary

In this short chapter, we've covered

- the origin of "masthead" and its use both in print and on the web

- a better way to present country and language selectors

- how to use a sprite to provide content for an image element

- how to organize text and an image within a container and get them to highlight properly

All of that adds up to how to make a masthead for a web page.

We want to emphasize one caveat that we've bumped into many times, both as visitors to various sites and in dealings with business people. Don't try to do too much with the masthead. Once you go beyond a logo, a shopping cart, and basic contact information, the masthead starts to get too busy. At that point, you start to weaken your branding and make it harder for your customers to find essential information.

Last but not least, an overly busy masthead can be a real performance drag, especially if you try to customize it for each customer. If you must customize the masthead (we've been there), test extensively and optimize in every possible way to reduce the page-load time. Also, don't save testing for the end of the development process. Early on, it's a problem; at the last minute, it's a crisis, and no one needs that heartburn. To paraphrase a famous Chicago politician: Test early, test often. That's good advice in general but especially so when you add customization to the masthead. Remember that every page gets the masthead, so a poorly performing masthead is a nightmare.

CHAPTER 9

■ ■ ■

Footer

Many sites have a footer. Usually, it's a place to put legal information (such as copyright and trademark notices) and some content that applies to every page. Everyone who has surfed the web for more than ten minutes knows that, if you don't find the Contact and About links in the header, look in the footer.

Another use for a footer, one that we're going to embrace, is as a place to hold the site map. Since the footer is present on every page, the site map is always present, too. That makes navigation easier for those visitors who think in terms of site maps, and it's still nicely out of the way for the visitors who like to search or browse to find the content they like.

Because the footer is pretty simple and this chapter would be very short otherwise, we're also going to use this chapter to introduce the idea of using SVG on a web site. SVG can provide a nice boost to page loading, as we'll discover later in the chapter.

Let's start by looking at what we have in mind for the footer. Then we'll talk about how to make it happen. Figure 9-1 shows the footer for our sample site, `http://clikz.us`

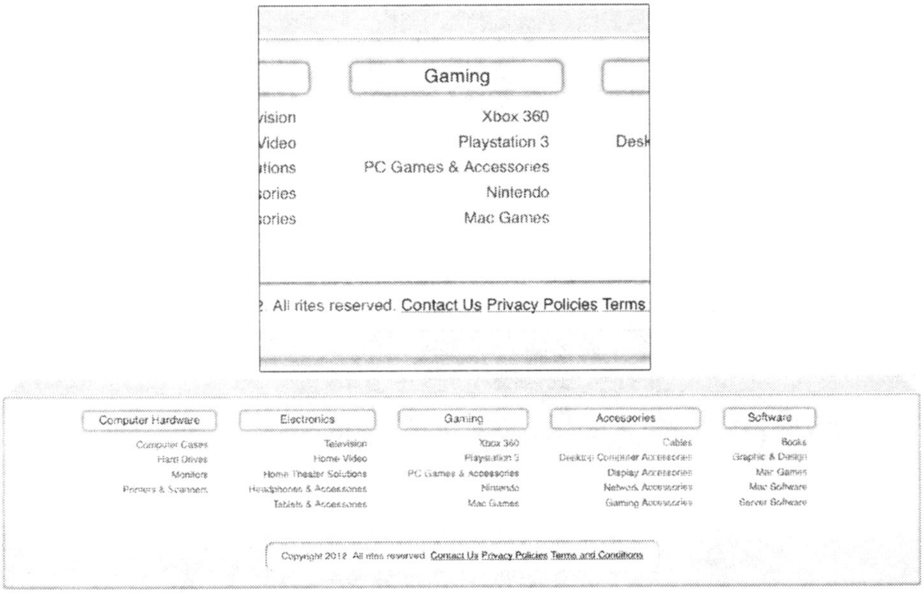

Figure 9-1. The footer for our sample site

Making the Footer

There are a bunch of ways to make a footer: coding each link by hand, generating the links through a number of different server-side mechanisms, and even using a JavaScript template. (We recommend against using a JavaScript template, though; it doesn't yield the best performance and isn't friendly to search bots). In this case, we're going to store the footer content in a separate file on the server. That same file also contains the content for the site's menu, which brings us to the first performance boost for the footer.

To create all the links in the site map, we're not going to create new content. Instead, we're going to use CSS to restyle the content that we already have in the menu. In addition to the performance gain from not downloading the same information twice, we also get a nice boost to developer performance. When you add an item to the menu, it automatically appears in the site map, too. That saves the trouble of adding the item twice and removes the possibility of a bug because you remember one place and forget the other. We're strongly opposed to typing the same content twice, not just because we're lazy, but because replicating by hand is often a source of error.

For the sake of this illustration, let's assume a PHP-powered site. Consequently, the navigation information (whether menu or site map) is in a file that contains some special markup that's meaningful to a PHP rendering engine. We could easily have chosen a number of other technologies, including .Net (through partial views), JavaServer Pages, JavaServer Faces, and others.

So first we must remove the navigation HTML from the main template and put it into another file. In this case, we put the code into an includes folder and called the file siteNavigation.php. In order to have the styling be different for the menu and the site map, we need a way to set a unique selector to match in our CSS. We create the unique selector by setting a variable above the PHP include and use that variable in our HTML. Listing 9-1 shows the contents of siteNavigation.php. The first line (which we have made bold) shows where we set the selector that applies styles to create either the menu or the site map. We also made bold the line where we set some assistive text that helps screen readers provide a much less painful experience for visitors whose eyesight is problematic.

Listing 9-1. The Contents of siteNavigation.php, with Variables Highlighted

```
<ul class="navMainUL <?php echo $navContext ?> clearfix" role="navigation">
  <li class="visuallyhidden">
    <h3 class="assistive-text"><?php echo $assistiveNav?></h3>
    <div class="skip-link">
      <a class="assistive-text" href="#content" title="Skip to primary content">Skip to primary
content</a>
    </div>
  </li>
  <li class="nmLI first">
    <a href="javascript:;" class="nmA">Computer Hardware </a>
    <div class="nmSlideout zeroHeight">
      <ul class="nmUL-L2 ">
        <li class="nmLI-L2">
          <a href="" class="nmA-L2">Computer Cases</a>
        </li>
        <li class="nmLI-L2">
          <a href="" class="nmA-L2">Hard Drives</a>
        </li>
        <li class="nmLI-L2">
          <a href="" class="nmA-L2">Monitors</a>
        </li>
```

```
      <li class="nmLI-L2 nmLast">
        <a href="" class="nmA-L2">Printers &amp; Scanners</a>
      </li>
    </ul>
  </div>
</li>
<li class="nmLI">
  <a href="javascript:;" class="nmA">Electronics</a>
  <div class="nmSlideout zeroHeight">
    <ul class="nmUL-L2 ">
      <li class="nmLI-L2">
        <a href="" class="nmA-L2">Television</a>
      </li>
      <li class="nmLI-L2">
        <a href="" class="nmA-L2">Home Video</a>
      </li>
      <li class="nmLI-L2 nmLast">
        <a href="" class="nmA-L2">Home Theater Solutions</a>
      </li>
      <li class="nmLI-L2 nmLast">
        <a href="" class="nmA-L2">Headphones &amp; Accessories</a>
      </li>
      <li class="nmLI-L2 nmLast">
        <a href="" class="nmA-L2">Tablets &amp; Accessories</a>
      </li>
    </ul>
  </div>
</li>
<li class="nmLI">
  <a href="javascript:;" class="nmA">Gaming</a>
  <div class="nmSlideout zeroHeight">
    <ul class="nmUL-L2 ">
      <li class="nmLI-L2">
        <a href="" class="nmA-L2">Xbox 360</a>
      </li>
      <li class="nmLI-L2">
        <a href="" class="nmA-L2">Playstation 3</a>
      </li>
      <li class="nmLI-L2 nmLast">
        <a href="" class="nmA-L2">PC Games &amp; Accessories</a>
      </li>
      <li class="nmLI-L2">
        <a href="" class="nmA-L2">Nintendo</a>
      </li>
      <li class="nmLI-L2">
        <a href="" class="nmA-L2">Mac Games</a>
      </li>
    </ul>
  </div>
</li>
<li class="nmLI">
```

```
      <a href="javascript:;" class="nmA">Accessories</a>
      <div class="nmSlideout zeroHeight">
        <ul class="nmUL-L2 ">
          <li class="nmLI-L2">
            <a href="" class="nmA-L2">Cables</a>
          </li>
          <li class="nmLI-L2">
            <a href="" class="nmA-L2">Desktop Computer Accessories</a>
          </li>
          <li class="nmLI-L2">
            <a href="" class="nmA-L2">Display Accessories</a>
          </li>
          <li class="nmLI-L2">
            <a href="" class="nmA-L2">Network Accessories</a>
          </li>
          <li class="nmLI-L2">
            <a href="" class="nmA-L2">Gaming Accessories</a>
          </li>
        </ul>
      </div>
    </li>
    <li class="nmLI last">
      <a href="javascript:;" class="nmA">Software</a>
      <div class="nmSlideout zeroHeight">
        <ul class="nmUL-L2 ">
          <li class="nmLI-L2">
            <a href="" class="nmA-L2">Books</a>
          </li>
          <li class="nmLI-L2">
            <a href="" class="nmA-L2">Graphic &amp; Design</a>
          </li>
          <li class="nmLI-L2">
            <a href="" class="nmA-L2">Mac Games</a>
          </li>
          <li class="nmLI-L2">
            <a href="" class="nmA-L2">Mac Software</a>
          </li>
          <li class="nmLI-L2">
            <a href="" class="nmA-L2">Server Software</a>
          </li>
        </ul>
      </div>
    </li>
    <li class="nmLI searchWrap">
      <input type="search" id="searchInput" class="searchInput" placeholder="Site Search" />
      <button class="searchBtn siteGrad">
        Search
      </button>
    </li>
  </ul>
```

Those two variables are all we need The $navContext variable identifies which set of styles to use (either menu or site map). The $navContext variable can have a value of either nmDropDown or footerNav. Given those values, we can create two very different layouts of the same information. We also set the value of the $assistiveNav variable to some text that is meaningful for screen readers, so that visitors who use screen readers know they've encountered a menu or site map and have a chance to skip it. Every web designer should have to listen to their sites in a screen reader. After hearing a hundred navigation links each time you visit another page, you'll soon be ready to head-butt the screen.

Setting the variables is a simple task. To set the proper values for the menu, put the code in Listing 9-2 just below the masthead.

Listing 9-2. *Setting Variable Values for the Menu*

```
<div class="navSpacer">
  <?php
    $navContext = "nmDropDown";
    $assistiveNav = "Main Navigation";
    include ("includes/siteNavigation.php");
  ?>
</div>
```

To set the proper values for the menu, put the code in Listing 9-3 at the top of the footer.

Listing 9-3. *Setting Variable Values for the Footer*

```
<div class="footerTopHolder">
  <?php
    $navContext = "footerNav";
    $assistiveNav = "Footer Navigation";
    include ("includes/siteNavigation.php");
  ?>
</div>
```

So in each instance we're defining a section of the code that gets processed by the server. That's what an instruction in the form of <?php //serverside code goes here ?> does. In this case, we're setting the appropriate variables for the section (menu or footer) and then outputting the contents of siteNavigation.php (populated with the proper section-specific values) directly below the variable declarations. What we get are distinct class names that let us properly style the HTML for each of the two use cases. For example, if we want to style the level 1 anchor tags differently in the menu and in the footer, we can use the CSS shown in Listing 9-4.

Listing 9-4. *Styling Level 1 Anchor Tags Differently in the Menu and the Footer*

```
.nmDropDown .nmA {
  /* only styles the main navigation; */
}
.footerNav  .nmA{
  /* only styles the footer navigation; */

}
```

As we mentioned earlier in the chapter, this mechanism lets us maintain just .siteNavigation.php (rather than two sources or two blocks of content in the same file) and share the content in that one file between the main site navigation and the footer.

In addition to the performance benefits mentioned earlier in this chapter, making the site map prominent offers another substantial benefit to both the visitors to the site and the business that runs the site. Users can see the site's taxonomy at a glance. But what if someone says, "Well, isn't that what a site map does?" The answer is that the benefit may be less obvious. Suppose a certain link is potentially very interesting to visitors, but that link is within a category that users think is just ho-hum. With a highly visible site map, visitors are more likely to click on that link. Without the site map, visitors would never find it, and the business would miss an opportunity to sell that product. That's a losing proposition for all parties. Visitors fail to find an interesting product, the business loses sales, and the web developer misses an opportunity to get visitors to the right content. So, yes, it's obvious, but the benefits can be significant.A final advantage of having all the links in the footer is that it provides a backup to a JavaScript-based main navigation (such as we use to show drop-down menus for navigation). If your site uses a JavaScript-based menu but visitors have JavaScript turned off, they won't find anything and will surf to some other site very quickly. The result? You just lost an opportunity. Also, search bots often don't traverse JavaScript-based menus. For both cases, having a site map that offers an alternative way to connect visitors and search bots to content keeps you in the game.

Styling the Footer

So much for theory. Let's look at the code behind styling the footer and the site map it contains. Listing 9-5 shows all of the CSS code needed to style the footer. It's a whopper of a listing, so bear with us. We'll explain what each piece does later in the chapter.

Listing 9-5. The CSS That Styles the Footer

```
.siteGrad {
  background: #e6272b; /* Old browsers */
  /* IE9 SVG, needs conditional override of 'filter' to 'none' */
  background: url(data:image/svg+xml;base64,PD94bWwgdmVyc2lvbj0iMS4wIiA/Pgo8c3ZnIHhtbG5zPSJodHRw
Oi8vd3d3LnczLm9yZy8yMDAwL3N2ZyIgd2lkdGg9IjEwMCUiIGhlaWdodD0iMTAwJSIgdmlld0JveD0iMCAwIDEgMSIgcHJl
c2VydmVBc3BlY3RSYXRpb249Im5vbmUiICAgeG1sbnM6eGxpbms9Imh0dHA6Ly93d3cudzMub3JnLzE5OTkveGxpbmsiPgogIDxsaW5lYXJHcmFkaWVudCBpZD0iZ3JhZC11Y2dnLWdlbmVyYXRlZCIgeDE9IjAlIiB5MT0iMCUiIHgyPSIwJSIgeTI9IjEwMCUiPgogICAgPHN0b3Agb2Zmc2V0PSIwJSIgc3RvcC1jb2xvcj0iI2U2MjcyYiIgc3RvcC1vcGFjaXR5PSIxIi8+CiAgICA8c3RvcCBvZmZzZXQ9IjE1JSIgc3RvcC1jb2xvcj0iI2YxMjgyZCIgc3RvcC1vcGFjaXR5PSIxIi8+CiAgICA8c3RvcCBvZmZzZXQ9IjI3JSIgc3RvcC1jb2xvcj0iI2YyMjkyZSIgc3RvcC1vcGFjaXR5PSIxIi8+CiAgICA8c3RvcCBvZmZzZXQ9IjUwJSIgc3RvcC1jb2xvcj0iI2UzMjYyYiIgc3RvcC1vcGFjaXR5PSIxIi8+CiAgICA8c3RvcCBvZmZzZXQ9Ijc3JSIgc3RvcC1jb2xvcj0iI2NhMjIyNiIgc3RvcC1vcGFjaXR5PSIxIi8+CiAgICA8c3RvcCBvZmZzZXQ9Ijg1JSIgc3RvcC1jb2xvcj0iI2M2MjEyNSIgc3RvcC1vcGFjaXR5PSIxIi8+CiAgICA8c3RvcCBvZmZzZXQ9IjEwMCUiIHN0b3AtY29sb3I9IiNjNjIxMjUiIHN0b3Atb3BhY2l0eT0iMSIvPgogIDwvbGluZWFyR3JhZGllbnQ+CiAgPHJlY3QgeD0iMCIgeT0iMCIgd2lkdGg9IjEiIGhlaWdodD0iMSIgZmlsbD0idXJsKCNncmFkLXVjZ2ctZ2VuZXJhdGVkKSIgLz4KPC9zdmc+);
  background: -moz-linear-gradient(top, #e6272b 0%, #f1282d 15%, #f2292e 27%, #e3262b 50%, #ca22
26 77%, #c62125 85%, #c62125 100%);/* FF3.6+ */
  background: -webkit-gradient(linear, left top, left bottom, color-stop(0%, #e6272b), color-
stop(15%, #f1282d), color-stop(27%, #f2292e), color-stop(50%, #e3262b), color-stop(77%, #ca2226)
, color-stop(85%, #c62125), color-stop(100%, #c62125));/* Chrome,Safari4+ */
  background: -webkit-linear-gradient(top, #e6272b 0%, #f1282d 15%, #f2292e 27%, #e3262b 50%, #c
a2226 77%, #c62125 85%, #c62125 100%);/* Chrome10+,Safari5.1+ */
  background: -o-linear-gradient(top, #e6272b 0%, #f1282d 15%, #f2292e 27%, #e3262b 50%, #ca2226
 77%, #c62125 85%, #c62125 100%);/* Opera 11.10+ */
  background: -ms-linear-gradient(top, #e6272b 0%, #f1282d 15%, #f2292e 27%, #e3262b 50%, #ca222
6 77%, #c62125 85%, #c62125 100%);/* IE10+ */
```

```
    background: linear-gradient(top, #e6272b 0%, #f1282d 15%, #f2292e 27%, #e3262b 50%, #ca2226 77
%, #c62125 85%, #c62125 100%);/* W3C */
      filter: progid:dximagetransform.microsoft.gradient(startColorstr='#e6272b', endColorstr='#c6212
5', GradientType=0);/* IE6-8 */

}
.mainFooter {
  clear: both;
  padding: 18px 0;
  text-align: center;
}
.mainFooter .row {
  overflow: visible;
}
nav.mainFooterWrap {
  box-shadow: 0px 3px 4px rgba(0, 0, 0, 0.2), inset 0px 0px 3px #888888;
  -webkit-border-radius: 3px;
  -moz-border-radius: 3px;
  border-radius: 3px;
  -moz-background-clip: padding;
  -webkit-background-clip: padding-box;
  background-clip: padding-box;
  background: #fafafa;/* Old browsers */

  /* IE9 SVG, needs conditional override of 'filter' to 'none' */
  background: url(data:image/svg+xml;base64,PD94bWwgdmVyc2lvbj0iMS4wIiA/Pgo8c3ZnIHhtbG5zPSJodHRw
Oi8vd3d3LnczLm9yZy8yMDAwL3N2ZyIgd2lkdGg9IjEwMCUiIGhlaWdodD0iMTAwJSIgdmlld0JveD0iMCAwIDEgMSIgcHJl
c2VydmVBc3BlY3RSYXRpbz0ibm9uZSI+CiAgPGxpbmVhckdyYWRpZW50IGlkPSJncmFkLVVjZ2ctZ2VuZXJhdGVkIiBncmFk
aWVudFVuaXRzPSJ1c2VyU3BhY2VPblVzZSIgeDE9IjAlIiB5MT0iMCUiIHgyPSIwJSIgeTI9IjEwMCUiPgogICAgPHN0b3Ag
b2Zmc2V0PSIwJSIgc3RvcC1jb2xvcj0iI2ZhZmFmYSIgc3RvcC1vcGFjaXR5PSIxIi8+CiAgICA8c3RvcCBvZmZzZXQ9IjE1
JSIgc3RvcC1jb2xvcj0iI2ZhZmFmYSIgc3RvcC1vcGFjaXR5PSIxIi8+CiAgICA8c3RvcCBvZmZzZXQ9IjI3JSIgc3RvcC1j
b2xvcj0iI2ZhZmFmYSIgc3RvcC1vcGFjaXR5PSIxIi8+CiAgICA8c3RvcCBvZmZzZXQ9IjUwJSIgc3RvcC1jb2xvcj0iI2Zm
ZmZmZiIgc3RvcC1vcGFjaXR5PSIxIi8+CiAgICA8c3RvcCBvZmZzZXQ9Ijc3JSIgc3RvcC1jb2xvcj0iI2Y5ZjlmOSIgc3Rv
cC1vcGFjaXR5PSIxIi8+CiAgICA8c3RvcCBvZmZzZXQ9Ijg1JSIgc3RvcC1jb2xvcj0iI2Y5ZjlmOSIgc3RvcC1vcGFjaXR5
PSIxIi8+CiAgICA8c3RvcCBvZmZzZXQ9IjEwMCUiIHN0b3AtY29sb3I9IiNmOWY5ZjkiIHN0b3Atb3BhY2l0eT0iMSIvPgog
IDwvbGluZWFyR3JhZGllbnQ+CiAgPHJlY3QgeD0iMCIgeT0iMCIgd2lkdGg9IjEiIGhlaWdodD0iMSIgZmlsbD0idXJsKCNn
cmFkLVVjZ2ctZ2VuZXJhdGVkKSIgLz4KPC9zdmc+);
  background: -moz-linear-gradient(top, #fafafa 0%, #fafafa 15%, #fafafa 27%, #ffffff 50%, #f9f9
f9 77%, #f9f9f9 85%, #f9f9f9 100%);/* FF3.6+ */
  background: -webkit-gradient(linear, left top, left bottom, color-stop(0%, #fafafa), color-
stop(15%, #fafafa), color-stop(27%, #fafafa), color-stop(50%, #ffffff), color-stop(77%, #f9f9f9)
, color-stop(85%, #f9f9f9), color-stop(100%, #f9f9f9));/* Chrome,Safari4+ */
  background: -webkit-linear-gradient(top, #fafafa 0%, #fafafa 15%, #fafafa 27%, #ffffff 50%, #f
9f9f9 77%, #f9f9f9 85%, #f9f9f9 100%);/* Chrome10+,Safari5.1+ */
  background: -o-linear-gradient(top, #fafafa 0%, #fafafa 15%, #fafafa 27%, #ffffff 50%, #f9f9f9
 77%, #f9f9f9 85%, #f9f9f9 100%);/* Opera 11.10+ */
  background: -ms-linear-gradient(top, #fafafa 0%, #fafafa 15%, #fafafa 27%, #ffffff 50%, #f9f9f
9 77%, #f9f9f9 85%, #f9f9f9 100%);/* IE10+ */
  background: linear-gradient(top, #fafafa 0%, #fafafa 15%, #fafafa 27%, #ffffff 50%, #f9f9f9 77
%, #f9f9f9 85%, #f9f9f9 100%);/* W3C */
    filter: progid:dximagetransform.microsoft.gradient(startColorstr='#fafafa', endColorstr='#f9f9f
```

```
9', GradientType=0);/* IE6-8 */


}
.footerNav {
  display: inline-block;
  padding-top: 20px;
}
.footerNav .nmLI {
  float: left;
  margin-right: 30px;
}
.footerNav .nmA {
  color: #777;
  box-shadow: 0 0 3px #999;
  font-size: 14px;
  display: block;
  padding: 2px 20px;
  -webkit-border-radius: 4px;
  -moz-border-radius: 4px;
  border-radius: 4px;
  -moz-background-clip: padding;
  -webkit-background-clip: padding-box;
  background-clip: padding-box;
  box-shadow: 0 0 3px rgba(0, 0, 0, 0.5), inset 0 0 2px rgba(0, 0, 0, 0.5);
  background: #ffffff;/* Old browsers */
  /* IE9 SVG, needs conditional override of 'filter' to 'none' */
  background: url(data:image/svg+xml;base64,PD94bWwgdmVyc2lvbj0iMS4wIiA/Pgo8c3ZnIHhtbG5zPSJodHRw
Oi8vd3d3LnczLm9yZy8yMDAwL3N2ZyIgd2lkdGg9IjEwMCUiIGhlaWdodD0iMTAwJSIgdmlld0JveD0iMCAwIDEgMSIgcHJl
c2VydmVBc3BlY3RSYXRpbz0ibm9uZSI+CiAgPGxpbmVhckdyYWRpZW50IGlkPSJncmFkLXVjZ2ctZ2VuZXJhdGVkIiBncmFk
aWVudFVuaXRzPSJ1c2VyU3BhY2VPblVzZSIgeDE9IjAlIiB5MT0iMTAwJSIgeDI9IjEwMCUiIHkyPSIwJSI+CiAgICA8c3Rv
cCBvZmZzZXQ9IjAlIiBzdG9wLWNvbG9yPSIjZmZmZmZmIiBzdG9wLW9wYWNpdHk9IjEiLz4KICAgIDxzdG9wIG9mZnNldD0i
MTUlIiBzdG9wLWNvbG9yPSIjZjlmOWY5IiBzdG9wLW9wYWNpdHk9IjEiLz4KICAgIDxzdG9wIG9mZnNldD0iNTAlIiBzdG9w
LWNvbG9yPSIjZmZmZmZmIiBzdG9wLW9wYWNpdHk9IjEiLz4KICAgIDxzdG9wIG9mZnNldD0iNzElIiBzdG9wLWNvbG9yPSIj
ZjhmOGY4IiBzdG9wLW9wYWNpdHk9IjEiLz4KICAgIDxzdG9wIG9mZnNldD0iODUlIiBzdG9wLWNvbG9yPSIjZmZmZmZmIiBz
dG9wLW9wYWNpdHk9IjEiLz4KICAgIDxzdG9wIG9mZnNldD0iMTAwJSIgc3RvcC1jb2xvcj0iI2Y4ZjhmOCIgc3RvcC1vcGFj
aXR5PSIxIi8+CiAgPC9saW5lYXJHcmFkaWVudD4KICA8cmVjdCB4PSIwIiB5PSIwIiB3aWR0aD0iMSIgaGVpZ2h0PSIxIiBm
aWxsPSJ1cmwoI2dyYWQtdWNnZy1nZW5lcmF0ZWQpIiAvPgo8L3N2Zz4=);
  background: -moz-linear-gradient(45deg, #ffffff 0%, #f9f9f9 15%, #ffffff 50%, #f8f8f8 71%, #ff
ffff 85%, #f8f8f8 100%);/* FF3.6+ */
  background: -webkit-gradient(linear, left bottom, right top, color-stop(0%, #ffffff), color-
stop(15%, #f9f9f9), color-stop(50%, #ffffff), color-stop(71%, #f8f8f8), color-stop(85%, #ffffff)
, color-stop(100%, #f8f8f8));/* Chrome,Safari4+ */
  background: -webkit-linear-gradient(45deg, #ffffff 0%, #f9f9f9 15%, #ffffff 50%, #f8f8f8 71%,
#ffffff 85%, #f8f8f8 100%);/* Chrome10+,Safari5.1+ */
  background: -o-linear-gradient(45deg, #ffffff 0%, #f9f9f9 15%, #ffffff 50%, #f8f8f8 71%, #ffff
ff 85%, #f8f8f8 100%);/* Opera 11.10+ */
  background: -ms-linear-gradient(45deg, #ffffff 0%, #f9f9f9 15%, #ffffff 50%, #f8f8f8 71%, #fff
fff 85%, #f8f8f8 100%);/* IE10+ */
  background: linear-gradient(45deg, #ffffff 0%, #f9f9f9 15%, #ffffff 50%, #f8f8f8 71%, #ffffff
85%, #f8f8f8 100%);/* W3C */
```

```css
  filter: progid :dximagetransform.microsoft.gradient(startColorstr='#ffffff',
endColorstr='#f8f8f8', GradientType=1);/* IE6-8 fallback on horizontal gradient */

}
.footerNav .ie9 .nmA {
  filter: none;
}
.footerNav .nmSlideout {
  height: auto;
  padding: 10px;
}
.footerNav .nmUL-L2 {
  padding-bottom: 20px;
}
.footerNav .nmA-L2 {
  color: #888;
  font-size: 12px;
  text-align: right;
  display: block;
  padding-bottom: 2px;
}
.footerNav .nmA-L2:first-word {
  color: #00F;
  font-weight: bold;
}
.footerNav .searchWrap {
  display: none;
}
.mainFooterUL {
  display: inline-block;
}
.mfLI {
  float: left;
  padding: 0 10px;
  border-right: 1px solid #999;
}
.mfLI.mfLast {
  border: 0;
}
.mfA {
  font-size: 12px;
  color: #999;
}
.mainFooterWrap {
  text-align: center;
  padding-bottom: 20px;
}
.legalWrap {
  background: #FFF;
  display: inline-block;
  padding: 10px 20px;
```

```
  -webkit-border-radius: 10px;
  -moz-border-radius: 10px;
  border-radius: 10px;
  -moz-background-clip: padding;
  -webkit-background-clip: padding-box;
  background-clip: padding-box;
  box-shadow: inset 1px 1px 2px rgba(0, 0, 0, 0.5);
}
.legalText {
  margin: 0;
  font-size: 12px;
  color: #777;
}
.legalText a {
  color: #555;
  text-decoration: underline;
}
```

Most of that code is pretty straightforward and similar to other things we've done. However, we want to point out a couple of things about the footer layout code. We'll start with the double box-shadow in our `.footerNav .nmA` ruleset, as shown in the following line:

```
box-shadow: 0 0 3px rgba(0, 0, 0, 0.5), inset 0 0 2px rgba(0, 0, 0, 0.5);
```

That line has three items to which we draw your attention. First, we used RGBA because that lets us set a transparency value through the Alpha (A) value. In this case, we've set the transparency at 50 percent (0.5). The result is black shadows with 50 percent transparency, which makes them dark gray and lets the items in the background show through the shadows.

Second, we used an inset value, which makes the box seem to recede into the page, thanks to the light source seeming to come from the upper left. (The light source could come from anywhere, but upper left is the norm.) The inset effect is visible around the copyright notice.

The keyword *inset*, tells the browser we want a shadow on the inside of the box. This can be used to make the inside of the box appear inset, meaning depressed, with a shadow being cast in the elevation difference, usually with the light simulated to come from the top left. We've set this effect around the copyright notice. The effect is defined by the following line within the `.legalWrap` class:

```
box-shadow: 1px 1px 2px rgba(0,0,0,.5);
```

▨ **Tip** The general format of a box shadow is as follows: box-shadow : `horizontal_offset vertical_offset blur_radius color;`

However, we didn't want the subheads for the navigation to appear sunken. In fact, we wanted the opposite effect: a bit of elevation. To achieve that appearance, we set the shadow to help define the edges and give the link a small amount of height. So we set the following shadow in the `.footerNav .nmA` class:

```
Box-shadow: 0 0 2px rbga(0,0,0,.5);
```

This makes an equal shadow of 2 pixels around the entire inside of the boxes that hold the categories in the site map. It creates a kind of bevel effect.

The third item to notice is that we have multiple shadow definitions separated by a comma. You can add as many shadows as you like, separating each from the others with a comma. To get an idea of how crazy it can get, visit another Paul Irish site to see how he uses shadows on text: `http://mothereffingtextshadow.com/`

We recommend caution with shadows, no matter where you apply them, unless you're making a site to demonstrate shadows. Wild shadows can make reading and navigation harder for the visitor. Still, when used well, they can draw the visitor's eye to important places, so they're a good idea.

SVG

As we mentioned at the beginning of the chapter, the footer can be a bit boring. To give it a bit more zip, we've added a little progressive enhancement via SVG (Scalable Vector Graphics). SVG can be pretty useful for certain things. However, Internet Explorer didn't include support for SVG until version 9. So we employ our usual trick of feature detection through Modernzr and only show the SVG if the browser knows what to do with it. SVG really shines on mobile devices that run the WebKit browser (iPhone, Android, Palm). However, we need to support older browsers, too, so we'll use progressive enhancement yet again to ensure that all visitors get a page that looks as good as their browsers can let a page look.

Before we get to the implementation, we need to explain a few things about SVG. SVG is stored as a dialect of XML that corresponds to a schema defined by the World Wide Web Consortium. The current recommendation (version 1.1) can be found at the W3 web site: `http://www.w3.org/TR/SVG11/`

SVG allows creation of complex shapes that then scale correctly to any size. A few years ago, Jay used SVG to create a four-foot-tall metal sign for a client. Because it was SVG, he could use a color laser to print off drafts of the sign on ordinary letter-size paper. Once the client was happy with the design, he gave the file to a metal-fabricating company, which used the image to create the sign. Because SVG scales to any size, Jay didn't have to worry about the sign looking good when rendered four feet tall. The client is happy with it, and the sign is still on the side of a building in Austin, Texas.

The secret to SVG's ability to endlessly scale is in how it's rendered. SVG (or any other vector image format) doesn't define a bunch of pixels, as raster image formats do. Instead, it describes various shapes and the relationships between them. If you ever took a geometry class, you know exactly how SVG works. It uses the same mathematical relationships between and within simple shapes (circles, triangles, squares, rectangles, and other polygons) to render images at any size. Complex shapes, such as letters in a font, are rendered as sets of simpler shapes, but that's a detail that the rendering engine handles (good thing, too, or SVG would be too much of a pain to use). Whether you need a logo on a web page, a four-foot-tall metal sign, a billboard, or a message on the side of a blimp, SVG scales such that the image prints correctly (without pixelation or other unfortunate printing artifacts) at that size.

A designer can create the XML to define an SVG image by hand, and that works well enough for simple images. However, it's generally easier to use a nice drawing tool and then save the result as SVG. Fortunately, Adobe Illustrator, CorelDraw, Inkscape, and various others can all save as SVG. Additionally, the Google Code project includes an SVG drawing tool. It's at `http://svg-edit.googlecode.com/svn/branches/2.5.1/editor/svg-editor.html`. Finally, Apache, through its XML Graphics Project, maintains a simple tool that's handy for experimenting with SVG. It's called Batik, and it's at `http://xmlgraphics.apache.org/batik/`. Jay used Batik to make that metal sign.

So where's the SVG in our footer? It's the top piece that provides the illusion of depth to the footer section. The idea is to create the illusion of a counter on which the customer's product sits. Mostly, though, we made it to show you some simple SVG.

The SVG that we use in the footer defines the simple shape (a light gray bar with inward-sloping ends) shown in Figure 9-2.

Figure 9-2. The SVG image in the footer.

Listing 9-6 shows the code that generates the SVG image and the div element that contains it.

Listing 9-6. The footerTopHolder div Element

```
<div class="footerTopHolder">
  <svg version="1.1" xmlns="http://www.w3.org/2000/svg" x="0px" y="0px" width="100%"
height="19px" viewBox="0 0 1133 19" preserveAspectRatio="none">
    <path fill="#F3F3F3" d="M0,19L19,0h1094l19,19H0z"/>
  </svg>
</div>
```

Before we plunge into the details of using an SVG element, let's consider the benefit of doing so. In this case, the SVG takes 182 bytes. A PNG image of the same size (1133 × 19) takes 290 bytes. Better still, we saved an HTTP request, because the SVG content is in the HTML. Both of those factors give us better performance than we could get with an image.

Now let's take a minute to look at the svg element. The opening tag of the svg element includes a number of attributes that we need for various reasons. We need the id attribute so that we can use JavaScript to modify the image. We'll get to that later in the chapter. We need the version and xmlns attributes to identify for the browser what kind of image we're creating. The x and y attributes define the origin of the shape. The width attribute, since it's set to 100 percent, specifies that the image should occupy all the available width. The height attribute specifies that the height should be 19 pixels.

■ **Tip** The viewBox attribute defines the minimum and maximum height and width for the rendering engine. As a rule, it should match the height and width of the elements that are children of the svg element. In our case, we have just one child element, so we set the size of our viewBox attribute to the size of the child element, which we have to derive mathematically. (We'll show how to do it when we get to the child element.)

Also, setting the viewBox defines the ratio of height to width. As different visitors use browsers with different widths (or if people change the widths of their browsers), that ratio remains the same. Consequently, the height of the bar gets smaller as the width gets smaller. In this case, we don't want that; we want the height of the bar to remain 19 pixels, no matter how wide the bar is. To do that, we have to use the preserveAspectRatio attribute with a value of none, which means we're not preserving the aspect ratio. Setting the preserveAspectRatio to none makes the image fill all available space, which gives us the effect we want. If that all seems less than clear, please bear with us. When we get to the finished product and show the resulting image, which we'll do later in the chapter, the interplay of the various elements should be much clearer.

The path element contains two attributes. The obvious one of the two is the fill attribute, which specifies the fill color. Since we're using a solid and opaque fill, we don't need other fill-related attributes, such as fill-rule or fill-opacity. The d (short for 'data') attribute has content that is more complex. It specifies the path that creates the shape we want. It defines four points through the following string: "M0,19L19,0h1094l19,19H0z". The trick to understanding how that string defines a path is in knowing what the letters within the path mean. Table 9-1 describes the various path-definition instructions (each of which is a single character) and their meanings.

Table 9-1. Basic SVG Path Instructions

Instruction	Meaning
M	moveto, absolute: Move the cursor to the absolute coordinates following the character.

M	moveto, relative: Move the cursor to the relative coordinates following the character
L	lineto, absolute: Draw a line from the current cursor position to the new cursor position, given in absolute coordinates
L	lineto, relative: Draw a line from the current cursor position to the new cursor position, given in relative coordinates
H	horizontal lineto, absolute: Draw a horizontal line from the current cursor position to the new cursor position, given in absolute coordinates
H	horizontal lineto, relative: Draw a line from the current cursor position to the new cursor position, given in relative coordinates
V	vertical lineto, absolute: Draw a line from the current cursor position to the new cursor position, given in absolute coordinates
V	vertical lineto, relative: Draw a line from the current cursor position to the new cursor position, given in relative coordinates
Z	closepath: closes the path, which enables filling
Z	closepath: closes the path, which enables filling

▪ **Note**   We've covered just the basic commands. Other commands, for defining more complex shapes, also exist. See the W3 SVG specification for more detail. You can find the SVG specification at `http://www.w3.org/TR/SVG/Overview.html`

If you work your way through the path string, you can see that it sets an initial location (`M0, 19`), draws four lines, and finally closes the path (with the z instruction). Table 9-2 describes the instructions in more detail.

Table 9-2. SVG Path Instruction Details

Instruction	Meaning
M0,19	Move the cursor to the absolute coordinates 0, 19.
L19,0	Draw a line, using absolute coordinates, from the current cursor location (0, 19) to the new cursor location (19, 0). This instruction defines the sloping line on the left side.
h1094	Draw a horizontal line, using relative coordinates from the current cursor location (19, 0) to the new cursor location (1114, 0). (1114, 0 is an absolute location and is the result of 20 + 1094.) This instruction defines the top edge of the image.
l19,19	Draw a line, using relative coordinates from the current cursor location (1114, 0) to 1133, 19. (1133, 19 is an absolute location and is the result of 1114 + 19, 0 + 19.) This instruction defines the sloping line on the right side.
H0	Draw a horizontal line, using absolute coordinates from the current cursor location (1133, 19) to the new cursor location (0, 19). This instruction defines the bottom edge of the image.
Z	Close the path.

By calculating the absolute cursor positions, as we did in Table 9-2, you can figure out how big the viewBox attribute of the svg element has to be. Of course, we actually worked backwards from a desired width of 1133, which is the width of the 1140 grid with a small margin.

To make sure the containing div.footerTopHolder appears when SVG is available, we add the code shown in Listing 9-7. Again, we're relying on Modernzr to test for SVG support, and then we're adding either svg or no-svg to the class attribute, depending on what Modernizr finds.

Listing 9-7. Removing the SVG Image for Browsers That Can't Display It

```
.no-svg .footerTopHolder {
                display:none;
}
```

As we mentioned earlier in this section, the SVG takes 182 bytes. A PNG image of the same size (1133 × 19) takes 290 bytes. More importantly, we saved an HTTP request, because the SVG content is in the HTML. Both of those factors yield better performance than we could get with an image.

In addition to the size advantage, there's another benefit from using SVG: The height can be forced to remain the same even though the width changes. It's not something you'd often want to do, but it does make for an interesting demonstration of another of SVG's advantages. Because we set width ="100%" and height ="19px", the browser ensures that the height remains 19 pixels as the width changes.

Traditionally if we used an image here and our browser window got smaller and our nice responsive site adapted to that smaller size, you'd expect something like the difference between Figures 9-3 and 9-4.

Figure 9-3. Original size

Figure 9-4. Smaller size (50%)Using SVG, while specifying a specific height and a percentage width, produces an image whose height does not change, as shown in Figure 9-5. Also, because the SVG rendering engine within the browser is rendering a mathematical construct (it's geometry, remember?), it never, ever produces any unfortunate rendering artifacts, such as pixelation.

Figure 9-5. Smaller size with fixed height

Again, it's not a technique to reach for often, but it sure is handy when you need it.JavaScript Interaction

Now let's consider the last benefit of using SVG. You can interact with the image via JavaScript. Using jQuery makes this kind of interaction very easy. Just use the .attr method and reset the various values within the SVG. Listing 9-8 shows a simple example of the kind of thing you can do to an SVG image.

Listing 9-8. Modifying an SVG Image with JavaScript

```
$("#footerTop").attr("width", "200px");
$("#footerTop").find("path").attr("fill", "#0000FF");
```

And now it's 200 pixels wide and blue, as shown in Figure 9-6.

Figure 9-6. *The footer bar after it's been changed with JavaScript*

Focus your attention on the ends of the lines. See how the angle is no longer 45 degrees? That's because we changed the width attribute of the svg element but didn't change the values of the d attribute within the path element. The effect is that of a vanishing point somewhere near the top of the monitor, which is the effect we had in mind.

We've just scratched the surface of what can be done with SVG. Far more interesting (and much too large a topic for this book) is using SVG in conjunction with the canvas element. SVG and the canvas element offer a real alternative to complex Flash functionality, experience, and interaction. We don't hate Flash (Michael was a Flash developer for a long time), but we don't recommend Flash today if content has to go mobile.

More Than Simple Shapes

We want to share one last thought about SVG. In the example on our sample web site, we use a very simple shape. However, SVG is capable of rendering far more complex images. By using a program such as Adobe Illustrator, you can make some amazing SVG art. The issue is usually balancing complexity and size. The more complex the graphic, the more code needed to get it to render properly. Sometimes, it makes more sense to use an image if scaling or printing isn't a concern.

That being said, though, let's look at some interesting functionality that happens to be built into Illustrator. It can turn complex images (even photographs) into SVG. However, the size of these files is usually prohibitively large. Just for fun, Michael used Live Trace in Illustrator to make an SVG image of himself. You can play with an interactive demo that lets you change the size of the image at http://clikz.us/svg.html. Now see if you can enlarge Michael's head to match his ego. This image requires a file size of 600 kilobytes (600 kb), proving that SVG is not always a good choice for a complex image (especially a photograph).

Figure 9-7. *Michael's self-portrait*

Summary

In this chapter, we described the footer that we use on our sample site: `http://clikz.us`.

In the course of doing so, we demonstrated the following:how to reuse content to make both a menu and a site map.how to highlight important parts of the footer with shadows.how to use SVG on a web site.

In the course of describing how to use SVG as content within a web page, we demonstrated that

- For simple images, SVG uses fewer bytes and reduces the number of HTTP requests, both of which make for better page-load times and less network traffic.

- SVG can be manipulated by JavaScript, letting you change an image in response to events on the page; this technique can make for some great interactive pages.

- SVG is not the best way to render complex images, especially photographs, though you can have some fun doing it.

We won't discuss the footer any further in this book. However, you can see it in action on every page of our sample site: `http://clikz.us`.

This chapter concludes our description of the items used on every page of our site. From here, we'll plunge into creating and using reusable web controls, as described in Chapter 5.

CHAPTER 10

■ ■ ■

Fractal Design Patterns

"Fractal" may seem a bit odd (especially since Jay has written about fractals in the strict mathematical sense in another book). In this case, though, we're using the term somewhat metaphorically. By strict mathematical definition, a fractal is a geometric shape that has symmetry of scale, meaning that you can zoom in to an arbitrary depth and see the same pattern repeated. Figure 10-1 shows a fractal tree that Jay created by writing a Java class. It represents our notion of building many pages from a few reusable components.

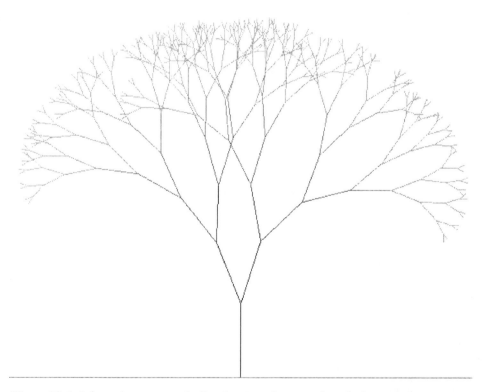

Figure 10-1. A fractal tree, to symbolize the recursive container design pattern

While we're not presenting mathematically derived fractals, we are going to describe a design pattern that includes repeating the same pattern to whatever depth we need (sometimes four or more levels deep). In other words, we're going to describe a recursive container pattern.

We mentioned the basic idea in Chapter 5 in the course of laying out the theoretical underpinnings of how we build large-scale web sites. In this chapter, we're going to explore the idea in more detail. In the remaining chapters within this section of the book, we're going to present a number of the fractal-type patterns as reusable components that we use throughout our sample site. Of course, you're also welcome to use them in your own work.

Reusable components (we call them controls, after the notion of user-interface controls) provide a number of benefits:

- Faster page development time

- Faster bug fixing

- Increased consistency

- Fewer patterns

- Greater acceptance

- Increased quality

We discuss each of these benefits in detail later in this chapter.

In Chapter 5 we showed a single bit of content that we then reused in a variety of ways by changing the CSS associated with the content. In that fashion, we derived a building block that we could put in a number of places. As just noted, we call those building blocks controls.

Defining a Control

Let's more closely define what a control is. A control is an HTML fragment with associated CSS and possibly JavaScript that is reusable and configurable. Configuration can include changing the content of a control. Let's consider the simplest of our controls, the Label control, as an example:

```
<span title="A description of this label" class="labelControl anotherClass">I'm a fun label
control</span>
```

We'll use a bit of PHP to make this into something reusable. Although we've chosen PHP to illustrate these principles, they're very basic concepts that work nicely for almost any server-side language. We chose PHP because it's a scripting language, which makes describing concepts a little easier than doing so would be in an object-oriented language such as Java or C# (though we've used both of those to do this kind of work).

Now, back to our control. We can create a common function that will construct our label for us:

Listing 10-1. *The PHP Function Behind the Label Control*

```php
<?php
function label($innerText, $titleText, $addClasses) {
  var $payload = '<span title=' . $titleText . ' ';
  $payload .= 'class="labelControl';
  if ($addClasses != null) {
    $payload .= ' ' . $addClasses;
  }
  $payload .= '">';
```

```
    $payload .= $innerText . '</span>';
    echo $payload;}
?>
```

> ■ **Note**   In PHP, the '.' character is the string concatenation character, serving the same function as the '+'
> character in many other languages. Similarly, the '.=' operator concatenates the string after the operator with the
> string value of the variable before the operator and assigns the result to the variable. The '.=' operator is the
> equivalent of the '+=' operator in many other languages, such as Java and C#.

To call this control on our pages, we'd put the following in the HTML where we want the label to go:

```
<?php label("I'm a fun label control", "A description of this label", "anotherClass"); ?>
```

As you can see, the label function is a very simple string builder wherein we replace inner text values
with the function's arguments. If the builder of the page specifies additional classes, we put them in.
Otherwise, the only class is `labelControl`. The echo statement is PHP's way of sending the function's
output to the HTML where this function is called.

You might think, "This is such a simple piece of HTML, why go to all the trouble of making a control."
Why? Because doing this, even for simple code such as a label, has certain advantages:

- Code consistency
- Simpler updates
- Greater readability
- Clear intentions

Code Consistency

You've now locked in a solid piece of HTML that can be used across your site and that will have a
consistent and predictable structure. You won't have other developers using particular (and possibly
peculiar) patterns of their own.

Simpler Updates

Because you've abstracted this code to a function, you have a central point from which to make changes
that will be in place throughout your site. You'll also have the option of adding functionality and structure.
As we'll mention later in this chapter, you can have segregated CSS and JS to match each control. As all of
the pertinent code is in one place, this greatly accelerates updates.

Greater Readability

Although you're obscuring the HTML of the control when you instantiate it, you don't have to look at all
the extra clutter. This benefit is especially helpful in larger, more complex controls.

Clear Intentions

Provided you use descriptive names for your controls, your intent is clear to other developers—and to yourself when you revisit this code at a later date.

■ **Tip**   Since these names won't be inserted into the HTML, you can use even long descriptive names without worrying about increasing the byte count (hence bandwidth usage) of the page.

Now that we've laid out the simplest possible control, let's move on to the fractal part of our pattern: controls within controls within controls.

Going Fractal: A Case Study

We've mentioned elsewhere that we worked together on a major e-commerce site (one of the five most active e-commerce sites in the world, in fact). More specifically, we worked on a framework team for this site. More than 20 teams used this framework to accelerate their development. We provided everything from general page layout intentions to controls that ran the gamut from simple link controls to complex mini-apps. What made this framework successful, besides having a truly great group of developers and visionary leadership, was the fractal design pattern.

While abstracting repeating patterns to controls added tremendous agility and speed, what made it exponential was that each of these patterns consisted of smaller patterns. For example, let's talk about a common e-commerce control, a faceted navigation pane, such as the one shown in Figure 10-2. This control lets visitors filter search results by a variety of criteria.

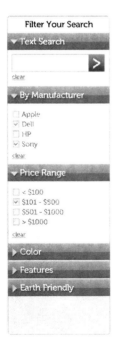

Figure 10-2. A faceted navigation control

What's important to us is that this control is made up of smaller reusable controls: link controls, label controls, checkbox controls, accordion controls, and so on. Consequently, faceted navigation becomes one of those just-mentioned mini-apps. Also, the faceted navigation pane is itself a component within a larger control—namely, the side navigation control that was itself contained in an overall page layout control. Figure 10-3 shows the major controls (most of which consist of other controls) within the faceted navigation control.

Figure 10-3. *Controls within the faceted navigation control*

This seemingly endless (and so fractal in character) nesting of controls within controls pays off in many ways. The most obvious is that you don't have to rewrite code every time you need a control whose elements are already controls. For the teams that subscribed to our framework, their job was greatly simplified. They were able to write a single line of code and pass arguments (generally in the form of a Model object within the .NET MVC framework) to get consistent, pixel-perfect elements with which to build a new page.

The obvious benefits include:

- Faster page development time

- Faster bug fixing

- Increased consistency

We describe each benefit in detail in the following sections.

Faster Page Development Time

We saw increased speed (from months to days, in one case) for making pages. Consequently, our client teams were getting new products onto the web site much more quickly, which made the businesspeople (and everyone else, too) happy.

Faster Bug Fixing

We could easily point out where a team that used the framework had somehow misused it. Prior to the framework, it seemed like each of our 20-plus client teams excelled in finding their own ways to make messes. Sometimes, of course, the error was ours, generally in some edge case that we had never anticipated. Since we were working with a limited number of components that we knew well, we could generally fix these bugs quickly (often within a day).

Increased Consistency

As the framework began to gain adoption by the organization's development teams, pages increasingly resembled one another. That resemblance made finding products and information a lot easier for the customers. It also made it easier for the development teams to set expectations for the businesspeople; they could have conversations that amounted to "Your new page will look like this existing page." Finally, because we were working with a separate design organization (another department within the company but separate from development), the designers were happy to see their designs gain greater use by the various development teams.

Then, as we worked more with the teams who used the framework, we started to see benefits we hadn't expected:

- Fewer patterns
- Greater acceptance
- Better-than-expected page-load times
- Increased quality

Again, we'll describe each of these unexpected benefits in detail in the following sections.

Fewer Patterns

We really started to see every aspect of the site as a repeatable pattern, which had the effect of letting us reduce patterns. We would often identify designs that were very similar to one another, yet each one was supported by its own dedicated set of HTML, CSS, and JavaScript. We were able to approach our stakeholders (business interests, that separate design team, and the developers who used the framework) and ask, "Can you use our existing control instead of your own control?" Most of the time, the stakeholders weren't aware of the existing control. Since we only asked that question when the custom control was very similar to a framework control, the stakeholders would usually agree.

Greater Acceptance

We weren't in a position to force people to use our controls. Our team had been constituted as a team that was equal to the existing teams, so we had no particular authority. Consequently, part of our job was basically sales. One of our best sales tools was getting the client teams to realize that it was in their interest to have their requirements instituted quickly, and the framework offered the fastest way to make new pages that would meet the requirements of the various business units (we're talking about a company with over 80,000 employees—there were a lot of business interests beating on the web development teams). Also, they understood that consistency within a large site is desirable, which gave us another entry point for our sales conversation.Better-Than-Expected Page-Load Times

Naturally, we expected some improvement in page-load times, since we were writing our reusable components in such a way that HTTP requests would drop and JavaScript and CSS would see much more reuse. However, even the members of the framework team were surprised by the extent of the improvement. In one case, we saw page-load time drop to a third of what it had been before that client team used the framework. If you look around the web today, you can find sites that have CSS files larger than 1 megabyte (we shake our heads in disbelief every time we find one, but there they are). By developing a framework of reusable components, including 8 page-layout intentions (which are essentially the master components that hold all the other components) and 40 or so controls to use within those layouts, we achieved a gzipped and minimized CSS file that is just about 50 kilobytes in size.

Increased Quality

The final less obvious benefit was quality. Because we were able to reduce all the content across thousands of pages (tens of thousands, in fact) down to fewer than 50 controls, we were able to put a lot of time into making those controls rock solid. We focused on both reliability and usability. A team that switched to using our framework could rely on the controls working the same way every time. Also, we were one of the few teams with a dedicated quality group within our team; for every two developers, we had a QA person, and each QA person was an experienced web developer in his or her own right. Then we documented the framework as an API, providing clear, meaningful names for all the controls and their arguments and settings. Finally, we provided a sample site that showed how to implement each of the controls, including all of each one's variations (we call them treatments). Finally, each control had a link to the design department's definition of the control. With the link, our customer teams could verify that we had correctly implemented the control and get further guidance from the design team about how to use any given control. We had the time to do all of that because we had identified a fairly small set of controls that we needed to support.

While we happily admit to being proud of our work on this large corporation's framework team, the point isn't simply to blow our own horn. The message we want you to take away from this history lesson is that adopting reusable components and then using them on every page can provide substantial benefits for your organization in both its business and development concerns.

Now that we've provided a high-level overview of how a reusable framework does its thing, let's move on to two related items that we've discovered improve performance (both page-load time and developer performance) further still: (1) segregating CSS and JavaScript and (2) combining CSS and JavaScript.

Segregating CSS and JavaScript

In essence, we adopted a "divide first and combine later" strategy for managing complexity within our CSS and JavaScript files. While it may sound odd, it turned out to be highly effective. So let's move on to the details of how it worked.

In conjunction with the fractal concept, the team also adopted a pattern of making small CSS and JS files that are associated with each control. For example, a link control would also have a `link.css` file and a `link.js` file. We would then use a combiner (which we'll get to later in this chapter) to stitch these files together with other relevant CSS and JavaScript files.

The big gain from this approach came in the form of defect resolution and maintenance. By being able to affect many patterns in a single code base, we made fixing defects and making change requests to our files a relative snap. And by having segregated CSS and JavaScript files, we didn't have to pour through a giant combination of CSS and JavaScript looking for relevant code. Especially when you're on a team (or multiple teams, as in our case) of folks writing code, it's hard to predict what kind of selectors they'll use to affect their CSS/JavaScript. It's easy to find something if the selector is definitive, but some people will use a descendant selector, such as that shown in Listing 10-2.

Listing 10-2. *Example of a Descendant Selector*

```
<style>
  .main div ul a {
    color: #999;
  }
</style>
```

They'll use a style such as that shown in Listing 10-2 to define the appearance of HTML content such as that shown in Listing 10-3.

Listing 10-3. *HTML Example for the Descendant Selector Example*

```
<div class="main">
  <p class="desc">This is a great idea </p>
  <div class="reasonsWhy">
    <ul>
      <li><a href="reason1.html" class="theReasons">Reason #1</a></li>
      <li><a href="reason2.html" class="theReasons">Reason #1</a></li>
    </ul>
  </div>
</div>
```

The relationship of CSS and HTML shown in Listings 10-2 and 10-3 is bad for a number of reasons. For one thing, it's slower than it could be, due to the use of a descendant selector in the CSS. (As we mentioned in Chapter 3, since descendant selectors cause the rendering engine to traverse the DOM tree, they are always slower than selecting by ID or by class.) The issue that makes debugging very hard, though, is trying to find that selector when an error arises. Consider a large set of CSS all contained in a single file. How many rules will you have to read to find the right one? And how often will you read a rule and, because it is very similar to many other rules, not realize that it's actually the match for the problem you're trying to find? That kind of thing burns a lot of time and is very frustrating.

But just because it's a bad idea doesn't mean a teammate might not do it. So to avoid the whole problem, even if your teammates are using poor selectors, use small CSS files that contain just the rules you need for a particular component. At least then you'll have a chance (because it should be much less code) of quickly finding the right selector as you comb through the code. Additionally, you can be fussy about your CSS preferences, whether it's the way you order your nondestructive rules (rules that don't affect specificity) or using particular parent/child structures for semantic reasons.

Finally, with big CSS files, a team can quickly lose discipline when rush situations arise (and they always do) and it becomes untenable to rearrange the files later. Once you reach that point, you're stuck with constantly maintaining that huge file. With smaller files, the bugs are easier to find, and the fixes are easier to make, but you have to have the discipline to carve up your code into small chunks. Once you've done it a few times and see the benefits, you won't have much trouble finding the discipline.

Combining CSS and JavaScript

It's great to make lots of little files at development time, but it's a disaster at runtime. So what do you do? You combine all the little files into one big file that you send with every page.

There are lots of solutions for minimizing and combining files. For our e-commerce example we used the Google Code Project's Minify utility. Its tagline reads: "Combines, minifies, and caches JavaScript and CSS files on demand to speed up page loads." You can download it from `http://code.google.com/p/minify/`

■ **Note** The Minify utility works only for PHP. You can find similar utilities for other languages. Yahoo's YUI compressor (available at http://developer.yahoo.com/yui/compressor/) is written in Java, for example.

The Minify utility provides the following benefits:

- It combines and minifies multiple CSS or JavaScript files into a single download.

- It uses an enhanced port of Douglas Crockford's JSMin library and custom classes to minify CSS and HTML.

- It caches server-side (files/apc/memcache) to avoid doing unnecessary work.

- It responds with an HTTP 304 (Not Modified) response when the browser has an up-to-date cache copy.

- Most modules are lazy loaded as needed (304 responses use minimal code).

- It automatically rewrites relative URIs in combined CSS files to point to valid locations.

- With caching enabled, Minify is capable of handling hundreds of requests per second on a moderately powerful server.

- For content encoding, it uses gzip, based on request headers. Since caching allows doing so, it serves gzipped files faster than Apache's mod_deflate option!

- It provides test cases for most components.

- It allows easy integration of third-party minifiers.

- It has separate utility classes for HTTP encoding and cache control.Minify works by sending your CSS and JS files, respectively, as query parameters to the PHP script. The following line of code shows an example for CSS:

```
<link type="text/css" rel="stylesheet" href="/min/b=css&amp;f=reset.css,1140.
css,mainNavDropDown.css,mainHead.css,breadcrumbs.css,sidebox.css,productStack.css,base.
css,footer.css" />
```

The following line of code shows an example for JavaScript:

```
<script href="/min/f=common.js,link.js,mainNavDropDown.js" ></script>
```

Just put those code lines in the same place you'd put the files. Of course, we know CSS is best in the head and JS in the bottom, but you have full flexibility to choose what seem to you the best places.

The only real downside to combining is that it can make debugging more difficult with Firebug or a similar browser tool. Because of the minimization (removing spaces and shortening identifiers) and because of all the files being combined, reading the code can be a real pain. To avoid that problem during development, we use separate references to the CSS and JavaScript files. Listing 10-4 shows an example.

Listing 10-4. Separate Links to CSS Files

```
<!-- <link rel="stylesheet" href="css/reset.css">
<link rel="stylesheet" href="css/1140.css">
<link rel="stylesheet" href="css/mainNav.css">
<link rel="stylesheet" href="css/mainHead.css">
<link rel="stylesheet" href="css/breadcrumbs.css">
<link rel="stylesheet" href="css/sidebox.css">
<link rel="stylesheet" href="css/productStack.css">
<link rel="stylesheet" href="css/base.css"> -->
<!-- <link type="text/css" rel="stylesheet" href="/min/b=css&amp;f=reset.css,1140.
css,mainNavDropDown.css,mainHead.css,breadcrumbs.css,sidebox.css,productStack.css,base.
css,footer.css" /> -->
```

When we debug, we remove the comment around the individual links and add the comment around the combined link, as shown in Listing 10-5.

Listing 10-5. Link to a Combined CSS File

```
<!-- <link rel="stylesheet" href="css/reset.css">
<link rel="stylesheet" href="css/1140.css">
<link rel="stylesheet" href="css/mainNav.css">
<link rel="stylesheet" href="css/mainHead.css">
<link rel="stylesheet" href="css/breadcrumbs.css">
<link rel="stylesheet" href="css/sidebox.css">
<link rel="stylesheet" href="css/productStack.css">
<link rel="stylesheet" href="css/base.css">
-->
<!-- <link type="text/css" rel="stylesheet" href="/min/b=css&amp;f=reset.css,1140.
css,mainNavDropDown.css,mainHead.css,breadcrumbs.css,sidebox.css,productStack.css,base.
css,footer.css" /> -->
```

That arrangement gives us code we can much more readily debug. Of course, we remove the individual links when a page goes to production.

Summary

This chapter covered the fractal, or recursive container, pattern of placing controls within controls and then placing those controls within other controls, and so on to any level of depth one might consider. We also presented a case study from our own experience to demonstrate the benefits to both business and development teams that use this approach. Finally, we discussed the details of dividing CSS and JavaScript files into small pieces at development time and combining them at runtime.

Over the course of the next several chapters, we'll show some concrete examples of this approach. We'll start with some of the simpler controls (links and buttons) and work up to tables and tabs and product listings. Along the way, we'll continue to discuss the details of using controls within controls, because the more complex controls contain the simpler controls. The code we'll present and the sample site where we'll show how it all works isn't as complex as the site we mentioned in the case study, but it's enough to get you started on better controlling the complexity of your sites.

CHAPTER 11

■ ■ ■

Link Control

You might be thinking, do we really need a control for a link? Isn't it just easier to write a single line of HTML to take care of this task? While we're fans of not using something complex when something simple will work, we also know we can gain significant benefits by making a link control. For one thing, we can improve the site's usability. For another, we can greatly improve developer performance (we often call it developer velocity) for ourselves and for our teammates.

As with all of our controls, we create a function that we can then call from within the HTML. That function inserts the proper HTML for a link. We'll include a number of parameters for controlling various aspects of the link (internal vs. external links, e-mail links, and so on)

While our approach may seem overly complex, we're going to isolate that complexity so that our teammates can get consistently styled links without ever having to tangle with the complexity. As we mentioned in Chapter 10, isolating functionality in a control lets you greatly improve that functionality, as time permits, without interrupting your development team. And when the design department decides that the links have to look different, you can change them in one place rather than change every link on your site. For us, that's a huge benefit, because we hate repetitive (i.e., boring) tasks, and that kind of search-and-replace operation just about always generates bugs. (We always seem to miss a few, don't we?) **Note** We want to point out one often overlooked thing about links: the web wouldn't exist without them. As we all know but usually don't think about, HTTP stands for HyperText Transfer Protocol. The essence of hypertext is linking one bit of content to another bit of content in an ever-expanding web of information. Without the humble link element, we wouldn't have a World Wide Web, and we wouldn't have jobs (or at least we'd have different jobs). Thus, the seemingly trivial link element is actually the basis of much of our lives.

So without further ado, let's see how a link control works and what benefits it gives us.

The Function

Let's consider what we want our link control to do. Of course, a bare minimum is to generate an anchor tag with an href attribute and a string to describe what the link is, as shown in the following HTML element:

```
<a href="somepage.html">descriptive text</a>
```

If that's all the control did, we wouldn't waste our time (or yours) with something so simple. Instead, we'll make our link control justify the time we spend developing it by making it provide the following options:

- Set the href attribute and the descriptive text and throw an exception if either of those is not set. Let's face it: A link isn't a link without those two items.

141

- Add CSS classes.

- Add an ID.

- Add a type of link: internal, external, e-mail, or help.

- Set a tooltip message.

- Control whether the link is output to the page or returned as a value to another function.

- Gain progressive enhancement when we detect more capable browsers.

That's more like it. Now we've got requirements for a flexible control that allow us to address a lot of use cases. Also, as we mentioned earlier, we can let a team of developers share this productivity boon while ensuring consistency across the entire site. Those are important requirements, too. So now that we know a bit of the requirements of our control, let's write some code.

We're going to use PHP again, but you could just as easily make it work in Java or .NET or just about any programming language that people use for web development. Basically, the core of the code is a function that builds a string and outputs it to the page or returns the string to another function.

As you read the next listing, consider the data-link-type attribute that we insert. It's a custom attribute that we have created to pass along data for use by a CSS rule. (If you want to jump ahead, Listing 11-6 shows what we do with this custom attribute.) While it is a custom attribute, data-link-type also follows the HTML5 specification *3.2.3.8 Embedding custom non-visible data with the data-* attributes.*

Table 11-1 describes the parameters of the mLink function.

Table 11-1. Parameters of the price function

Parameter	Description
text	The text content of the link
href	The destination of the link
type	The type of link (internal, external, e-mail, or help)
class	Additional classes that you want to add to the link
echo	"echo" indicates that the function should insert the HTML into the page; "return" indicates that the function should return the HTML as a string to another function. The return value lets other controls embed the link control as part of a larger control, as we'll see in the rest of the book.
id	Optional. The value of the id attribute for this link. If the value does not exist, the id attribute does not get inserted.
tooltipMessage	Optional. The message that should pop up when a visitor's mouse hovers over the link.

Listing 11-1 shows the PHP code for our link control.

Listing 11-1. The PHP Code for Our Link Control

```php
<?php
  function mLink($text, $href, $type, $class, $echo, $id, $tooltipMessage) {
```

```
// A link with an href attribute and a way to describe what is about to
// happen seems pretty important, so we'll make it mandatory. While
// there's cases for omitting these, we'll keep this code clean and
// handle those other cases in a different manner.

// We'll use a try-catch block so that we can do
// something if we don't get the values we require.
try {
  if (($text == NULL || $text =="") || ($href == NULL || $href =="")){
    throw new Exception("At least one Link is missing descriptive text and/or an href");
  }
} catch (Exception $e){

  // We've chosen to display our exception in eye-jarring colors that
  // really stick out. It makes for immediate feedback as you develop,
  // but it can backfire on you. Choosing to do it in the DOM is risky
  // as it can be seen by visitors if bad data are passed to your live
  // site. You have the option here of choosing how you learn about the
  // exception. You could just as easily write this to a log or send it
  // to a browser that has a console (Chrome, Firefox with the Firebug
  // plugin, IE8+), by un-commenting the following line:
  // echo '<script>if(console.log){console.log(' . $e->getMessage() . ');}</script>';
  // In that case, you'd probably want to comment out our eye-watering
  // error message:
  echo '<span style="color: #995cb1;background:#a8ff85;font-weight: bold">' .
$e->getMessage() . '</span>';
  }

// Let's start building our string, starting with the first bit of the
// opening tag for our link and an href attribute:
$output = "<a href='" . $href . "'";

// The following ternary operator checks to see that our $type argument
// has a value, and if it does we'll add the "data-link-type" attribute
// along with the value of $type (we'll see later what the $type does):
$output .= ( ($type == NULL || $type == "") ? "" : " data-link-type='" . $type . "'");
// Add an ID if there's one present, with yet another ternary operator.
$output .= ( ($id == NULL || $id == "") ? "" : " id='" . $id . "'");
// Add our generic link class:
$output .= " class='link";
// Another ternary to pass in a class if there's one set:
$output .= ( ($class == NULL || $class=="") ? "" : " " . $class);
// Descriptive text for the link:
$output .= "'>" . $text;
// Add the link icon and, if $tooltipMessage has a value,
// we'll add an attribute to drive the CSS:
/*
 * For folks who like ternary operators, here's a single-line way to add the icon and message:
    $output .= ( ($type == NULL || $type == "") ? "" : "<span class='linkIcon'" . ( $type ==
"help" ? " data-tooltip-message='" . $tooltipMessage . "'" : "" ) . "></span>");
*/
```

```
    // We include the other way for greater readability (
      if ($type != NULL && $type != "")
        $output .= <span class='linkIcon'"
      if (type == "help")
        $output .= " data-tooltip-message='" . $tooltipMessage . "'";
      $output .= "></span>"
        $output .= "</a>";

        // (If the ternary operators are too hard to follow, try breaking them up
        // into if-else blocks.) Sometimes, we need to return the link string to
        // other functions for further processing. Other times (most of the time,
        // really), we want to output the link where it's being called in the HTML.
        // So we pass a string in for the $echo argument that defaults to echoing
        // the output if anything besides "return" is passed. In this way we can
        // not set it for most of our uses. Here's a (commented) ternary operator
        // that would do the job:
        // ($echo != "return") ? echo $output : return $output;
        // Here's the replacement for that ternary operator, in case you're tired
        // of ternary operators:
        if ($echo != "return") {
          echo $output;
        } else {
          return $output;
        }
    }
?>
```

As you saw, we added a lot of comments to describe the basic functionality. To implement this in our HTML we'd write the following code where we want a basic link to be inserted:

```
<?php mLink("Regular Link", "page.html"); ?>
```

You'd get a link element that looks similar to the following element:

```
<a href="page.html" class="link">Regular Link</a>
```

But that's boring, so what else we can do with our function? As it happens, a lot, as Listing 11-2 shows.

Listing 11-2. Various Invocations of the mLink Function

```
<?php mLink("Regular Link", "page.html"); ?><br/><br/>
<?php mLink("Internal Link", "page.html", "internal"); ?><br/><br/>
<?php mLink("External Link", "http://somesite.com", "external"); ?><br/><br/>
<?php mLink("Email Link", "mailto:me123@thefakeemail.com", "email"); ?><br/><br/>
<?php mLink("Help Link", "javascript:;", "help", NULL, NULL, NULL, "Can it really be this
easy?"); ?>
```

Listing 11-3 shows the elements that would end up in the HTML result.

Listing 11-3. HTML Result Elements for Listing 11-2:

```
<a href='page.html' class='link'>Regular Link</a><br/><br/>
<a href='page.html' data-link-type='internal' class='link'>Internal with Icon<span
class='linkIcon'></span></a><br/><br/>
```

```
<a href='http://somesite.com' data-link-type='external' class='link'>External Link<span
class='linkIcon'></span></a><br/><br/>
<a href='mailto:me123@thefakeemail.com' data-link-type='email' class='link'>Email Link<span
class='linkIcon'></span></a><br/><br/>
<a href='javascript:;' data-link-type='help' class='link'>Help Link<span class='linkIcon' data-
tooltip-message='Can it really be this easy?'></span></a>
```

Notice that we didn't set the id attribute, add additional classes, or specify to return to another function rather than echo the HTML document. In each of those cases, specifying the indicated parameter generates the corresponding attribute, which seems easy enough.

Figure 11-1 shows what those elements would look like in a browser.

Regular Link

Internal with Icon 🖼

External Link 🔼

Email Link ✉

Help Link ⑦

Figure 11-1. How the links look

■ **Note** You can see how the links in Figure 11-1 look in a browser at http://clikz.us/BookExamples/linkControl.php

---

Styling the Links

We use CSS to generate the icons that go with the links and otherwise control the appearance of the various incarnations of the link control. You might have little use for an icon for an internal link. In many sites, most of the links are internal and it would add too much clutter to show them all this way. Conversely, you might find the external link treatment to be much more informative for your users. It's a good usability standard to let visitors know when they're leaving your site, which they may have come to trust, and going to another domain, which they may not trust. E-mail links are also indicative of the results of clicking on that link. Finally, we'll use the help icon ("?"); it seems to have become a de facto convention for adding additional information about a particular link or piece of information.

Because we've standardized these types of links, we can use very specific CSS and JavaScript to give us additional functionality. For example, if CSS animations are available, visitors see a nice animation of the links transforming from their current color to a green color in a throbbing manner. This creates a very application-like feel. We'll show you that animation later in this chapter.

We can make tooltips appear if a visitor's mouse hovers above the icons by the links. For the internal, external, and e-mail links, the tooltip message is static. However, for the help links, we can create a custom message. The custom message is the function's last argument, $tooltipMessage. Figure 11-2 shows the links with their tooltips.

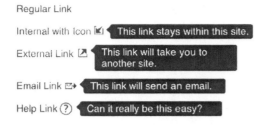

Figure 11-2. *The link icons and their meanings*

We also built our controls to be able to ignore unnecessary arguments (except for href and descriptive text, which we think are necessary). For performance reasons, we don't want to generate any HTML that isn't expressly needed.

Rather than a single huge listing, we've broken it up into a number of smaller listings, each with an introduction. We've also added comments to the more complex rules (such as the rule that controls the animation).

Listing 11-4 shows the bare-bones link rule.

Listing 11-4. *The basic link rule*

```
a.link {
  display: inline-block;
  color: #14699F;
  padding: 0;
}
```

Listing 11-5 shows how to get the "throb" animation. Because we want it to work on every browser that can possibly support it, it's a long listing.

Listing 11-5. *Styling the Throb Hover Effect*

```
/*
 * This hover state calls a keyframe, called "throb", declared below
 * this ruleset with duration, iteration count, easing (timing
 * function), and fill-mode, which tells the animation to end on the
 * 100% properties if the hover state is left.
 */
a.link:hover {
  text-decoration: none;
  -webkit-animation-name: throb;
  -webkit-animation-duration: 1s;
  -webkit-animation-iteration-count: infinite;
  -webkit-animation-timing-function: linear;
  -webkit-animation-fill-mode: forwards;

  -moz-animation-name: throb;
  -moz-animation-duration: 1s;
  -moz-animation-iteration-count: infinite;
  -moz-animation-timing-function: linear;
  -moz-animation-fill-mode: forwards;
```

```
  animation-name: throb;
  animation-duration: 1s;
  animation-iteration-count: infinite;
  animation-timing-function: linear;
  animation-fill-mode: forwards;
}
/*
 * Our keyframe "throb" makes the link above start with its original
 * blue color and transition to green with a smooth animation. Then
 * back to blue. It repeats infinitely so long as the link is in the
 * hover state. The percentages are based on the animation-duration
 * defined in the ruleset above it. So in this case 100% will be one
 * second long.
 */
@-webkit-keyframes throb {
  0% {
    color: #14699F;
  }
  50% {
    color: #169f1d;
  }
  100% {
    color: #14699F;
  }
}
@-moz-keyframes throb {
  0% {
    color: #14699F;
  }
  50% {
    color: #169f1d;
  }
  100% {
    color: #14699F;
  }
}
@keyframes throb {
  0% {
    color: #14699F;
  }
  50% {
    color: #169f1d;
  }
  100% {
    color: #14699F;
  }
}
```

A reminder of the visual effect and functionality that we're trying to achieve might help at this point. Figure 11-3 shows a table full of nonsense content that contains various kinds of links. The header row has help links, the second column has external links, and the last column has e-mail links.

Austin irony leggings ⑦	Tattooed small batch ⑦	Pork belly hoodie ⑦	Keytar sartorial ⑦
Squid four loko biodiesel messenger bag	cosby sweater semiotics ⬈	Photo booth kogi yr cray lo-fi	Boo@Scare.com ✉
Jean shorts artisan hoodie	trust fund williamsburg ⬈	VHS farm-to-table american	This@That.com ✉
Small batch DIY dreamcatcher	chillwave mumblecore ✉	Carles dreamcatcher	Hi@Goodbye.com ✉
Pork belly 3 wolf moon seitan bushwick	iphone beard ⬈	mustache butcher	Random@Deliberate.com ✉
Etsy stumptown butcher	wes anderson pork ✉	messenger bag master	Here@There.com ✉

Figure 11-3. A table showing different kinds of links

Listing 11-6 defines a hover effect that appears for visitors whose browsers don't support the throb effect.

Listing 11-6. Creating a Hover Effect When We Can't Make It Throb

```
/*
 * If a browser doesn't support CSS3 animations we still want to show a hover state.
 */
.no-cssanimations a.link:hover {
  color: #169f1d;
}
```

Listing 11-7 sets some common properties (position and padding-right) for all the types of links (other than the simple link).

Listing 11-7. Setting Common Properties for Links (Other Than the Simple Link)

```
/*
 * This looks for all anchors with an attribute of "data-link-type"
 * and a class of "link". We'll use this to set common CSS
 * properties for link controls that have a "data-link-type"
 * attribute set. This saves repeating the properties in each type.
 */
a[data-link-type].link {
  position: relative;
  padding-right: 23px;
}
```

Listing 11-8 shows how we set properties for the span that holds the link icon. Again, these properties don't apply to the simple link, because it has no icon.

Listing 11-8. Setting Properties for Link Icons

```
/*
 * Same as 11-6 but for the "linkIcon" span we inserted in the link
 * control for our link $types
```

```
 */
a[data-link-type].link .linkIcon {
  background-image: url(/images/sprites/clikz-sprite.png);
  background-repeat: no-repeat;
  width: 16px;
  height: 16px;
  position: absolute;
  right: 3px;
  top: 0;
}
```

Listing 11-9 shows a neat trick (well, *we* think it's neat). The idea is to insert an element when the visitor's mouse hovers over the link icon. It's a bit tricky because it relies on setting borders on three sides of an element. People naturally want to set borders on all four sides but that would be wrong for our purpose. The end result is a triangle that highlights the link icon—a handy way to visually connect the tooltip message and the icon it's describing.

Listing 11-9. Highlighting the Current Link Icon with a Triangle

```
/*
 * This is a little trickier. We're creating a nested element inside
 * the "linkIcon" span by adding the pseudo :before class only when
 * you hover on the "linkIcon" span. This :before is used to make
 * the triangle that appears to the right of our tooltip message.
 * The effect is accomplished by setting only three sides of the
 * border, with the top and bottom being transparent. The background
 * of the triangle is set by defining the right border color.
 */
a[data-link-type].link .linkIcon:hover:before {
  content: "";
  position: absolute;
  right: -6px;
  top: 3px;
  width: 0;
  height: 0;
  z-index: 99;
  border-top: 5px solid transparent;
  border-right: 6px solid #14699F;
  border-bottom: 5px solid transparent;
}
```

Listing 11-10 defines the container for the tooltip message. We use the pseudo :after class to create a space for and style the message.

Listing 11-10. Creating a Container for and Styling the Tooltip Message

```
/*
 * This is the container for our tooltip message. As above, we use a
 * pseudo class but this time it's the :after class. We also add a
 * ".tooltipMessage" selector as a fallback if the :after pseudo
 * class isn't available (as in older browsers).
 */
```

```
a[data-link-type].link .linkIcon:hover:after, .tooltipMessage {
  content: '';
  background: #14699F;
  width: 200px;
  position: absolute;
  z-index: 99;
  right: -206px;
  -webkit-border-radius: 3px;
  -moz-border-radius: 3px;
  border-radius: 3px;
  -moz-background-clip: padding;
  -webkit-background-clip: padding-box;
  background-clip: padding-box;
  color: white;
  padding: 2px 5px 3px 10px;
-moz-box-sizing: border-box;
  box-sizing: border-box;

  min-height: 16px;
}
```

Listing 11-11 defines the position and tooltip content of an internal link.

Listing 11-11. *Defining the Position and Tooltip Content of an Internal Link*

```
/*
 * INTERNAL LINK
 */
/*
 * This positions the background image we declared in the ruleset
 * above, "a[data-link-type].link .linkIcon", so we can see the
 * proper icon.
 */
a[data-link-type="internal"].link .linkIcon {
  background-position: -137px -54px;
}
/*
 * Here we set the text of our tooltip.
 */
a[data-link-type="internal"].link .linkIcon:hover:after {
  content: "This link stays within this site.";
}
```

Listing 11-12 defines the position and tooltip content of an external link.

Listing 11-12. *Defining the position and Tooltip Content of an External Link*

```
/*
 * EXTERNAL LINK
 */
a[data-link-type="external"].link .linkIcon {
  background-position: -159px -53px;
```

```
}
a[data-link-type="external"].link .linkIcon:hover:after {
  content: "This link will take you to another site.";
}
```

Listing 11-13 defines the position and tooltip content of an e-mail link.

Listing 11-13. Defining the Position and Tooltip Content of an e-mail Link

```
/*
 * EMAIL LINK
 */
a[data-link-type="email"].link .linkIcon {
  background-position: -116px -54px;
}
a[data-link-type="email"].link .linkIcon:hover:after {
  content: "This link will send an email.";
}
```

Listing 11-14 defines the position and tooltip content of a help link. Because we want the tooltip content for a help link to be the content that our developers pass to the function, we use CSS's seldom-seen content function to put that content into the tooltip—another handy trick.

Listing 11-14. Defining the Position and Tooltip Content of a Help Link

```
/*
 * HELP LINK
 */
a[data-link-type="help"].link .linkIcon {
  background-position: -92px -54px;
}
/*
 * We're using a rarely seen function of CSS that really works only for
 * the content property: attr (name of an attribute for which we want
 * the value). This attribute has to be on the selector for our ruleset.
 */
a[data-link-type="help"].link .linkIcon:hover:after {
  content: attr(data-tooltip-message);
}
```

Listing 11-15 shows our "if all else fails" rule. If we can't do anything else, we'll hide the tooltip message that will be created by JavaScript if the :after and :before functionality isn't available, as you'll see in the next section.

Listing 11-15. Styling the Fallback Condition

```
/*
 * This is also for our fallback, so we start with a hidden state
 * that we'll show with some JavaScript.
 */
.tooltipMessage {
  display: none;
}
```

Using JavaScript When CSS Fails Us

With CSS, it's amazing how much we can do to make our code very efficient. The CSS used here also performs very well, because the browser handles it natively rather than as extra functionality defined by scripting. However, if this more modern CSS is not supported, we still want to retain our tooltip functionality, at least for the help links. Of course, by using the method below, you can also retain the description on the static links. Or you can default to your own favorite method for displaying tooltips. Just be sure to add the check with Modernizr (if(!Modernizr.generatedcontent){}) around your function calls, regardless of how you add failover capability.

To supplement our HTML, we've heavily leaned on CSS for functionality. However, when the CSS doesn't work (because someone has an old or otherwise not very functional browser), we've used Modernizr to trigger a JavaScript solution. (If that visitor also doesn't use JavaScript, we're stuck, but since those visitors are probably used to very plain web sites, ours won't look bad by comparison.)

To add the tooltip functionality without CSS's help, we created a jQuery plug-in. You could certainly use other ways, but we like jQuery.Listing 11-16 shows the script that contains the jQuery plug-in and how to invoke it with Modernizr.

Listing 11-16. A jQuery Plug-in That Uses Modernizr to Invoke It

```
<script>
  (function($) {

    //Attach this method to jQuery
    $.fn.extend({

      //Your plugin's name goes here
      tooltip : function() {

        //Iterate over the matched elements
        return this.each(function() {

          //plug-in code goes here
          var t = $(this),
            message = t.attr("data-tooltip-message");

          t.find(".linkIcon").append("<div class='tooltipMessage'>"
              + message + "</div>");
          var tooltipMessage = t.find(".tooltipMessage");

          t.hover(function(){
            tooltipMessage.show();
          },function(){
            tooltipMessage.hide();
          })
        });
      }
    });
  })(jQuery);

  if(!Modernizr.generatedcontent){
    $("a[data-tooltip-message]").tooltip();
```

```
  }
</script>
```

We've written a jQuery plug-in to handle help tooltip functionality when generatedcontent functionality is not available (that is, when the pseudo :after and :before classes are not available). We use the plug-in to approximate the :after functionality by inserting a div element and assigning it the class of tooltipMessage, which we added to the same rule that handled the tooltip via CSS. Then we'll add the value from the data-tooltip-message attribute, which we set with the link control.

Then all we need to do is wrap our tooltip plug-in in an if statement that runs when the generatedcontent functionality isn't available. Through the plug-in, we attach our tooltip div to any anchor that has a data-tooltip-message attribute.

Summary

In this chapter, we built a link control we can use all over our site. Doing so provides the following benefits:

- Ensures consistency across the site; this helps visitors navigate and makes the site more attractive.

- Increases developer productivity (or velocity, if you like).

- Uses encapsulation, so that developers don't have to code their own solutions every time they want a link that's a bit more than just a link. Encapsulation further increases velocity and reduces the chances of bugs arising.

To make our link control, we created three pieces. First, we created a function that replaces code in the web page with the final HTML that goes to the user's browser. This function accepts several parameters that developers can use to add a number of optional features to their links. The function also supports five different kinds of links (through its type parameter). If our development team ever needs yet another kind of link, we can add to the function rather than force our team to create its own solutions (again, we want to avoid that for consistency and quality reasons).

Second, we created a number of CSS rulesets to style the link. This styling includes not just controlling the appearance of the link but also positioning and styling the tooltip text that goes with all but the simplest kind of link. In keeping with the philosophy of progressive enhancement, we added an animation hover for the links for browsers that support CSS3 animations and a standard hover for older browsers.

Third, we used JavaScript to add a failover capacity for browsers that can't display tooltips through CSS. We'd hate to lose our tooltips (especially on the help links), so we added one more bit of progressive enhancement to ensure that just about everyone gets at least the tooltips, even if they don't get animations or other fancy effects.

Again, that may seem like a lot of work for a link. But think of the number of links on the average e-commerce site. Shouldn't they all look and work the same? We think so, and this is how we achieve those goals.

CHAPTER 12

■ ■ ■

Sidebox Control

Now that you've seen the relatively simple link control, let's look at controls within controls and the developer productivity that such structures offer. The sidebox (or inset) is a staple of most multicolumn sites. A sidebox is usually located to the left or right of the main content area in a site. This control can be pretty versatile in that it can contain many different types of information: links, information callouts, navigation, surveys, and various others. Figure 12-1 shows a typical sidebox, one intended to highlight new arrivals at our store:

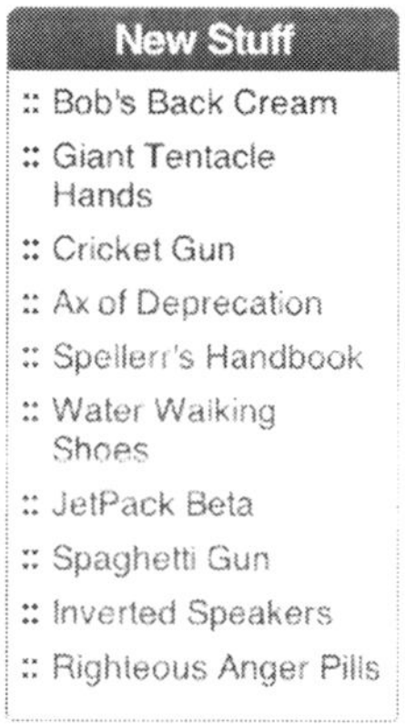

New Stuff

:: Bob's Back Cream
:: Giant Tentacle Hands
:: Cricket Gun
:: Ax of Deprecation
:: Spellerr's Handbook
:: Water Walking Shoes
:: JetPack Beta
:: Spaghetti Gun
:: Inverted Speakers
:: Righteous Anger Pills

Figure 12-1. A sidebox with a list of links to new products

The Content

Although it has many uses, the sidebox control always has certain features—in particular, a header and a bounding box—regardless of its content. Let's start developing our control by specifying those two features (see Figure 12-2).

Figure 12-2. A blank inset control

The structure of the sidebox is pretty basic, as may be seen in Listing 12-1.

Listing 12-1. The HTML of a Sidebox

```
<nav class="sideBox">
  <h1 class="sbH1 accentGradient gradient siteGrad">Sidebox Head</h1>
  <div class="sbBody">
    <!--Our sidebox contents go here -->
  </div>
</nav>
```

As you can see, it's just a nav element serving as a container for the header (an h1 element) and the other content (in the div element). We specify a number of classes to control the appearance of our sidebox control, and we'll talk about those next.

The Styling

The CSS for a sidebox control is pretty basic, except that we've added some shadows to the H1 to give the sidebox a little visual appeal. We've used our old friends, the :after and :before pseudo-classes (on the h1 element) to accomplish this effect. To avoid another HTTP request, we've encoded the images as base64 and included them in the CSS.

We'll describe each class and pseudo-class separately, to keep the listing from being huge and hard to follow. Listing 12-2 shows the .sideBox class, which specifies the bottom margin (to keep the content from bumping into the heading).

Listing 12-2. The .sideBox Class

```
.sideBox {
  margin-bottom: 10px;
}
```

Listing 12-3 shows the .sbH1 (short for sidebox H1) style, which specifies the many properties of the H1 element. In addition to ho-hum properties such as font size and color, we also specify rounded corners for the sidebox control. Specifying the rounded corners takes up most of the listing, because we have to get it to work for every browser that can support rounded corners.

Listing 12-3. The .sbH1 Class

```
.sbH1 {
  font-size: 16px;
  color: white;
  padding: 3px;
  text-align: center;
  letter-spacing: -0.05em;
  -webkit-border-top-right-radius: 5px;
  -webkit-border-bottom-right-radius: 0;
  -webkit-border-bottom-left-radius: 0;
  -webkit-border-top-left-radius: 5px;
  -moz-border-radius-topright: 5px;
  -moz-border-radius-bottomright: 0;
  -moz-border-radius-bottomleft: 0;
  -moz-border-radius-topleft: 5px;
  border-top-right-radius: 5px;
  border-bottom-right-radius: 0;
  border-bottom-left-radius: 0;
  border-top-left-radius: 5px;
  -moz-background-clip: padding;
  -webkit-background-clip: padding-box;
  background-clip: padding-box;
  position: relative;
  margin: 0;
}
```

Listing 12-4 shows the .sbH1:before pseudo-class. This class specifies the placement of the image that provides the appearance of a rounded shadow to the left of the box containing the header. It also provides the image, as a block of data encoded in base64.

Listing 12-4. The sbH1:before class

```
.sbH1:before {
  content: "";
  background: url(data:image/png;base64,
```
iVBORw0KGgoAAAANSUhEUgAAAAcAAAAZCAMAAADKUMQKAAAAGXRFWHRT
b2Z0d2FyZQBBZG9iZSBJbWFnZVJlYWR5ccllPAAAA+dpVFhOWE1MOmNvbS5hZG9iZS54bXAAAAAAADw/eHBhY2tldCBiZWdp
bj0i77u/IiBpZD0iVzVNME1wQ2VoaUh6cmVTek5UY3prYmlkSj8+IDx4OnhtcG1ldGEgeG1sbnM6eD0iYWRvYmU6bnM6bWV0
YS8iIHg6eG1wdGs9IkFkb2JlIFhNUCBDb3JlIDUuMC1jMDYwIDYxLjEzNDc3NywyMDEwLzAyLzEyLTE3OjMyMjowMCAgICAg
ICAgIj4gPHJkZjpSREYgeG1sbnM6cmRmPSJodHRwOi8vd3d3LnczLm9yZy8xOTk5LzAyLzIyLXJkZi1zeW50YXgtbnMjIj4g
PHJkZjpEZXNjcmlwdGlvbiByZGY6YWJvdXQ9IiIgeG1sbnM6eG1wPSJodHRwOi8vbnMuYWRvYmUuY29tL3hhcC8xLjAvIiB4
bWxuczpxcz0iaHR0cDovL3B1cmwub3JnL2RjL2VsZW1lbnRzLzEuMS8iIHhtbG5zOnhtcE1NPSJodHRwOi8vbnMuYWRvYmUu
Y29tL3hhcC8xLjAvbW0vIiB4bWxuczpzdFJlZj0iaHR0cDovL25zLmFkb2JlLmNvbS94YXAvMS4wL3NUeXBlL1Jlc291cmNl
UmVmIyIgeG1wOkNyZWF0b3JUb29sPSJBZG9iZSBQaG90b3Nob3AgQ1M1IE1hY2ludG9zaCIgeG1wOkNyZWF0ZURhdGU9IjIw
MTItMDQtMjhUMTA6MzA6NDYtMDU6MDAiIHhtcDpNb2RpZnlEYXRlPSIyMDEyLTA2LTE4VDIxOjE1OjU1LTA1OjAwIiB4bXA6
TWV0YWRhdGFEYXRlPSIyMDEyLTA2LTE4VDIxOjE1OjU1LTA1OjAwIiBkYzpmb3JtYXQ9ImltYWdlL3BuZyIgeG1wTU06SW5z
dGFuY2VJRD0ieG1wLmlpZDoyMjQyNzc2NUIxQUYxMUUxOEJFFOD1BMDkxM0UyQOFDNCIgeG1wTU06RG9jdW1lbnRJRD0ieG1w

LmRpZDoyMjQyNzc2NkIxQUYxMUUxOEJFODlBMDkxMoUyQOFDNCI+IDx4bXBNTTpEZXJpdmVkRnJvbSBzdFJlZjppbnNOYW5j
ZU1EPSJ4bXAuaWlkOjIyNDI3NzYzQjFBRjE4RTE4QkU4OUEwOTEzRTJDQUMOIiBzdFJlZjpkb2N1bWVudElEPSJ4bXAuZGlk
OjIyNDI3NzYOQjFBRjExRTE4QkU4OUEwOTEzRTJDQUMOIi8+IDwvcmRmOkRlc2NyaXBOaW9uPiA8L3JkZjpSREY+IDwveDp4
bXBtZXRhPiA8P3hwYWNrZXQgZW5kPSJyIj8+ADj9TgAAADBQTFRF/v7+7e3t/Pz83d3dzMzM9/f3u7u79fX1+vr61NTUrKys
4eHhw8PD5eXl8fHxsrKy+VpLHQAAAF1JREFUeNp8TtsWgDAIOnRry13+/29jtE5v+QIHEZROCEfPQoxNKkshatdpHAcluFCaE
5QDGAF7ZQxPRFGH/+Plnfu4nC5DfjM1vD+LXmbixTrYscPNl2392uuQWYABfdwN7BXQddQAAAABJRU5ErkJggg==);

```
    width: 7px;
    height: 25px;
    position: absolute;
    z-index: 2;
    top: 0;
    right: -7px;
}
```

Listing 12-5 shows the .sbH1:after pseudo-class. This class specifies the placement of the image that provides the appearance of a rounded shadow to the right of the box containing the header. If you're wondering why we use an SVG image here, it's to create a particular shadow effect. We could have tried using different border radius settings, but there's no guarantee it would work on any given browser. Also, this method uses no more bandwidth than all the properties that'd be needed to get the border radius technique to work on as many browsers as possible. Since SVG is more likely to work in more places, it becomes the best choice to get the desired appearance. As you read the listing, you can ignore the SVG data, since it's a block of data encoded in base64 and not meant to be human-readable anyway.

Listing 12-5. The sbH1:after class

```
.sbH1:after {
    content: "";
```

    background: url(data:image/png;base64,iVBORwOKGgoAAAANSUhEUgAAAcAAAAZCAMAAADKUMQKAAAAGXRFWHRT
b2Z0d2FyZQBBZG9iZSBJbWFnZVJlYWR5ccllPAAAA+dpVFhOWE1MOmNvbS5hZG9iZS54bXAAAAAAADw/eHBhY2tldCBiZWdp
bj0i77u/IiBpZD0iVzVNME1wQ2VoaUh6cmVTek5UY3prY1Ij8+IDx4OnhtcG1ldGEgeG1sbnM6eD0iYWRvYmU6bnM6bWV0O
YS8iIHg6eG1wdGs9IkFkb2JlIFhNUCBDb3JlIDUuMC1jMDYwIDYxLjEzNDc3NywgMjAxMC8wMi8xMi0xNzozMjowMCAgICAg
ICAgIj4gPHJkZjpSREYgeG1sbnM6cmRmPSJodHRwOi8vd3d3LnczLm9yZy8xOTk5LzAyLzIyLXJkZi1zeW50YXgtbnMjIj4g
PHJkZjpEZXNjcmlwdGlvbiByZGY6YWJvdXQ9IiIgeG1sbnM6eG1wPSJodHRwOi8vbnMuYWRvYmUuY29tL3hhcC8xLjAvIiB4
bWxuczpkYz0iaHR0cDovL3B1cmwub3JnL2RjL2VsZW1lbnRzLzEuMS8iIHhtbG5zOnhtcE1NPSJodHRwOi8vbnMuYWRvYmUu
Y29tL3hhcC8xLjAvbW0vIiB4bWxuczpzdFJlZj0iaHR0cDovL25zLmFkb2JlLmNvbS94YXAvMS4wL3NUeXBlL1Jlc291cmNl
UmVmIyIgeG1wOkNyZWF0b3JUb29sPSJBZG9iZSBQaG90b3Nob3AgQ1M1IE1hY2ludG9zaCIgeG1wOkNyZWF0ZURhdGU9IjIw
MTItMDQtMjhUMTA6MzA6NDYtMDU6MDAiIHhtcDpNb2RpZnlEYXRlPSIyMDEyLTA2LTE4VDIxOjE2OjEwLTA1OjAwIiB4bXA6
TWVOYWRhdGFEYXRlPSIyMDEyLTA2LTE4VDIxOjE2OjEwLTA1OjAwIiB4bYzpmb3JtYXQ9ImltYWdlL3BuZyIgeG1wTUO6SW5z
dGFuY2VJRD0ieG1wLmlpZDoyMjQyNzc2OUIxQUYxMUUxOEJFODlBMDkxMoUyQOFDNCIgeG1wTUO6RG9jdW1lbnRJRD0ieG1w
LmRpZDoyMjQyNzc2QUIxQUYxMUUxOEJFODlBMDkxMoUyQOFDNCI+IDx4bXBNTTpEZXJpdmVkRnJvbSBzdFJlZjppbnNOYW5j
ZU1EPSJ4bXAuaWlkOjIyNDI3NzYzQjFBRjExRTE4QkU4OUEwOTEzRTJDQUMOIiBzdFJlZjpkb2N1bWVudElEPSJ4bXAuZGlk
OjIyNDI3NzY4QjFBRjExRTE4QkU4OUEwOTEzRTJDQUMOIi8+IDwvcmRmOkRlc2NyaXBOaW9uPiA8L3JkZjpSREY+IDwveDp4
bXBtZXRhPiA8P3hwYWNrZXQgZW5kPSJyIj8+lSD+3wAAADBQTFRF+fn529vb/v7+8fHxxMTE9fX1sLCw+/v7vb2970zsOdHR
5ubm4uLizc3N1tbW6enp6eXkiwAAAF9JREFUeNqMzksSwCAIA9AgWj/Qev/bltBx39UbJWJQSuloihBtGnhUE6pb7hDqq6LO
NvOedEulak+9EOOjr/FLW8yf97kvnZL7M5j/RoA92tejY/rKnjGgbJTGxSvAAHW1A9LlrBDQAAAAAE1FTkSuQmCC);

```
    width: 7px;
    height: 25px;
    position: absolute;
    z-index: 2;
    top: 0;
    left: -7px;
```

```
}
.sbBody {
  -webkit-border-top-right-radius: 0;
  -webkit-border-bottom-right-radius: 3px;
  -webkit-border-bottom-left-radius: 3px;
  -webkit-border-top-left-radius: 0;
  -moz-border-radius-topright: 0;
  -moz-border-radius-bottomright: 3px;
  -moz-border-radius-bottomleft: 3px;
  -moz-border-radius-topleft: 0;
  border-top-right-radius: 0;
  border-bottom-right-radius: 3px;
  border-bottom-left-radius: 3px;
  border-top-left-radius: 0;
  -moz-background-clip: padding;
  -webkit-background-clip: padding-box;
  background-clip: padding-box;
  border: 1px solid #C62125;
  padding-bottom: 10px;
  border-top: 0;
  font-size: 13px;
  box-shadow: 0 2px 3px #AAA;
}
```

■ **Tip**   Separating Content from Presentation

We want to mention a programming paradigm (a pattern) that we've used with great success in other places: MVC. MVC stands for Model-View-Controller (a common design pattern for web sites). MVC does a great job of separating content from presentation. We met on a project for which the mandate was to convert a very large web site from ASP.NET and webforms to Microsoft MVC. There was so much business logic tangled up in the webforms code that we gave up trying to convert it and started afresh with a new design. That radical step let us put the presentation in the View code (where it belongs) and put the business logic in the model (again, where it belongs). Following the best practices for the MVC pattern, we had very "skinny" controllers that basically just provided a number of entry points into the controls. The mantra for MVC is "fat model, skinny controller."

Each control had a number of "treatments," which were more or less minor variations on the control. For example, we had a sidebox control that didn't have a header. That version of the control had its own method in the controller class for the sidebox control. All the controller did was pass the model (which held the data) to another class that rendered the HTML elements that constitute the control. The rendering classes were data-agnostic. So long as the data conformed to certain parameters (mostly, it had to be present, but some controls demanded a list or other particular data structure), the rendering classes would turn the data into HTML.

If the control had special features, we moved the logic for those features into the model class. A prime example was the tab control, which rendered a series of tabs. The tabs could be ordered in a number of ways: alphabetical,

159

reverse alphabetical, original order (most common), and so on. The model used an enumeration that told the rendering class how to order the tabs. Moving that logic into the models let the rendering class (and so the whole control, really) be as dumb as the proverbial box of rocks. And really dumb controls let us stay away from trying to understand business logic.

Another great feature of MVC is the ability to use partial views (often just called "partials"). Through partial views, the view that specifies a control's appearance can include a partial view that handles some part of the content for the parent view. We'll do something very similar for the sidebox control, because doing so is how we let the `sidebox` function be content-agnostic. Through partials, the sidebox control can handle any kind of content. We'll get to that in the next section, "The Functions."

It may sound as if we were trying to avoid helping the business teams. The reverse is actually true. Very good separation of business and development concerns let us get more done, and it also enabled the business teams to get more done. We provided extensive API documentation and a fully worked example site where other teams could see the controls in action. We even put in each possible variation (that is, each treatment) for every control. It was quite a site.

Lots of people recommend separating presentation from content and keeping business logic out of web code. Our experience definitely validates that approach.

The Functions

We told the story of how we worked to separate content from presentation so that understanding what we're about to do here will be easier. We're going to follow those principles in the function we use to render this version of the sidebox control. So long as we get a value for the header and a partial view (which defines how to render its own content) for the content, we don't care at all what's in either of those parameters. The fact that this sidebox control can render many different kinds of content makes it tremendously useful.

■ **Note**   The partial that renders the content can contain one or more paragraphs. Consequently, the sidebox control can just as easily be used on a blog as on an e-commerce site. Again, when the presentation doesn't have to care about the content, the usefulness of the controls increases tremendously.

Table 12-1 shows the parameters accepted by the `sidebox` function.

Table 12-1. Parameters for the sidebox function

Parameter	Description
$title	Contains the contents of the header.
$content	Contains the path to the contents of the body. This has to be a partial view.

$class	Contains any additional classes to apply to the control. Can be empty.

In our example, we'll render the partial view through another function. Various platforms handle partials in different ways. PHP and other scripting languages tend to use another function (although PHP includes can consist of just plain HTML). Object-oriented platforms such as Microsoft MVC (which uses a number of languages) and Spring (which uses Java) tend to use a class as a partial view. Listing 12-6 shows the entry point for the sidebox control.

Listing 12-6. The Sidebox Control Entry Point

```php
<?php
  function sidebox($title, $content, $class){
    $path = $_SERVER['DOCUMENT_ROOT'];
    $sbTitle = $title;
    $sbContent = $path.$content; // The path to the partial view
    $classadd = ($class == null ? "" : $class);
    include $path."/includes/sideBox.php";
  }
?>
```

The first line of the sidebox function defines a variable that contains the root of the site. The next three lines create variables to hold the title, the path to the partial view that will display the content for us, and the additional classes (if any). The final line specifies where to find the HTML for the sidebox control. In other words, the last line defines the main view for the control. The main view holds the title and then calls the partial view (specified in the $content parameter) to render the content.

▓ **Note** In this case, the value of the $content parameter would be new_to_store.php, which is the file that defines the content for this sidebox. We'll get to that file later in this chapter.

Listing 12-7 shows sideBox.php (which we put in the "includes" directory).

Listing 12-7. The Content of sidebox.php

```php
<nav class="sideBox sbMainSubNav <?php echo $classadd; ?>">
  <h1 class="sbH1 accentGradient gradient siteGrad"><?php echo $sbTitle ?></h1>
  <div class="sbBody">
    <?php include $sbContent ?> // Here's where we call on the partial view to render the
content
  </div>
</nav>
```

As you can see, we pass the title and CSS class names into the appropriate places in the HTML. Then we're also including the path to the content that goes into the control. Through this method, the sidebox control can contain any content without the logic of the content being in the control. This approach also gives us ways to be clever with the content to help speed up development, as we did with the content of the sidebox in Figure 12-1. Here we're going to use the link control from Chapter 11 and a for loop to do the work for us. To do that, we're going to create a function to define the content and then use another function to render the content.

Listing 12-8 shows how we create the content as a set of arrays within an outer array. We do that in a separate file named new_to_store.php.

Listing 12-8. new_to_store.php, Which Contains the Content for the Sample Sidebox Control

```php
<?php
  $newToStoreArray = array(
    array("Bob's Back Cream", "javascript:fakelink(this);", NULL, "sbA-L2"),
    array("Giant Tentacle Hands","javascript:fakelink(this);", NULL, "sbA-L2"),
    array("Cricket Gun","javascript:fakelink(this);", NULL, "sbA-L2"),
    array("Ax of Deprecation","javascript:fakelink(this);", NULL, "sbA-L2"),
    array("Speller's Handbook","javascript:fakelink(this);", NULL, "sbA-L2"),
    array("Water Walking Shoes","javascript:fakelink(this);", NULL, "sbA-L2"),
    array("JetPack Beta","javascript:fakelink(this);", NULL, "sbA-L2"),
    array("Spaghetti Gun","javascript:fakelink(this);", NULL, "sbA-L2"),
    array("Inverted Speakers","javascript:fakelink(this);", NULL, "sbA-L2"),
    array("Righteous Anger Pills","javascript:fakelink(this);", NULL, "sbA-L2")
  );
  echo buildLevel2List($newToStoreArray);
?>
```

Most of Listing 12-8 is just the construction of a set of arrays within an outer array. We created it this way to simulate the kind of data we'd generally expect to receive from a database. For the sample site, though, we use only static data, since we're focusing on front-end technologies and don't want to clutter the book by dealing with a database. That data could just as easily be XML or whatever, so long as its something for which you can write a function (or method, if you use an object-oriented language) to parse. The last line calls the rendering function. While not strictly MVC, new_to_store.php basically creates our model. In strict MVC, we wouldn't have the call to the next function; the controller would pass the model to the rendering code for us.

Now that we have the data, we pass the data to another function that will build the HTML (an unordered list) that serves as the content of the sample sidebox control. We could have included the HTML-building function in new_to_store.php. However, we want to separate data from presentation. Also, we may have other uses for a function that builds a list. Because of those concerns, we decided to abstract the list-building code into its own function. Listing 12-9 shows the function that creates an HTML list.

Listing 12-9. Creating an Unordered List to Serve as Content

```php
function buildLevel2List($linkArray){
  $StringBuilder .= '<ul class="sbUL-L2">';

  for ($i=0, $size = sizeof($linkArray); $i < $size; $i++) {
    $StringBuilder .= '<li class="sbLI-L2">';
    $StringBuilder .= mLink($linkArray[$i][0], $linkArray[$i][1], $linkArray[$i][2],
$linkArray[$i][3], "return");
    $StringBuilder .= '</li>';
  }
  $StringBuilder .= '</ul>';
  return $StringBuilder;
}
```

We're using a string-building algorithm to create a collection of HTML elements that we'll then insert into the larger collection of HTML elements that constitute the sidebox control. String building offers the best way to create markup. Creating an object for each element leads to greater memory usage and much slower performance for no gain. That observation applies to strictly object-oriented languages such as Java and C#, too. Creating HTML as a string offers the best performance in any language we've encountered so far. (Jay first learned this truism when he was a contributor to the Apache FOP project and has validated it repeatedly over the years.)

The first line creates the opening tag of an unordered list (UL) element. Then the for loop traverses the outer loop. For each inner array within the outer array, the for loop creates an li element. Each li element contains an instance of the link control (described in detail in Chapter 12, "Link Control"). To provide the parameters to the link controls, we individually select the bits of data we need as we process each member of the data.

■ **Note** We had to provide a value of "return" as the last parameter to the link control. Otherwise, the link control would echo its own HTML, making a mess of our list. That's why the link control has that last parameter that controls whether to directly echo its output or return its output to another function, as we're doing here.

Now we have a sidebox control that offers an extreme amount of flexibility. While we didn't use an MVC framework, we thought about that pattern while we wrote this control, because we wanted to be careful to separate content from presentation. Thanks to that separation, we can now create any number of sideboxes, each with different kinds of content, from a single control. That saves the trouble of writing custom code for each sidebox and avoids all the bugs that go with writing code to handle each sidebox. Finally, we now have a single place where we can make improvements or add new features to our sidebox control. If a design team began beating down the door to get us to include sideboxes that didn't have headers, we could accommodate them pretty quickly. Also, if we think of ways to make sideboxes perform better or be more robust, we can make those improvements in one set of code objects and see the benefits across the web site.

We'd be remiss if we didn't mention one last benefit of making and using controls rather than writing custom HTML and CSS for each design element on each page in a web site: By using an array of controls within another control, we've extended our flexibility and robustness further still. We know how our link control works because we use it all the time. Just as importantly, we know how it can break, and, should it break, we know right where to look to fix it. Ever have a bug and wonder where to even start looking for it? We sure have, and we hate that. Making and using controls lets us get away from that problem.

Summary

In this chapter, we provided another sample control to use on our sample web site and that you're free to use on your own sites if it suits your needs. You'll likely need to extend it a bit to get it to handle all the different kinds of sideboxes (or insets or whatever you want to call them) on your site. Still, it offers a starting point.

As we do with all controls, we showed how to define the HTML, the CSS, and the handler code for the control. In our examples, we use PHP. You could just as easily use C# or Java or any other language that can be used to render a web page. Similarly, we don't use a framework, but you could certainly use this control and the other controls we present with a framework—Spring or Microsoft MVC, for example.

Finally, we want to remind you to keep your content (that is, data) separate from your presentation. The more content-agnostic your controls can be, the more things you can do with them. Of course, sometimes a control makes sense only in the presence of a certain kind of data. We'll show you how to handle that problem in a later chapter, when we describe our product stack control.

CHAPTER 13

Button Control

Here's another seemingly simple piece of HTML to make into a control. However, while it may seem like an odd place to invest effort, doing so pays off in consistency, flexibility, and developer velocity. We'll stick with the fractal design pattern. That is, we'll use (reuse, really) the same HTML for each kind of button, use Boolean values on the server side to identify which kind of button to display, and create the presentation variations by dynamically setting a CSS class.

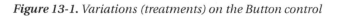 **Note** We often call each variation of a control a "treatment." For example, a button is a button, but two different buttons may differ greatly in appearance. The concept is rather like window treatments on a house. A window is a window, but blinds and curtains each give a window a very different look.

We've laid out a selection of buttons to illustrate the approach. However, as with the link control, almost any pattern is conceivable. On our sample site, we're going with the treatments shown in Figure 13-1.

Figure 13-1. Variations (treatments) on the Button control

You can view and interact with these buttons (in full color, too) at http://clikz.us/BookExamples/ buttonControl.php. In the online example, you can see that we've included some fancy interactions for our buttons. Namely, the button appears to depress on hover or throb with an inner glow, depending on which treatment we use. Those animations are pure eye candy, but they offer both a great way to take advantage of new browser capabilities and a superior experience. We'll also be sure to provide more traditional hover effects for visitors with older browsers. As always, we embrace progressive enhancement and try to ensure that all visitors get the best experience their browser can deliver.

Figure 13-1 showed several types of buttons. Let's briefly look at the differences. We've defined a class of button called Primary. We could have just as easily (and perhaps more descriptively) called it Blue button. However, this descriptive name would be a problem should updated requirements call for a change of color. Then we'd either have to look at a disconnected button name or replace a bunch of code to make it right. So we find it's far better to use terms that describe purpose rather than appearance. In this case, if we also had a green button, we might call that Secondary, or it could be specific to an action and so be called a Purchase button. For our example, all buttons are of the Primary family.

Button Types

We have Primary buttons only (as opposed to Secondary buttons, which we might use if we had More Info or See Also buttons), but we have several different treatments for them, as we describe in the rest of this section.

Primary

Let's start with our default button. Having all of the buttons in the Primary family descend from this default button allows us to have a bit of CSS abstraction that we can extend for the specific buttons should we need to. This treatment contains the hover interaction, which other button treatments may either use as is or override.

Figure 13-2. *The Primary button treatment*

Primary with Icon

The title says it all. We use the base primary button but add an icon. We'll go into how this works later in the chapter.

Figure 13-3. *The Primary with Icon button treatment*

Primary Glass

For this treatment, we create a glass effect on the primary button. To achieve the effect, we use a CSS gradient. If you find the glass effect hard to see in the screenshot (we do), please visit our sample site, http://clikz.us/BookExamples/buttonControl.php

[Primary Glass Button]

Figure 13-4. The Primary Glass button treatment

Primary Shadow

The Primary Shadow button treatment looks very similar to the Primary Glass button treatment, but we create the effect by using a different technique: a white inset shadow. This requires far less code than the gradient and allows some CSS animation options that complex gradients don't. We actually use the shadow method to generate the throb effect on hover.

[Primary Shadow Button]

Figure 13-5. The Primary Shadow button treatment

Primary Outset

Here we add a bit of visual interest by defining an outset shape (i.e., the shape is outside the button). We're using the :before pseudo-class to create the outer shape so that our markup stays clean.

[Primary Outset Button]

Figure 13-6. The Primary Outset button treatment

Primary Go

The Primary Go button treatment comes in handy when we need a small button for Search or for other places where interface elements get crowded. We can generate the circle by using the border-radius property; we'll get to the code later in this chapter.

Figure 13-7. The Primary Go button treatment

Primary Go Outset

The Primary Go Outset button treatment is a Go button with an outer image defined by the :before pseudo-class. It's useful where we need a small button with a bit more presence than a basic Go button.

Figure 13-8. The Primary Go Outset button treatment

Coding the Button Control

Let's examine the code behind the button control. It's probably familiar by now, since it uses the same techniques used in previous controls. We use the fractal design pattern here, so we make a string with some conditionals.

Table 13-1 describes the parameters of the price function.

Table 13-1. Parameters of the Price Function

Parameter	Description
text	The text on the button.
href	The destination for the button.
id	The value of the id attribute for this button. Because pages often have multiple buttons, this value should be unique within the page.
title	Optional. The value of the title attribute. If you don't specify a value for this attribute, the attribute does not get inserted.
type	Optional. The type of button (primary, primaryGlass, primaryShadow, primaryOutset, primaryGo, primaryGoOutset). If you don't specify one of those values, you get a plain HTML button.
class	Optional. Additional classes that developers who use the button control can add to the button.
icon	Optional. A value indicating whether to include an icon on the button. To add an icon, use TRUE as this argument's value. The iconClass argument specifies the actual argument.
iconClass	Optional. The name of the class that specifies the icon. If the icon argument contains anything other than TRUE, the icon won't appear on the button. If you set the icon argument to TRUE but don't specify a class name (or multiple class names) for this argument, no icon appears on the button.
htmlElement	Optional. Whether the inserted HTML element is a button element or an anchor (a) element. The default is an anchor element. To get a button element, specify button for the value of this parameter.

Listing 13-1 shows the PHP function that is the heart of our button control:

Listing 13-1. The Main Button Function

```php
<?php
// Our main button function.
function button($text, $href, $id, $title, $type, $class, $icon, $iconClass, $htmlElement) {
  $htmlEl = ($htmlElement == "button" ? "button" : "a");
```

```php
// Start string that contains the HTML output with
// the option to use an anchor tag or a button tag.
$output = "<" . $htmlEl;
// Put in our href attribute.
$output .= " href='" . $href . "'";
// Get a base class of button.
$output .= " class='button";
// If there's a type declared, get the proper classes that give our
// different treatments.
$output .= (($type != NULL || $type != "") ? " " . getTypeClasses($type) : "");
// If addition classes are present pass them in. This ability allows
// us greater flexibility.
$output .= (($class != NULL || $class != '') ? " " . $class . "'" : "'");
// If a title is declared, add it.
If ($title != NULL && $title != "") {
  $output .= " title='" . $title . "'";
}
$output .= ">";
$output .= $text;
if ($icon == TRUE) {
  $output .= "<span class='buttonIcon";
  if ($iconClass != NULL && $iconClass != "") {
    $output .= " " . $iconClass . "'></span>";
  }
}

// Finish the string by adding the closing tag (either </a> or </button>).
$output .= "</" . $htmlEl . ">";

echo $output;
}
// This function adds the appropriate classes based on the declared $type.
function getTypeClasses ($type) {
  switch ($type)
  {
  case "primary":
    return "primary";
    break;
  case "primaryGlass":
    return "primary glass";
    break;
  case "primaryShadow":
    return "primary shadow";
    break;
  case "primaryOutset":
    return "primary outset";
    break;
  case "primaryGo":
    return "primary go";
    break;
  case "primaryGoOutset":
```

```
      return "primary go outset";
      break;
  default:
      return "";
  }
}
?>
```

As we've mentioned before, the same purpose can be achieved in many different languages. We just happen to be using PHP (we had to use something, and we find PHP to be easy to read).

We're not up to anything fancy here. The only part that might seem odd is including the ability for a button to be an anchor element or a button element. If you need to put a button in a form, you might want to use a button element (so that it's easier to attach submit behavior and so on). Outside of a form, you might want to use an anchor element, because such a button has the same effect as an anchor element.

Again, you probably recognize the pattern by now. In order to instantiate our button control, we call the function with the desired arguments in the place we want the button to appear in our HTML. Listing 13-2 shows code that creates buttons.

Listing 13-2. *Creating the Buttons*

```
<?php button("Primary", "javascript:;", NULL, NULL, "primary")  ?><br/><br/>
<?php button("Primary Button with Icon", "#", NULL, NULL, "primary", "btn_checkmark", TRUE,
"icon_checkmark"); ?><br/><br/>
<?php button("Primary Glass Button", "javascript:;", NULL, NULL, "primaryGlass")  ?><br/><br/>
<?php button("Primary Shadow Button", "javascript:;", NULL, NULL, "primaryShadow")  ?><br/><br/>
<?php button("Primary Outset Button", "javascript:;", NULL, NULL, "primaryOutset")  ?><br/><br/>
<p>Primary Go Button</p>
<?php button("GO", "javascript:;", NULL, NULL, "primaryGo")  ?><br/><br/>
<p>Primary Go Outset Button</p>
<?php button("GO", "javascript:;", NULL, NULL, "primaryGoOutset")  ?><br/><br/>
```

Listing 13-3 shows the resulting HTML markup that gets inserted into the result document.

Listing 13-3. *The HTML that Results from the Function Calls*

```
<a href="javascript:;" class="button primary">Primary</a><br><br>
<a href="#" class="button primary btn_checkmark">Primary Button with Icon<span class="buttonIcon
icon_checkmark"></span></a><br><br>
<a href="javascript:;" class="button primary glass">Primary Glass Button</a><br><br>
<a href="javascript:;" class="button primary shadow">Primary Shadow Button</a><br><br>
<a href="javascript:;" class="button primary outset">Primary Outset Button</a><br><br>
<p>Primary Go Button</p>
<a href="javascript:;" class="button primary go">GO</a><br><br>
<p>Primary Go Outset Button</p>
<a href="javascript:;" class="button primary go outset">GO</a><br><br>
```

The CSS

As always, the CSS gets pretty dense because of all the vendor prefixes that enable things to work correctly in different browsers. The interesting parts are in the outset classes, where we use the :before pseudo-class with a combination of padding, offset position, and z-index to attain the outset effect. Basically, we generate an element by using the :before pseudo selector and make that element match the containing button in width, height, and border radius. We then added a 5-pixel padding all the way around, which made the whole treatment 10 pixels bigger than the button itself. To center the button within its wrapper, we added top and left values of –5 pixels. A z-index value of –1 puts the wrapper behind the button so that the button can be clicked.

Another technique we like is defining a background sprite for our buttonIcon ruleset via base64 encoding instead of a link to the sprite. This is a good technique for caching an image in CSS for future reuse; we've already used it in the sidebox control (see Chapter 12). If we need that sprite, we give the element a base class of buttonIcon, and we have it. This way, we get the best of two worlds: We avoid a costly HTTP request, and the image is cached.

Finally, it's worth noting that generating the Primary Glass button requires quite a bit of CSS, especially if it's going to look nice in Internet Explorer 9 with the additional SVG encoding. By contrast, the Primary Shadow button effect achieves a comparable look with a fraction of the code. We showed both ways to make you aware of the differences. We generally recommend using the shadow technique unless a client absolutely insists on the glass effect (there is a slight visual difference, and everyone's seen clients obsess over such things).

As with other controls, the CSS can seem a bit large. For the sake of readability, we split the CSS into multiple listings though it's a single block of code on our sample site. Listing 13-4 shows the first of the default button styles, which apply to all button treatments.

Listing 13-4. The First of the Default Button Styles

```
/*
 * Default button styles
 */
.button, .button:visited {
  padding: 4px 15px 5px 15px;
  -webkit-border-radius: 5px;
  -moz-border-radius: 5px;
  border-radius: 5px;
  -moz-background-clip: padding;
  -webkit-background-clip: padding-box;
  background-clip: padding-box;
  background-color: #1f81dd;
  color: white;
  display: inline-block;
  text-shadow: 0 0 4px rgba(0, 0, 0, 0.6);
  -webkit-box-shadow: inset 0 0 3px rgba(0, 0, 0, 0.6), 2px 2px 3px rgba(0, 0, 0, 0.4);
  -moz-box-shadow: inset 0 0 3px rgba(0, 0, 0, 0.6), 2px 2px 3px rgba(0, 0, 0, 0.4);
  box-shadow: inset 0 0 3px rgba(0, 0, 0, 0.6), 2px 2px 3px rgba(0, 0, 0, 0.4);
  text-decoration: none;
  font-size: 14px;
  position: relative;
  border: 1px solid rgba(0, 0, 0, 0.3);
}
```

Listing 13-5 shows the CSS that defines a button's appearance when a visitor's mouse hovers over it.

Listing 13-5. Default Button Hover Style

```
.button:hover {
  color: white;
```

```
  background-color: #24c61c;
  text-decoration: none;
  text-shadow: 0 0 4px rgba(255, 255, 255, 0.2);
  -webkit-box-shadow: inset 0 0 3px rgba(0, 0, 0, 0.6), 1px 1px 1px rgba(0, 0, 0, 0.4);
  -moz-box-shadow: inset 0 0 3px rgba(0, 0, 0, 0.6), 1px 1px 1px rgba(0, 0, 0, 0.4);
  box-shadow: inset 0 0 3px rgba(0, 0, 0, 0.6), 1px 1px 1px rgba(0, 0, 0, 0.4);
  top: 1px;
  left: 1px;
  -webkit-animation: shadowThrob 1s infinite;
  -moz-animation: shadowThrob 1s infinite;
  -o-animation: shadowThrob 1s infinite;
  animation: shadowThrob 1s infinite;
}
```

Listing 13-6 shows the style rule that applies when a visitor's browser doesn't support animation. In that case, we just change the background color.

Listing 13-6. The Default Hover Style for Browsers That Don't Support Animation

```
.no-cssanimations .button:hover {
  background: green;
}
```

Listing 13-7 shows the first rule that defines the appearance of the Primary button treatment. Just skip over the SVG block. It's base64-encoded data and not meant to be readable by a human.

Listing 13-7. The First Rule of the Primary Button Treatment

```
/*
 * Primary button
 */
.button.primary {
  background: #2c81da;
  background: url(data:image/svg+xml;base64,PD94bWwgdmVyc2lvbj0iMS4wIiA/Pgo8c3ZnIHhtbG5zPSJodHRw
Oi8vd3d3LnczLm9yZy8yMDAwL3N2ZyIgd2lkdGg9IjEwMCUiIGhlaWdodD0iMTAwJSIgdm
lld0JveD0iMCAwIDEgMSIgcHJlc2VydmVBc3BlY3RSYXRpbz0ibm9uZSI+CiAgPGxpbmVhckdyYWRpZW50IGlkPSJncmFkLX
VjZ2ctZ2VuZXJhdGVkIiBncmFkaWVudFVuaXRzPSJ1c2VyU3BhY2VPblVzZSIgeDE9IjAlIiB5MT0iMCUiIHgyPSIwJSIgeT
I9IjEwMCUiPgogICAgPHN0b3Agb2Zmc2V0PSIwJSIgc3RvcC1jb2xvcj0iIzJjODFkYSIgc3RvcC1vcGFjaXR5PSIxIi8+Ci
AgICA8c3RvcCBvZmZzZXQ9IjQ4JSIgc3RvcC1jb2xvcj0iIzViYWRmZiIgc3RvcC1vcGFjaXR5PSIxIi8+CiAgICA8c3RvcC
BvZmZzZXQ9IjEwMCUiIHN0b3AtY29sb3I9IiMyYzgyZGEiIHN0b3Atb3BhY2l0eT0iMSIvPgogIDwvbGluZWFyR3JhZGllbn
Q+CiAgPHJlY3Q+geD0iMCIgeT0iMCIgd2lkdGg9IjEiIGhlaWdodD0iMSIgZmlsbD0idXJsKCNncmFkLXVjZ2ctZ2VuZXJhdG
VkKSIgLz4KPC9zdmc+);
  background: -moz-linear-gradient(top, #2c81da 0%, #5badff 48%, #2c82da 100%);
  background: -webkit-gradient(linear, left top, left bottom, color-stop(0%, #2c81da),
color-stop(48%, #5badff), color-stop(100%, #2c82da));
  background: -webkit-linear-gradient(top, #2c81da 0%, #5badff 48%, #2c82da 100%);
  background: -o-linear-gradient(top, #2c81da 0%, #5badff 48%, #2c82da 100%);
  background: -ms-linear-gradient(top, #2c81da 0%, #5badff 48%, #2c82da 100%);
  background: linear-gradient(top, #2c81da 0%, #5badff 48%, #2c82da 100%);
  filter: progid:dximagetransform.microsoft.gradient(startColorstr='#2c81da',
endColorstr='#2c82da', GradientType=0);
}
```

Listing 13-8 shows the CSS rule for the Primary button in the active state.

Listing 13-8. *CSS Rule for the Primary Button in the Active State*

```
.button.primary:active {
  background: green;
}
```

Listing 13-9 shows the rule that defines the Primary button with a glass effect. Compare Listing 13-9 with Listing 13-10, which generates a very similar effect with much less code. Again, skip over the SVG block, since it's data rather than something meant to be meaningful to a human being. We include these blocks because we can't bring ourselves to put an incomplete listing in the book.

Listing 13-9. *Rule for the Glass Effect on the Primary Button*

```
/*
 * Primary button with Glass effect
 */
.button.primary.glass {
  background: #51a2ff;
  background: url(data:image/svg+xml;base64,PD94bWwgdmVyc2lvbj0iMS4wIiA/Pgo8c3ZnIHhtbG5zPSJodHRw
Oi8vd3d3LnczLm9yZy8yMDAwL3N2ZyIgd2lkdGg9IjEwMCUiIGhlaWdodD0iMTAwJSIgdmlld0JveD0iMCAwIDEgMSIgcHJl
c2VydmVBc3BlY3RSYXRpbz0ibm9uZSI+CiAgPGxpbmVhckdyYWRpZW50IGlkPSJncmFkLXVjZ2ctZ2VuZXJhdGVkIiBncmFk
aWVudFVuaXRzPSJ1c2VyU3BhY2VPblVzZSIgeDE9IjAlIiB5MT0iMCUiIHgyPSIwJSIgeTI9IjEwMCUiPgogICAgPHN0b3Ag
b2Zmc2VOPSIwJSIgc3RvcC1jb2xvcj0iIzUxYTJmZiIgc3RvcC1vcGFjaXR5PSIxIi8+CiAgICA8c3RvcCBvZmZzZXQ9IjQ4
JSIgc3RvcC1jb2xvcj0iIzM3OTVmNSIgc3RvcC1vcGFjaXR5PSIxIi8+CiAgICA8c3RvcCBvZmZzZXQ9IjUxJSIgc3RvcC1j
b2xvcj0iIzI1N2JkMSIgc3RvcC1vcGFjaXR5PSIxIi8+CiAgICA8c3RvcCBvZmZzZXQ9IjEwMCUiIHN0b3AtY29sb3I9IiMy
NTZlYmEiIHN0b3Atb3BhY2l0eT0iMSIvPgogIDwvbGluZWFyR3JhZGllbnQ+CiAgPHJlY3QgeD0iMCIgeT0iMCIgd2lkdGg9
IjEiIGhlaWdodD0iMSIgZmlsbD0idXJsKCNncmFkLXVjZ2ctZ2VuZXJhdGVkKSIgLz4KPC9zdmc+);
  background: -moz-linear-gradient(top, #51a2ff 0%, #3795f5 48%, #257bd1 51%, #256eba 100%);
  background: -webkit-gradient(linear, left top, left bottom, color-stop(0%, #51a2ff),
color-stop(48%, #3795f5), color-stop(51%, #257bd1), color-stop(100%, #256eba));
  background: -webkit-linear-gradient(top, #51a2ff 0%, #3795f5 48%, #257bd1 51%, #256eba 100%);
  background: -o-linear-gradient(top, #51a2ff 0%, #3795f5 48%, #257bd1 51%, #256eba 100%);
  background: -ms-linear-gradient(top, #51a2ff 0%, #3795f5 48%, #257bd1 51%, #256eba 100%);
  background: linear-gradient(top, #51a2ff 0%, #3795f5 48%, #257bd1 51%, #256eba 100%);
  filter: progid:dximagetransform.microsoft.gradient(startColorstr='#51a2ff',
endColorstr='#256eba', GradientType=0);
}
```

Listing 13-10 shows the rule that defines the Primary button with a shadow effect. Again, Listing 13-10 produces an effect similar to that created by Listing 13-9 but uses much less code.

Listing 13-10. *Rule for the Shadow Effect on the Primary Button*

```
/*
 * Primary Button with the Shadow Effect (approximates the Glass look)
 */
.button.shadow {
  background: #2c81da;
  -webkit-box-shadow: inset 0px 0px 4px rgba(0, 0, 0, 0.4), inset 0 12px 2px rgba(255, 255, 255,
0.4);
```

```
  -moz-box-shadow: inset 0px 0px 4px rgba(0, 0, 0, 0.4), inset 0 12px 2px rgba(255, 255, 255,
0.4);
  box-shadow: inset 0px 0px 4px rgba(0, 0, 0, 0.4), inset 0 12px 2px rgba(255, 255, 255, 0.4);
}
```

Listing 13-11 shows the first of the rules that create the Outset button treatment for the two buttons that have outset treatments. As we mentioned before, we create a 5-pixel border on all sides of the button, making a treatment that has 10 pixels more width and height than the actual button.

Listing 13-11. First Rule to Define the Outset Button Treatment

```
/*
 * Outset button styles
 */
.button.outset {
  content: "";
  display: inline-block;
  position: relative;
  -webkit-border-radius: 5px;
  -moz-border-radius: 5px;
  border-radius: 5px;
  -moz-background-clip: padding;
  -webkit-background-clip: padding-box;
  background-clip: padding-box;
  -webkit-box-shadow: inset 2px 2px 2px rgba(0, 0, 0, 0.3), inset 0 0 3px rgba(0, 0, 0, 0.4);
  -moz-box-shadow: inset 2px 2px 2px rgba(0, 0, 0, 0.3), inset 0 0 3px rgba(0, 0, 0, 0.4);
  box-shadow: inset 2px 2px 2px rgba(0, 0, 0, 0.3), inset 0 0 3px rgba(0, 0, 0, 0.4);
}
```

Listing 13-12 defines the hover state for the Outset button treatments.

Listing 13-12. The Hover State for the Outset Button Treatments

```
.button.outset:hover {
  top: 0;
  left: 0;
  -webkit-box-shadow: inset 50% 50% 0 #ffffff;
  -moz-box-shadow: inset 50% 50% 0 #ffffff;
  box-shadow: inset 50% 50% 0 #ffffff;
}
```

Listing 13-13 uses the :before pseudo selector syntax to generate an element before the button. We then use that element to create the area around the button. Also, we set the generated element's z-index property to –1 so that visitors can click the button.

Listing 13-13. Generating the Outset Element with the :before Pseudo Selector

```
.button.outset:before {
  content: "";
  width: 100%;
  height: 100%;
  display: block;
  z-index: -1;
```

```
   position: absolute;
   padding: 5px;
   background: #CCC;
   left: -5px;
   top: -5px;
   -webkit-border-radius: 5px;
   -moz-border-radius: 5px;
   border-radius: 5px;
   -moz-background-clip: padding;
   -webkit-background-clip: padding-box;
   background-clip: padding-box;
   -webkit-box-shadow: inset 0px 0px 4px rgba(0, 0, 0, 0.4), inset 0 10px 2px rgba(255, 255, 255,
0.4);
   -moz-box-shadow: inset 0px 0px 4px rgba(0, 0, 0, 0.4), inset 0 10px 2px rgba(255, 255, 255,
0.4);
   box-shadow: inset 0px 0px 4px rgba(0, 0, 0, 0.4), inset 0 10px 2px rgba(255, 255, 255, 0.4);
}
```

Listing 13-14 shows the style rule that defines the Go buttons, which are round and much smaller than the other buttons.

Listing 13-14. The Rule That Defines the Appearance of the Go Buttons

```
/*
 * Go Button Styles
 */
.button.go {
  font-size: 11px;
  width: 22px;
  height: 17px;
  -webkit-border-radius: 100%;
  -moz-border-radius: 100%;
  border-radius: 100%;
  -moz-background-clip: padding;
  -webkit-background-clip: padding-box;
  background-clip: padding-box;
  border: none;
  padding: 5px 0 0 0;
  text-align: center;

}
```

Listing 13-15 shows the rule that defines the Outset Go button.

Listing 13-15. Defining the Outset Go Button

```
/*
 * Go Button with outset treatment
 */
.button.go.outset:before {
  content: "";
  width: 100%;
  height: 100%;
```

```
  display: block;
  z-index: -1;
  position: absolute;
  padding: 3px;
  background: #CCC;
  left: -3px;
  top: -3px;
  -webkit-border-radius: 100%;
  -moz-border-radius: 100%;
  border-radius: 100%;
  -moz-background-clip: padding;
  -webkit-background-clip: padding-box;
  background-clip: padding-box;
  -webkit-box-shadow: inset 0px 0px 4px rgba(0, 0, 0, 0.4), inset 0 10px 2px rgba(255, 255, 255,
0.4);
  -moz-box-shadow: inset 0px 0px 4px rgba(0, 0, 0, 0.4), inset 0 10px 2px rgba(255, 255, 255,
0.4);
  box-shadow: inset 0px 0px 4px rgba(0, 0, 0, 0.4), inset 0 10px 2px rgba(255, 255, 255, 0.4);
}
```

Listing 13-16 shows the rules that define the throb effect. Visitors whose browsers don't support animations still get an effect when they their mouse pointer hovers over a button. They get the hover style defined in Listing 13-6.

Listing 13-16. *Defining the Throb Effect*

```
/*
 * Shadow Throb
 */
@-webkit-keyframes shadowThrob {
  0% {
    -webkit-box-shadow: inset 0px 0px 4px rgba(0, 0, 0, 0.4), inset 0 12px 2px rgba(255, 255,
255, 0);
    -moz-box-shadow: inset 0px 0px 4px rgba(0, 0, 0, 0.4), inset 0 12px 2px rgba(255, 255, 255,
0);
    box-shadow: inset 0px 0px 4px rgba(0, 0, 0, 0.4), inset 0 12px 2px rgba(255, 255, 255, 0);
  }
  50% {
    -webkit-box-shadow: inset 0px 0px 4px rgba(0, 0, 0, 0.4), inset 0 12px 2px rgba(255, 255,
255, 0.2);
    -moz-box-shadow: inset 0px 0px 4px rgba(0, 0, 0, 0.4), inset 0 12px 2px rgba(255, 255, 255,
0.2);
    box-shadow: inset 0px 0px 4px rgba(0, 0, 0, 0.4), inset 0 12px 2px rgba(255, 255, 255, 0.2);
  }
  100% {
    -webkit-box-shadow: inset 0px 0px 4px rgba(0, 0, 0, 0.4), inset 0 12px 2px rgba(255, 255,
255, 0);
    -moz-box-shadow: inset 0px 0px 4px rgba(0, 0, 0, 0.4), inset 0 12px 2px rgba(255, 255, 255,
0);
    box-shadow: inset 0px 0px 4px rgba(0, 0, 0, 0.4), inset 0 12px 2px rgba(255, 255, 255, 0);
  }
```

```
}
@-moz-keyframes shadowThrob {
  0% {
    opacity: 0.0;
  }
  50% {
    opacity: 0.5;
  }
  100% {
    opacity: 1.0;
  }
}
@-o-keyframes shadowThrob {
  0% {
    opacity: 0.0;
  }
  50% {
    opacity: 0.5;
  }
  100% {
    opacity: 1.0;
  }
}
@keyframes shadowThrob {
  0% {
    opacity: 0.0;
  }
  50% {
    opacity: 0.5;
  }
  100% {
    opacity: 1.0;
  }
}
```

Listing 13-17 shows the first of the rules that define the icon for the Primary with Icon button treatment. As we mentioned earlier in the chapter, the actual icon is an SVG image, which lets us avoid an HTTP request and take advantage of the browser's cache. For Internet Explorer 8 and earlier versions, we could add an image as a fallback. In this case, to hold down the size of an already large listing, we've not done so. As we've mentioned before, you should skip over the SVG image data.

Listing 13-17. Defining the Icon for Buttons That Have Icons

```
/*
 * Button Icons
 */
.buttonIcon {
  position: absolute;
  left: 2px;
  top: 2px;
  background-repeat: no-repeat;
```

```
    background-image: url(data:image/png;base64,iVBORw0KGgoAAAANSUhEUgAAAHEAAAAZCAYAAAG2cHnAAAAGX
RFWHRTb2Z0d2FyZQBBZG9iZSBJbWFnZVJlYWR5ccllPAAAA+dpVFh0WE1MOmNvbS5hZG9iZS54bXAAAAAAADw/eHBhY2tldC
BiZWdpbj0i77u/IiBpZD0iVzVNME1wQ2VoaUh6cmVTek5UY3prYzlkIj8+IDx4OnhtcG1ldGEgeG1sbnM6eD0iYWRvYmU6bn
M6bWV0YS8iIHg6eG1wdGs9IkFkb2JlIFhNUCBDb3JlIDUuMC1jMDYwIDYxLjEzNDc3NywyMDEwMC8wMi8xMi0xNzozMjowMC
AgICAgICAgIj4gPHJkZjpSREYgeG1sbnM6cmRmPSJodHRwOi8vd3d3LnczLm9yZy8xOTk5LzAyLzIyLXJkZi1zeW50YXgtbn
MjIj4gPHJkZjpEZXNjcmlwdGlvbiByZGY6YWJvdXQ9IiIgeG1sbnM6eG1wPSJodHRwOi8vbnMuYWRvYmUuY29tL3hhcC8xLj
AvIiB4bWxuczczpkYz0iaHR0cDovL3B1cmwub3JnL2RjL2VsZW1lbnRzLzEuMS8iIHhtbG5zOnhtcE1NPSJodHRwOi8vbnMuYW
RvYmUuY29tL3hhcC8xLjAvbW0vIiB4bWxuczpzdFJlZj0iaHR0cDovL25zLmFkb2JlLmNvbS94YXAvMS4wL3NUeXBlL1Jlc2
91cmNlUmVmIyIgeG1wOkNyZWF0b3JUb29sPSJBZG9iZSBQaG90b3Nob3AgQ1M1IE1hY2ludG9zaCIgeG1wOkNyZWF0ZURhdG
U9IjIwMTItMDYtMThUMjM6MjY6NDktMDU6MDAiIHhtcDpNb2RpZnlEYXRlPSIyMDEyLTA2LTIxVDAyOjM1OjU2LTE5OjAwIi
B4bXA6TWV0YWRhdGFEYXRlPSIyMDEyLTA2LTIxVDAyOjM1OjU2LTE5OjAwIiBkYzpmb3JtYXQ9ImltYWdlL3BuZyIgeG1wTU
06SW5zdGFuY2VJRD0ieG1wLmlpZDo5MzdGQ0Q5MO0UIxRUMxMUUxOEJFOD1BMDkxMOUyQOFDNCIgeG1wTU06RG9jdW1lbnRJRD
OieG1wLmRpZDo5MzdGQ0Q5MO0UIxRUMxMUUxOEJFOD1BMDkxMOUyQOFDNCI+IDx4bXBNTTpEZXJpdmVkRnJvbSBzdFJlZjppbn
N0YW5jZUlEPSJ4bXAuaWlkOjkzNODZDQzQ3QjJjFFQzExRTE4QkU4OUEwOTExRTJDQUMOIiBzdFJlZjpkb2N1bWVudElEPSJ4bX
AuZGlkOjkzNODZDQzQ4QjJjFFQzExRTE4QkU4OUEwOTFzRTJDQUMOIi8+IDwvcmRmOkRlc2NyaXB0aW9uPiA8L3JkZjpSREY+ID
wveDp4bXBtZXRhPiA8P3hwYWNrZXQgZW5kPSJyIj8+7zXkvQAABN9JREFUeNrsWmFkHEEUvjR1LOEOdZTTEPKrHCGEkCpHCO
EIRwghHCEkQighhJIKR/vnqpUqRwmpVAipVEiFUlKlXJUQQivVSDTyKzRa2zd8y8uY2d3ZnU1S8vjs3uzM25337Xvz5uO1uK
6bupL/W66F6NNOqBC2CN8ILo5baG+/MmMiOmKDxB7CMqFGOCSME+4SGnAcR3sN/XoiPKh7AUhKsoSnFvXlw1uRwqkCFcIOoV
9qvOMo4cjb+9G/otGngyczhuNMMcPulYT+IuGA8Mmizr6wfVWNVcIaoQm/hwnrhBP3rJygfQj9mjmjCuakjiAxynEzLwtHQf2/
qFff5A9+JlIHGOsEpoJNzAQ3H5SljCkcsi+jdi/JwBiSlm4CnLBp5iBKYSIHFEssNsDF1pwiCcYgTOIF6QMqEzLIlFhMQM4T
ahjgc7hiJHGuzgZsfoV8e4jCYU+5HIQ96UZQJnNPez4SmyTETUlQdhjsYTO2FrJ4hEEQp72bmQ94RcwAPkOM/FONHWg1BrQi
IncjKmgSc1a60tEtvYy8slynN3EwohwqkD/Wkdie2EzzgfwwPtwqu8Pq1IXJZxbGXXMujvYnwKi3yHIYk2iJz0SZZskJiGrV
TyyFBXhuUUKcnWwywv4USWdSTOsTC2iQcaOGR3riarHEDbJgtncxFI5MmIaXiaCEiSXIuJkkrqhrrKkmflmP1FbvFbMRexTGV
VJG4h7t6Egl9IUrxthZ94241GjHOhpyNEyu2GMNaEJQJtkNgGw6pkg9AVgUT+e4PpW2XnRckbh1Qk/iTcwlrmSutZNYBEvqV
YR5vQOwxSUzGMOi2FaB3GQm5TwpJYVKO9WEpUEiUrbZTIkJ1lVTrnY8+QeB17/mbCEaoOKVRiPGkLqBfw64esenEEvXHkIXR
UCX8JzxR9RnH9MfrHkTbo6kVF6gm71kHoV4yR+wWVMDtxnkZVxsFvcXzO+n4h/MC5sOUIu9bNxl16T+yAjh3OHZWuj6JdXN9
DuItyPwd7SR4q96SUfkOx97jbIe5RzdL9uSfW/DzxMq+J3Ujj12BMj7AKdFcYsQ767QZsiVxNKr+rmdsk26fJ8tRCkjQo/b6
vIPEADub1aYFtEslOSxazOwLKeivS2jSISXmTG5RS/xVkiFmD+3VqvMx7mZugl8uWZsOORUERPfrxPML75hUv5QhzsDMkcq8
J2ieuavaJO1I2GXWfWERYWdIYKo2ihO7aEoycMfT8kmYD/4LVRj1iWy1WfsZkUnxqp8Ke9/wqNhuschC1YrPO3rCNCBWbARC
4oJlY2KxvAfd3DNdgEao+BCwfRcv11wzCdjaAxAJeNN+yW8mndjqsePPTaNfVTkuGJHpfA2oxCORE1hThOMwWw5GSCloSZxt
DCKVpicQcvDVv6ytGHW953fJXDC+Ez1s2zDye13SfKObxUprjjqIMlkrAK7tAYBWOULDxPbGMOHQqTeoU7eWY3xOnWNaZhGE
qLJNODb2ZJzR9CRNo9aOwN/FtRfzPIyPMK5KR7Rhf9mcTNsgsooNp2c3BGrl4zgQakdjg82+3XlRDcoRXhHeE76jKZPFHngK
hRNhHNeVthP/YnLcOGPbPoDqyf87P2Ud4E2pCIf6yKMpNAyCsBQQeglBB7GvCx6s/p12chCHxSi65/BNgAM6z2oOaR+9QAAA
AAElFTkSuQmCC);
}
```

Listing 13-18 shows the two related classes that make room for and position the icon image.

***Listing 13-18.** Making Room for and Positioning the Icon*

```
/*
 * Checkmark Icon Button
 */
.icon_checkmark {
  background-position: -64px -2px;
  width: 20px;
  height: 21px;
}
.btn_checkmark {
  padding-left: 27px;
}
```

This CSS seems like a lot when you read through it in a book, but it's not really all that much in the big scheme of things. We've mentioned the sad fact that we've seen CSS files larger than a megabyte. Imagine trying to understand those monsters! Still, we hope *our* CSS makes sense to you. Also, we encourage you to visit our sample site for the button control and examine the CSS in action. The sample site for our button control is `http://clikz.us/BookExamples/buttonControl.php`

Summary

In this chapter, we created another control for an element that may not seem to deserve the effort. While we understand that first-glance assessment, we think a little thought will show why creating a control for buttons makes sense. The biggest reason is that buttons are all over the place. Most sites, especially e-commerce sites, have multiple buttons on almost every page. There's nearly always a way to buy something, customize something, start a chat session with a support person or sales agent, and so on and on. Given the sheer number of buttons around, we definitely want them all to look and behave consistently. A button control is a great way to get them to cooperate.

Second (but still a big benefit), we've created something that frees our teammates from having to think about how to make a button. If they use our control, they get a button guaranteed to meet the company's standards for appearance and behavior. Consequently, their development velocity increases; simply put, they get more done in less time. How can we not love that?

Third (but still important), maintenance is easier. Suppose a business consideration (such as a company-wide rebranding effort) necessitates changing every last button. We change one block of code, the control, and all the buttons on the site change.

Also, we feel compelled to mention the idea of encapsulation. Got a problem with buttons? Look no further than the button control. Troubleshooting is a *lot* faster when your problem is isolated in a control.

Taken all together, these benefits provide a lot of power and flexibility for not a lot of cost. And that's why we love our button control, even though it may seem like overkill at first glance.

CHAPTER 14

■ ■ ■

Price Control

The price control is really two controls, but we're putting them in the same chapter because they often go together. In addition to the actual price control, we have a shipping control. The price control contains price information—not just the final price but also base price, discounts, taxes, and so on. The shipping control contains shipping information.

Before getting started, we want to show an image of the finished controls. It's a single image because, again, the controls often go together.

Retail Price $1599.⁹⁹
Discount $100.⁰⁰
Your Price $1499.⁹⁹
▦ Estimated Ship Date:
   July 25, 2013

Figure 14-1. The price and shipping controls

If you want to see the price and shipping controls in action, look for them on the sample web site we created to support this book. For the sample price control, the address is `http://clikz.us/BookExamples/priceControl.php`

The Price Control

As with all of our other controls, this one is really a function and a set of CSS rules that get applied to the function's output. However, since it's hard to understand the rules without seeing the HTML, we start with the HTML generated by the function that is really the control.

One of the nagging problems with which we have seen many web developers struggle is creating a dot leader between a left-aligned element, such as a product name, and right-aligned content, such as a price. To help people get past that problem, the price control includes a dot leader that always flexes to fill the space between a left-aligned element and a right-aligned element.

The HTML

The HTML for the price control isn't complex. It's just a series of div elements and span elements, with a sup element to hold the currency and another sup element to hold the fractional part of the price.

■ **Note** The HTML that holds the price information includes a placeholder for shipping information.

Listing 14-1 shows the portion of the HTML that holds the price information for the price listing shown in Figure 14-1.

Listing 14-1. The Price Portion of the HTML Inserted by the Price Control

```
<div class="dottedPriceWrap">
  <div class="priceLabel">Retail Price</div>
  <div class="priceSubWrap">
    <div class="priceAmt">
      <sup class="currency">$</sup><span class="wholeNumber">1599.</span><sup
class="currency">99</sup>
    </div>
    <div class="dottedSpanner">.</div>
  </div>
</div>
<div class="dottedPriceWrap">
  <div class="priceLabel">Discount</div>
  <div class="priceSubWrap">
    <div class="priceAmt">
        <sup class="currency">$</sup><span class="wholeNumber">100.</span><sup
class="currency">00</sup>
    </div>
    <div class="dottedSpanner">.</div>
  </div>
</div>
<div class="dottedPriceWrap">
  <div class="priceLabel">Your Price</div>
  <div class="priceSubWrap">
    <div class="priceAmt">
      <sup class="currency">$</sup><span class="wholeNumber">1499.</span><sup
class="currency">99</sup>
    </div>
    <div class="dottedSpanner">.</div>
  </div>
</div>
```

The CSS

The CSS for the price control consists of just a few rules. We describe each one individually, so that we can talk about how each one works and how the rules fit together.

Along the way, we also describe how the dotted leader works. To get a dotted leader that works across various backgrounds (including gradients), we use a lesser-known effect that is part of the overflow:hidden property. Michael learned this from Nicole Sullivan's blog (www.stubbornell.org). If you're not familiar with Nicole Sullivan's fine CSS work, take some time to check out her ideas; it'll be time well spent.
Here's the tricky part of the overflow:hidden property, from the W3C CSS 2.1 specification:

The border box of a table, a block-level replaced element, or an element in the normal flow that establishes a new block formatting context (such as an element with 'overflow' other than 'visible') must not overlap any floats in the same block formatting context as the element itself.

Cascading Style Sheets Level 2 Revision 1 (CSS 2.1) Specification

What this breaks down to is that the overflow:hidden element next to a float takes up the remaining space. That's how we're getting the variable width of our dots to automatically take up the remaining space between the label and the amount. We're creating a nested overflow:hidden arrangement wherein we use the priceSubWrap to contain the amount and the div that contains the dotted delimiter. Figure 14-2 labels the various parts of the price control.

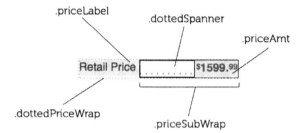

Figure 14-2. The parts of the price control

We use another base64-encoded image for the dots. However, because the base64 image won't work in Internet Explorer 6 or 7, we also include a link to the graphic for visitors who are using those browsers. We use the same technique for the calendar icon in the shipping stack.

So now let's start looking at the CSS rules. Listing 14-2 shows the first rule to be applied to the price stack. It sets position and width for a line that holds a description and a price.

Listing 14-2. Setting Position and Width for a Price

```
.dottedPriceWrap {
  position: relative;
  width: 200px;
}
```

Listing 14-3 shows the priceLabel rule, which styles the description part of a price line. In particular, it sets the float property to left (which makes the div element whose class is priceSubWrap appear next to the price label) and sets the padding.

Listing 14-3. Styling the Description of a Price

```
.priceLabel {
  float: left;
  padding-right: 4px;
}
```

Listing 14-4 specifies the actual delimiter (or leader). Here's where we set the value of the overflow property to hidden. The text-indent property ensures that the text within the div whose class is dottedSpanner does not appear. We had to put something in that div element or it would collapse and not show our delimiter, but we don't want that text to appear. As we discussed earlier in the chapter, the base64-encoded data contains the image that constitutes the dots for our dotted delimiter.

■ **Tip** This technique provides a dot leader that works against various backgrounds, including gradients.

Listing 14-4. Specifying the Delimiter (the Dots)

```
.dottedSpanner {
  overflow: hidden;
  line-height: inherit;
  text-indent: -999em;
 background
```

: url(data:image/gif;base64,R0lGODlhBwAFAJECAGZmZGJmZf///wAAACH/
C1hNUCBEYXRhWE1QPD94cGFja2V0IGJlZ2luPSLvu78iIGlkPSJXNU0wTXBDZWhpSHpyZVN6TlRjemtjOWQiPz4gPHg6eG1w
bWV0YSB4bWxuczp4PSJhZG9iZTpuczptZXRhLyIgeDp4bXB0az0iQWRvYmUgWE1QIENvcmUgNS4wLWMwNjAgNjEuMTM0Nzc3
LCAyMDEwLzAyLzEyLTE3OjMyOjAwICAgICAiPiA8cmRmOlJERiB4bWxuczpyZGY9Imh0dHA6Ly93d3cudzMub3JnLzE5
OTkvMDIvMjItcmRmLXN5bnRheC1ucyMiPiA8cmRmOkRlc2NyaXB0aW9uIHJkZjphYm91dD0iIiB4bWxuczp4bXA9Imh0dHA6
Ly9ucy5hZG9iZS5jb20veGFwLzEuMC8iIHhtbG5zOnhtcE1NPSJodHRwOi8vbnMuYWRvYmUuY29tL3hhcC8xLjAvbW0vIiB4
bWxuczpzdFJlZj0iaHR0cDovL25zLmFkb2JlLmNvbS94YXAvMS4wL3NUeXBlL1J1c291cmNlUmVmIyIgeG1wOkNyZWF0b3J3
b29sPSJBZG9iZSBQaG90b3Nob3AgQ1M1IFdpbmRvd3MiIHhtcE1NOkluc3RhbmNlSUQ9InhtcC5paWQ6NUZCQUFFNTUJBRjU3
MTFFMUE4NkZBBMzc4MEIwMDVGMEQiIHhtcE1NOkRvY3VtZW50SUQ9InhtcC5kaWQ6NUZCQUFFNUNBRjU3MTFFMUE4NkZBBMzc4
MEIwMDVGMEQiPiA8eG1wTU06RGVyaXZlZEZyb20gc3RSZWY6aW5zdGFuY2VJRDOieG1wLmlpZDo1RkJBQUU1OUFGNTcxMUUx
QTg2RkEzNzgwQjAwNUYwRCIgc3RSZWY6ZG9jdW1lbnRJRDOieG1wLmRpZDo1RkJBQUU1QUFGNTcxMUUxQTg2RkEzNzgwQjAw
NUYwRCIvPiA8L3JkZjpEZXNjcmlwdGlvbj4gPC9yZGY6UkRGPiA8L3g6eG1wbWV0YT4gPD94cGFja2V0IGVuZDOiciI/PgH/
/v38+/r5+Pf29fTz8vHw7+7t7Ovq6ejn5uXk4+Lh4N/e3dzb2tnY19bV1NPS0dDPzs3My8rJyMfGxcTDwsHAv769vLu6ubi3
trWos7KxsK+urayrqqmop6alpKOioaCfnp2cm5qZmJeWlZSTkpGQj46NjIuKiYiHhoWEg4KBgH9+fXx7enl4d3Z1dHNycXBv
bm1sa2ppaGdmZWRjYmFgX15dXFtaWVhXVlVUU1JRUE9OTUxLSklIR0ZFRENCQUA/Pjo8Ozo5ODc2NTQzMjEwLy4tLCsqKSgn
JiUkIyIhIB8eHRwbGhkYFxYVFBMSERAPDgOMCwoJCAcGBQQDAgEAACH5BAEAAAIALAAAAAAHAAUAAAIHjI6Ay+1XAAA7)
repeat-x bottom left;
}
```

    background: url(data:image/gif;base64,R0lGODlhBwAFAJECAGZmZGJmZf///wAAACH/C1hNUCBEYXRhWE1QPD94
cGFja2V0IGJlZ2luPSLvu78iIGlkPSJXNU0wTXBDZWhpSHpyZVN6TlRjemtjOWQiPz4gPHg6eG1wbWV0YSB4bWxuczp4PSJh
ZG9iZTpuczptZXRhLyIgeDp4bXB0az0iQWRvYmUgWE1QIENvcmUgNS4wLWMwNjAgNjEuMTM0Nzc3LCAyMDEwLzAyLzEyLTE3
OjMyOjAwICAgICAiPiA8cmRmOlJERiB4bWxuczpyZGY9Imh0dHA6Ly93d3cudzMub3JnLzE5OTkvMDIvMjItcmRmLXN5
bnRheC1ucyMiPiA8cmRmOkRlc2NyaXB0aW9uIHJkZjphYm91dD0iIiB4bWxuczp4bXA9Imh0dHA6Ly9ucy5hZG9iZS5jb20v
eGFwLzEuMC8iIHhtbG5zOnhtcE1NPSJodHRwOi8vbnMuYWRvYmUuY29tL3hhcC8xLjAvbW0vIiB4bWxuczpzdFJlZjOiaHR0
cDovL25zLmFkb2JlLmNvbS94YXAvMS4wL3NUeXBlL1J1c291cmNlUmVmIyIgeG1wOkNyZWF0b3J3b29sPSJBZG9iZSBQaG90
b3Nob3AgQ1M1IFdpbmRvd3MiIHhtcE1NOkluc3RhbmNlSUQ9InhtcC5paWQ6NUZCQUFFNUNBRjU3MTFFMUE4NkZBBMzc4MEIw
MDVGMEQiIHhtcE1NOkRvY3VtZW50SUQ9InhtcC5kaWQ6NUZCQUFFNUNBRjU3MTFFMUE4NkZBBMzc4MEIwMDVGMEQiPiA8eG1w
TU06RGVyaXZlZEZyb20gc3RSZWY6aW5zdGFuY2VJRDOieG1wLmlpZDo1RkJBQUU1OUFGNTcxMUUxQTg2RkEzNzgwQjAwNUYw
RCIgc3RSZWY6ZG9jdW1lbnRJRDOieG1wLmRpZDo1RkJBQUU1QUFGNTcxMUUxQTg2RkEzNzgwQjAwNUYwRCIvPiA8L3JkZjpE
ZXNjcmlwdGlvbj4gPC9yZGY6UkRGPiA8L3g6eG1wbWV0YT4gPD94cGFja2V0IGVuZDOiciI/PgH//v38+/r5+Pf29fTz8vHw
7+7t7Ovq6ejn5uXk4+Lh4N/e3dzb2tnY19bV1NPS0dDPzs3My8rJyMfGxcTDwsHAv769vLu6ubi3trWos7KxsK+urayrqqmo
p6alpKOioaCfnp2cm5qZmJeWlZSTkpGQj46NjIuKiYiHhoWEg4KBgH9+fXx7enl4d3Z1dHNycXBvbm1sa2ppaGdmZWRjYmFg
X15dXFtaWVhXVlVUU1JRUE9OTUxLSklIR0ZFRENCQUA/Pjo8Ozo5ODc2NTQzMjEwLy4tLCsqKSgnJiUkIyIhIB8eHRwbGhkY
FxYVFBMSERAPDgOMCwoJCAcGBQQDAgEAACH5BAEAAAIALAAAAAAHAAUAAAIHjI6Ay+1XAAA7) repeat-x bottom left;
```

}

Listing 14-5 shows the rule that specifies where to find the image for the dots for visitors who use IE6 or 7. It also specifies that the image should repeat horizontally across the entire line.

Listing 14-5. Specifying Dots for IE6 and IE7

```
.ie6 .dottedSpanner, .ie7 .dottedSpanner {
  background: url(/images/period.gif) repeat-x bottom left;
}
```

Listing 14-6 shows the rule that styles the amount part of a price line. In particular, it specifies that the price should float to the right and have a left padding of 2 pixels (to give a bit of space between the delimiter and the price value).

Listing 14-6. Styling the Price Value

```
.priceAmt {
  float: right;
  padding-left: 2px;
}
```

Listing 14-7 shows the priceSubWrap class. This class applies to the div that holds the price amount and the dotted delimiter. To make the delimiter image fill the space between the price label and the price value, this class sets the value of the overflow property to hidden. It also specifies that the value of the div element's position property is relative.

Listing 14-7. Styling the Wrapper Around the Price and Delimiter

```
.priceSubWrap {
  overflow: hidden;
  position: relative;
}
```

Listing 14-8 styles the currency symbol ($, £, , etc.) with a straightforward rule that specifies the symbol's size and position. We also use this style for the portion of the price to the right of the decimal point.

Listing 14-8. Styling the Currency Symbol

```
sup.currency {
  font-size: 70%;
  top: auto;
  position: relative;
  vertical-align: text-top;
  line-height: 125%;
}
```

The Control

The price function builds up a string that contains HTML elements and the values specified in the parameters, except for the $echo parameter. The $echo parameter indicates whether to insert the HTML string into the page that called the function or return to the HTML as a string to some other function.

> ■ **Note**   Usually, the values that go into these controls (and most others) would come from a database. For the sake of simplicity, we're not using a database on our sample site. Instead, we're just inserting values by hand, since our focus is HTML and CSS, not back-end work.

Table 14-1 describes the parameters of the price function.

Table 14-1. *Parameters of the Price Function*

Parameter	Description
label	The description portion of a price line. In our examples, we use values such as "Retail Price", "Discount", and "Your Price".
currencySymbol	The currency symbol to put before the price amount. In our examples, we use a dollar sign ($). You could just as easily use a British pound symbol (£), the euro symbol (€), or whatever currency symbol you need.
wholeNumber	The part of the currency value to the left of the decimal place. If the total amount were 12.34, this value would be 12.
remainder	The part of the currency value to the right of the decimal place. If the total amount were 12.34, this value would be 34.
echo	echo indicates that the function should insert the HTML into the page; return indicates that the function should return the HTML as a string to another function. The "return" value lets other controls embed the price control as part of a larger control, as the next chapter will show.

Listing 14-9 shows the PHP code that defines the price function.

Listing 14-9. *The Price Function*

```php
<?php
  function price($label, $currencySymbol, $wholeNumber, $remainder,  $echo) {
    $output = '<div class="dottedPriceWrap">';
    $output .= '  <div class="priceLabel">';
    $output .= $label;
    $output .= '  </div>';
    $output .= '  <div class="priceSubWrap">';
    $output .= '    <div class="priceAmt">';
    $output .= '      <sup class="currency">'. $currencySymbol . '</
sup><span>'.$wholeNumber.'</span><sup class="currency">'.$remainder.'</sup>';
    $output .= '    </div>';
    $output .= '  </div>';
    $output .= '  <div class="dottedSpanner">.</div>';
    $output .= '</div>';

    if($echo == "return"){
      return $output;
    } else {
      echo $output;
    }
```

```
    }
?>
```

The Shipping Control

As we mentioned at the start of the chapter, the shipping control is a separate control. however, because a shipping control often follows a price control, we're explaining the shipping control here. Starting with the HTML produced by the shipping control function will provide context that should help you make sense of the CSS rules and of the function that is the actual control.

The HTML

The HTML for the shipping control contains a single div with three spans. The spans let us create separate rules to style the shipping icon, the shipping label, and the shipping date. Listing14-10 shows the HTML that holds the shipping information.

Listing 14-10. The Shipping Portion of the HTML Inserted by the Price Control

```
<div class="shippingWrap">
  <span class="iconShipping"></span>
  <span class="shipLabel">Estimated Ship Date:        </span>
  <span class="shipDate">July 25, 2013</span>
</div>
```

By this point in the book, you're probably used to our style of HTML. We use simple elements with meaningful class names and then specify what to do with those elements through CSS (and JavaScript, when we can't get what we want with CSS). So let's examine the CSS that turns this content into the output we want for a price control.

The CSS

Since the shipping stack consists of one div and three spans, we need just four rules to style the shipping control.

Listing 14-11 shows the shippingWrap rule, which specifies the position and font-size of the shipping stack. It provides a left padding value of 22 pixels to make room for a calendar icon and a top margin value of 5 pixels to provide a little space between the price and the shipping information.

Listing 14-11. Styling the Shipping Information

```
.shippingWrap {
  position: relative;
  padding-left: 22px;
  font-size: 12px;
  margin-top: 5px;
}
```

Listing 14-12 shows the iconShipping rule, which defines the calendar icon we put to the left of the shipping information. We put an 18-pixel image into the left side of a 22-pixel space (the 22 pixels were defined by the shippingWrap rule; see Listing 14-11), which provides a 4-pixel space between the calendar icon and the shipping information. As with the dots in the delimiter, we use a block of base64-encoded data to specify the icon image.

Listing 14-12. Inserting the Calendar Icon

```
.iconShipping {
  width: 18px;
  height: 18px;
  position: absolute;
  left: 0;
  top: 1px;
  background-repeat: no-repeat;
  background-image: url(data:image/png;base64,
```
iVBORw0KGgoAAAANSUhEUgAAABIAAAASCAMAAABhEH5lAAAAGX
RFWHRTb2Z0d2FyZQBBZG9iZSBJbWFnZVJlYWR5ccllPAAABVhpVFhoWE1MOmNvbS5hZG9iZS54bXAAAAAAADw/eHBhY2tldC
BiZWdpbj0i77u/IiBpZD0iVzVNME1wQ2VoaUh6cmVTek5UY3prYzlkIj8+IDx4OnhtcG1ldGEgeG1sbnM6eD0iYWRvYmU6bn
M6bWV0YS8iIHg6eG1wdGs9IkFkb2JlIFhNUCBDb3JlIDUuMC1jMjYwIDYyLjEzNDc3NywyMjAxMC8wMi8xMi0xNzozMjowMC
AgICAgICAgIj4gPHJkZjpSREYgeG1sbnM6cmRmPSJodHRwOi8vd3d3LnczLm9yZy8xOTk5LzAyLzIyLXJkZi1zeW50YXgtbn
MjIj4gPHJkZjpEZXNjcmlwdGlvbiByZGY6YWJvdXQ9IiIgeG1sbnM6eG1wPSJodHRwOi8vbnMuYWRvYmUuY29tL3hhcC8xLj
AvIiB4bWxuczpkYz0iaHR0cDovL3B1cmwub3JnL2RjL2VsZW1lbnRzLzEuMS8iIHhtbG5zOnhtcE1NPSJodHRwOi8vbnMuYW
RvYmUuY29tL3hhcC8xLjAvbW0vIiB4bWxuczpzdEV2dD0iaHR0cDovL25zLmFkb2JlLmNvbS94YXAvMS4wL3NUeXBlL1Jlc2
91cmNlRXZlbnQjIiB4bWxuczpzdFJlZj0iaHR0cDovL25zLmFkb2JlLmNvbS94YXAvMS4wL3NUeXBlL1Jlc291cmNlUmVmIy
IgeG1wOkNyZWF0b3JUb29sPSJBZG9iZSBQaG90b3Nob3AgQ1M1IE1hY2ludG9zaCIgeG1wOkNyZWF0ZURhdGU9IjIwMTItMD
YtMTMtMjM6MjY6NDktMDU6MDAiIHhtcDpNb2RpZnlEYXRlPSIyMDEyLTA2LTIyVDE3OjQyOjUxLTA1OjAwIiB4bXA6TWV0YW
RhdGFEYXRlPSIyMDEyLTA2LTIyVDE3OjQyOjUxLTA1OjAwIiBkYzpmb3JtYXQ9ImltYWdlL3BuZyIgeG1wTU06SW5zdGFuY2
VJRDoieG1wLmlpZDpGRTVEQjQyRkI0OQjUxMUUxOEJFOD1BMDkxMOUyQOFDNCIgeG1wTU06RG9jdW1lbnRJRDoieG1wLmRpZD
pGRTVEQjQzMEIOQjUxMUUxOEJFOD1BMDkxMOUyQOFDNCIgeG1wTU06T3JpZ2luYWxEb2N1bWVudElEPSJ4bXAuZGlkOjAxOD
AxMTcOMDcyMDY4MTE0QTZEQjZBNUFBMERGQUNCIj4gPHhtcE1NOkhpc3Rvcnk+IDxyZGY6U2VxPiA8cmRmOmxpIHNORXZ0Om
FjdGlvbj0iY3JlYXRlZCIgc3RFdnQ6aW5zdGFuY2VJRDoieG1wLmlpZDowMTgwMTE3NDA3MjA20DExOEE2REI2QTVBQTBERk
FDQiIgc3RFdnQ6d2hlbj0iMjAxMi0wNi0xOFQyMzoyNjo0OSOwNTowMCIgc3RFdnQ6c29mdHdhcmVBZ2VudD0iQWRvYmUgUG
hvdG9zaG9wIENTNSBNYWNpbnRvc2giLz4gPC9yZGY6U2VxPiA8L3htcE1NOkhpc3Rvcnk+IDx4bXBNTTpEZXJpdmVkRnJvbS
BzdFJlZjppbnN0YW5jZUlEPSJ4bXAuaWlkOjAxODAxMTcOMDcyMDY4MTE0QTZEQjZNUFBMERGQUNCIiBzdFJlZjpkb2N1bW
VudElEPSJ4bXAuZGlkOjAxODAxMTcOMDcyMDY4MTE0QTZEQjZNUFBMERGQUNCIi8+IDwvcmRmOkRlc2NyaXB0aW9uPiA8L3
JkZjpSREY+IDwveDp4bXBtZXRhPiA8P3hwYWNrZXQgZW5kPSJyIj8+Ih6y4AAAABtQTFRF5eXljcP38fHx////1dXVJYnnLZ
TONp7/AAAAGCCkcgAAAAlOUk5T//////////8AU0Q4EgAAAD1JREFUeNpi4OBgYkACTBwcDBwMjOxIgBEowMTIhgIYgZrYWF
EAG1A3MxoACbGwoCAcQkNZIOoAggMRIMAA9OOD+65FZsYAAAAASUVORK5CYII=
```
);
}

Listing 14-13 specifies the location of an image for our calendar icon for visitors who use IE6 or IE7.

*Listing 14-13. Inserting the Calendar Icon for IE 6 and IE7*

```
.ie6 .iconShipping, .ie7 .iconShipping {
  background-image: url(/images/icon_calendar.png);
}
```

Listing 14-14 shows the shipLabel rule, which styles the phrase "Estimated Ship Date" such that it is a shade of gray and is a block. Since the shipLabel rule is on a span element, we have to make it display as a block to keep it on its own line.

Listing 14-14. Styling the Label Portion of the Shipping Block

```
.shipLabel {
  color: #777;
```
```

```
    display: block;
}
```

Now let's move on to the PHP portion of the control.

The Control

The `.shipDate` function does much the same thing as the `price` function. That is, it builds up a string containing HTML elements and, if the `$echo` parameter contains "echo", sends the content to the browser or, if the `$echo` parameter contains "return", sends the content to the function that called this function. However, it uses different parameters and creates two lines rather than one.

■ **Note** For the sake of describing the functions, we've separated them into two listings. On our sample site, http://clikz.com/BookExamples/priceControl.php, the two functions are in the same code block.

Table 14-2 describes the parameters of the shipDate function.

Table 14-2. Parameters of the shipDate Function

Parameter	Description
shipDateLabel	The value of the first line. In our examples, it is "Estimated Ship Date".
shipDate	The actual date on which the customer's order should ship. This is a string parameter rather than a date object. Consequently, formatting the date is up to the developer who calls the function.
echo	echo indicates that the function should insert the HTML into the page; "return" indicates that the function should return the HTML as a string to another function. return lets other controls embed the price control as part of a larger control, as the next chapter will show.

As the description of the `shipDate` parameter indicates, the parameter is just a string. If you want to ensure you always get the same date format, split it into three parameters: year, month, date. You can even add a fourth parameter to specify the format of the date if you want an even more flexible control. As we're pretending that all of our (fictional) customers are in the United States, we'll just use a typical US date format and be done.

Listing 14-15 shows the PHP code that defines the `shipDate` function.

Listing 14-15. The shipDate Function

```php
<?php
  function shipDate($shipDateLabel, $shipDate, $echo){
  $output = '<div class="shippingWrap">';
  $output .= '  <span class="iconShipping"></span>';
  $output .= '  <span class="shipLabel">';
  $output .= $shipDateLabel;
  $output .= '</span>';
  $output .= '  <span class="shipDate">';
  $output .= $shipDate;
  $output .= '</span>';
```

```php
    $output .= '</div>';

    if($echo == "return"){
    return $output;
    }else {
    echo $output;
    }
}
?>
```

Using the Controls

To use the controls, you must insert php tags into your web page. Each price and shipping control requires a separate php tag. Consider the example we've used throughout this chapter. Figure 14-3 shows our sample price stack (consisting of three price controls and one shipping control). It's exactly the same image as Figure 14-1, repeated here for your convenience.

Retail Price $1599.⁹⁹
Discount $100.⁰⁰
Your Price $1499.⁹⁹
　Estimated Ship Date:
　July 25, 2013

Figure 14-3. A simple price stack (again)

To create our sample price stack, we need four php tags, each of which calls either the price control or the shipping control. Listing 14-16 shows the function calls that create the price stack shown in Figure 14-3.

Listing 14-16. Using the Price and Shipping Controls

```php
<?php price("Retail Price", "$", "1599", "99"); ?>
<?php price("Discount", "$", "100", "00"); ?>
<?php price("Your Price", "$", "1499", "99"); ?>
<?php shipDate( "Estimated Ship Date:", "July 25, 2013") ?>
```

Summary

The price control is really two controls, one to produce an individual line within a price stack and one to create shipping information. This separation of concerns provides a number of benefits. For one thing, you can stack up any number of price stack lines (perhaps to show various discounts or fees). For another thing, you can put the shipping information at either the top or the bottom of the price stack (even between price lines, if you can think of a good reason to do so). You can also leave out one control or the other, having price lines by themselves or a shipping block by itself.

We'll use both the price control and the shipping control in the next chapter, wherein we describe the product control (or product stack, as we usually call it). As we keep repeating, most of our controls consist of other controls, though often with additional information. Remember the fractal metaphor: If you zoom in to a closer view of a fractal image, you see a very similar image. Similarly, if you look inside one of our controls, you're likely to find more controls.

CHAPTER 15

■ ■ ■

Product Control

In previous chapters, we have alluded to the product control, which uses other controls for much of its content. Because it is a stack of other controls and its usual layout is vertical, with one item of information stacked upon another, we normally call it the product stack. The control can also have a more horizontal layout, wherein content appears in two differently sized columns. As we do with other controls, we call the variations of the product control treatments. It has two treatments: vertical and horizontal.

Before we get to this control, let's take a minute to recall the reason we're making all these controls: improved performance. The biggest performance gain undoubtedly goes to the developers. Rather than create their own product listings, they can use our control and get a product listing in a fraction of the time it would take them to code everything. Also, because the controls encapsulate their code into an easy-to-find place, debugging is easier and faster—another performance improvement for developers. Visitors get to see a performance boost, too. When every product looks a bit different, distinguishing the differences becomes a challenge. But since there is a guarantee of consistency from one product listing to the next, distinctions are easy to spot, and visitors can find the product or products they want in a hurry. Finally, if the visitors find what they want more easily, not only may they buy more, but they'll tell their friends what a good site they've found. That's a big win for the business.

The product control uses the link control (to provide a help link), the price control, and the button control. It also adds an image of the product and some text that might entice a customer to buy the product. (In our case, we've used nonsense text, but then we're not really trying to sell anything.)

If you want to see the product stack on a web page, you can find it at our sample site: `http://clikz.us/BookExamples/productControl.php`

Figure 15-1 shows the product control in use. In its vertical orientation, it takes up an entire page (and that's after we shrank it a bit so that we could get the caption on the page with the image). Because a product control presents a lot of information, it takes a lot of room.

**The Worlds Best
Laptop**

Retail Price $1599.⁹⁹
Discount $100.⁰⁰
Your Price $1499.⁹⁹

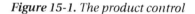 Estimated Ship Date ⑦
July 25, 2013

Sartorial williamsburg small
batch helvetica mixtape
wayfarers. Art party biodiesel
before they sold out authentic.

- Squid pinterest carles,
  fingerstache forage
  scenester.

- Pinterest carles,
  fingerstache forage
  scenester.

- Carles, fingerstache forage
  scenester.

[Buy Me]

Figure 15-1. The product control

The horizontal layout of the product control takes the same amount of space but is a bit friendlier for a book layout. We find that the vertical layout works best on a web page, where we can put a number of product controls next to one another to help customers compare products. That said, the horizontal layout has its web uses, too, especially when it's the only product control on the page.

Figure 15-2 shows the horizontal layout of the product control.

The Worlds Best Laptop

Retail Price $1599.⁹⁹
Discount $100.⁰⁰
Your Price $1499.⁹⁹

Sartorial williamsburg small batch helvetica
mixtape wayfarers. Art party biodiesel before
they sold out authentic.

- Squid pinterest carles, fingerstache forage
  scenester.

- Pinterest carles, fingerstache forage
  scenester.

- Carles, fingerstache forage scenester.

Estimated Ship Date ⑦
July 25, 2013

Buy Me

Figure 15-2. The horizontal layout of the product control

Much of the content in the product control, whether vertical or horizontal, probably looks familiar. The help link (the question mark in a circle) is the same help link seen in Chapter 11. The shipping block (the calendar icon, the "Estimated Ship Date" text, and the actual date) is the same shipping block seen in Chapter 13. The three lines of price information are also the same as those seen in Chapter 13. The "Buy Me" button is an instance of the button control described in Chapter 12.

Now that you've seen what a product control looks like, it's time to learn how to make it work. Let's start with how to put one in a web page.

Inserting the Control

To specify the horizontal or vertical treatment for the product control, we call a PHP function from within our page and specify two arguments: a data source and a treatment. We'll get to the data source later. For now, just think of it as a blob of data that we process within the control at runtime.

The name of the vertical treatment is pcTreatment1 (for product control Treatment 1). It's not the most original or descriptive name, but it follows our usual naming convention. The name of the horizontal treatment (you've probably already guessed it) is pcTreatment2.

For our sample page, we first create the vertical layout and then the horizontal layout, with a couple of blank lines between to provide a bit of white space. Listing 15-1 shows the code for creating the two different treatments of a product control within a web page.

Listing 15-1. Putting Product Controls on a Page

```
<h1>pcTreatment1</h1>
<?php
  productStack(json_decode($productJSON), "pcTreatment1");
?>
<br/>
<br/>
<h1>pcTreatment2</h1>
<?php
  productStack(json_decode($productJSON), "pcTreatment2");
?>
```

Now that you know what the input looks like, let's consider the output.

The HTML Produced by the Control

The control creates HTML where it is used within a page. We provide that HTML so that you can see what the control produces at runtime. The HTML is embedded in the control, as we'll show later, but it's a lot easier to read on its own and with all the values in place.

As you read through Listing 15-2, pay attention to the class names. The trick to making this kind of control lies in the class names. The HTML elements really just contain data. As an experienced user of CSS knows, you can make entirely different layouts from the same elements, given different CSS rules. That's how we achieve the different treatments for our controls. We rely on the class names to give us entry points for controlling the layout of any given treatment. Consequently, the whole show depends on the class names.

▨ **Note**   Listing 15-2 shows the resulting HTML of just the vertical treatment. The listing's big as it is, so we didn't make it bigger still by adding the horizontal treatment. Also, the only difference between the treatments within the HTML is `pcTreatment1` versus `pcTreatment2`. All the other differences between the two treatments are in the CSS rules.

Listing 15-2 shows the HTML for the vertical treatment, with all the values in place. We've added a few comments to point out the other controls within the product control. To make those comments easy to find, we set them in bold type.

Listing 15-2. The HTML Created by the Product Control for the Vertical Treatment

```
<article class="productControlWrap pcTreatment1">
  <img src="/images/laptop1.jpg" alt="This is a picture" class="pcImage"><h2 class="pcTitle">The
Worlds Best Laptop</h2>
<!-- Here's the top of a price stack -->
  <div class="pcPriceStack">
    <div class="dottedPriceWrap">
      <div class="priceLabel">
        Retail Price
      </div>
      <div class="priceSubWrap">
        <div class="priceAmt">
          <sup class="currency">$</sup><span class="wholeNumber">1599.</span><sup
class="currency">99</sup>
        </div>
        <div class="dottedSpanner">
          .
        </div>
      </div>
    </div>
    <div class="dottedPriceWrap">
      <div class="priceLabel">
        Discount
```

```
        </div>
        <div class="priceSubWrap">
          <div class="priceAmt">
            <sup class="currency">$</sup><span class="wholeNumber">100.</span><sup
class="currency">00</sup>
          </div>
          <div class="dottedSpanner">
            .
          </div>
        </div>
      </div>
      <div class="dottedPriceWrap">
        <div class="priceLabel">
          Your Price
        </div>
        <div class="priceSubWrap">
          <div class="priceAmt">
            <sup class="currency">$</sup><span class="wholeNumber">1499.</span><sup
class="currency">99</sup>
          </div>
          <div class="dottedSpanner">
            .
          </div>
        </div>
      </div>
    </div>
  </div> <!-- End of price stack control -->
  <!-- Here's the shipping stack,
       which is not within the price stack -->
  <!-- Remember, the price control can create produce price lines
          and shipping blocks independently of one another. -->
  <div class="pcShippingStack">
    <div class="shippingWrap">
      <!-- Note the anchor element; that is the help link control -->
      <span class="iconShipping"></span><span class="shipLabel"><a href="javascript:;" data-
link-type="help" class="link">Estimated Ship Date<span class="linkIcon" data-tooltip-
message="You will receive a definitive date during checkout"></span></a> </span><span
class="shipDate">July 25, 2013 </span>
    </div>
  </div> <!-- End of shipping stack -->
  <div class="pcDescWrap">
    <div class="pcDescText">
      Sartorial williamsburg small batch helvetica mixtape wayfarers. Art party biodiesel before
they sold out authentic.
    </div>
    <ul class="pcDescBullets">
      <li class="pcDescLI">
        Squid pinterest carles, fingerstache forage scenester.
      </li>
      <li class="pcDescLI">
        Pinterest carles, fingerstache forage scenester.
      </li>
```

```
    <li class="pcDescLI">
      Carles, fingerstache forage scenester.
    </li>
  </ul>
<!-- Here's a button control, constituted as a link, since it's not in a form -->
</div><a href="/addToCart.php" class="button primary shadow">Buy Me</a>
</article>
```

The listing would be bigger still if we didn't use controls within controls. Without nested controls, we'd have to include all the elements for each of the contained controls. The ability to compress code helps a lot, both in keeping the code for each page smaller and in helping us read the code we have. We can look at the attributes of the anchor elements within Listing 15-2 and know instantly that one is a pop-up help link and the other is a Buy button. The code, type="help", gives a pretty big clue, as does class="button primary shadow" followed by Buy Me. As with most code in any language, learning to spot things within the code is just a matter of practice. If you worked with controls all day, as we do, you'd spot them in a flash, too.

The CSS

As with all the other controls, the CSS does the job of arranging the product control in an attractive manner (we hope). In the present case, we've got two treatments for which we need to arrange the same content (not counting class names). Since some of the rules apply to both treatments, we end up with three logical sections within the CSS: the rules that apply to both treatments, the rules that apply to just the vertical treatment (pcTreatment1), and the rules that apply to just the horizontal treatment (pcTreatment2). We'll give each rule group its own listing.

Listing 15-3 shows the CSS rules that apply to both the vertical and the horizontal treatments of the product control.

Listing 15-3. CSS Rules for Both Treatments of the Product Control

```
/*
 * Starting with the base definition that are shared
 * across all of the productControls. Besides the treatment
 * for the image, we're basically reseting margins and setting
 * initial font-sizes for consistency. We want to keep the styling
 * light so we reduce the number of times we have to override
 * the styles in the treatment specific sections.
 */
.productControlWrap {
  position: relative;
  font-size: 14px;
}
.pcImage {
  -webkit-box-shadow: 2px 2px 3px 0 rgba(0, 0, 0, 0.3);
  -moz-box-shadow: 2px 2px 3px 0 rgba(0, 0, 0, 0.3);
  box-shadow: 2px 2px 3px 0 rgba(0, 0, 0, 0.3);
  border: 1px solid #999;
  border: 1px solid rgba(0, 0, 0, 0.3);
}
.pcTitle {
```

```
  font-size: 18px;
  margin: 0;
  line-height: 110%;
  color: #1f81dd;
}
.priceLabel {
  color: #555;
}
.priceAmt {
  color: green;
  font-weight: bold;
}
.pcDescBullets {
  margin: 0;
  padding-left: 20px;
}
```

Listing 15-4 shows the CSS rules that apply only to the vertical treatment of the product control. The listing makes more sense if you remember that the name of the vertical treatment is pcTreatment1.

Listing 15-4. CSS Rules for only the Vertical Treatment of the Product Control

```
/*
 * Styles to affect the pcTreatment1 look.
 *
 */
.pcTreatment1 {
  width: 200px;
  color: #333333;
}
.pcTreatment1 .pcImage {
  width: 200px;
  height: 200px;
  margin-bottom: 10px;
}
.pcTreatment1 .pcTitle {
  margin-bottom: 10px;
}
.pcTreatment1 .shippingWrap {
  margin-bottom: 10px;
}
.pcTreatment1 .pcDescText {
  margin-bottom: 10px;
  line-height: 150%;
}
.pcTreatment1 .pcDescLI {
  margin-bottom: 10px;
}
```

Listing 15-5 shows the CSS rules that apply only to the horizontal treatment of the product control. The listing makes more sense if you remember that the name of the horizontal treatment is pcTreatment2.

Listing 15-5. CSS rules for only the Horizontal Treatment of the Product Control

```
/*
 * Styles to affect the pcTreatment2 look.
 *
 */
.pcTreatment2 {
  width: 300px;
  padding-left: 230px;
  color: #333333;
}
.pcTreatment2 .pcImage {
  width: 200px;
  height: 200px;
  position: absolute;
  left: 0;
  top: 0;
  -webkit-box-shadow: 0 4px 4px 0px rgba(0, 0, 0, 0.4);
  -moz-box-shadow: 0 4px 4px 0px rgba(0, 0, 0, 0.4);
  box-shadow: 0 4px 4px 0px rgba(0, 0, 0, 0.4);
}
.pcTreatment2 .pcTitle {
  font-size: 24px;
  margin-bottom: 20px;
}
.pcTreatment2 .pcPriceStack {
  width: 200px;
  margin-bottom: 10px;
}
.pcTreatment2 .shippingWrap {
  position: absolute;
  left: 0;
  top: 220px;
}
.pcTreatment2 .shipLabel .link {
  color: #333333;
}
.pcTreatment2 .shipLabel .link:visited {
  color: #333333;
}
.pcTreatment2 .pcDescText {
  margin-bottom: 10px;
  line-height: 150%;
}
.pcTreatment2 .pcDescLI {
  margin-bottom: 10px;
}
.pcTreatment2 .button {
  position: absolute;
  left: 0;
  top: 270px;
```

}

Because these rules aren't complex, there's no need to describe each one separately, as we've done in other chapters. This is in fact another benefit of building controls from other controls: The complexity can be hidden. We're using the CSS rules for the link, price, and button controls, but we don't have to concern ourselves with those rules because they are part of those controls, which we just use (rather than define) here. It's great to know that once a control is working, we can use it in just the same way that someone linking controls together to make a page would use controls. That's the power of encapsulation. What great stuff!

The Data for the Product Control

The product control requires enough information that trying to provide strings through function parameters would be really awkward and likely lead to errors. Instead, we pass in a data object. In our case, we choose to use a JSON (JavaScript Object Notation) object, because JSON is an established standard, one we know well and use a lot.

If you aren't familiar with JSON, take a few minutes to learn the basics. JSON's home on the web is http://www.json.org (it's a bit dense for a quick overview, however). You may find the JSON tutorial at W3 Schools (http://www.w3schools.com/json/default.php) more accessible for a quick reading.

Examine our data source and you'll see that we create a bunch of name-value pairs. Each pair is separated from the others by a comma. Within each name-value pair, the name is separated from the value by a colon. Each value, whether a name or a value, is a string and so is enclosed in quotation marks.

Look closely and you should also see a couple of different grouping mechanisms. For example, the priceStack name has a collection of data as its value. Within that collection are further collections enclosed within brace characters. That's a way to encode the idea that the data for the price stack control consists of a collection of values and that each of those values consists of the data that define a price line within the price stack control. JSON is pretty handy, once you learn to read its syntax.

Of course, the trick to dealing with all the bits of data is parsing them so that they end up in the right places. We'll get to that in the next section, where we describe the PHP code for the control.

Listing 15-6 shows the JSON object that contains the data for our product control.

Listing 15-6. A JSON Object Containing Data for the Product Control

```php
<?php
  $productJSON = '{
    "title":"The Worlds Best Laptop",
    "img":"/images/laptop1.jpg",
    "imgAlt" : "This is a picture",
    "priceStack" : [
    {"label":"Retail Price", "currencySymbol" : "$", "wholeNumber": "1599", "remainder":"99"},
    {"label":"Discount", "currencySymbol" : "$", "wholeNumber": "100", "remainder":"00"},
    {"label":"Your Price", "currencySymbol" : "$", "wholeNumber": "1499", "remainder":"99"}
    ],
    "shipDate": {"shipLabel":"' . mLink("Estimated Ship Date", "javascript:;", "help", NULL,
"return", NULL, "You will receive a definitive date during checkout") . '", "shipDate":"July 25,
2013"},
    "descText": "Sartorial williamsburg small batch helvetica mixtape wayfarers. Art party
biodiesel before they sold out authentic.",
    "descBullets": [
    {"bulletText": "Squid pinterest carles, fingerstache forage scenester."},
```

```
        {"bulletText": "Pinterest carles, fingerstache forage scenester."},
        {"bulletText": "Carles, fingerstache forage scenester."}
        ],
        "button" : {"text": "Buy Me", "href": "/addToCart.php", "type": "primaryShadow"}
    }';
?>
```

Now that you've seen the control's output and its CSS and its data, it's time to see the PHP code that does all the work.

The Control

While it makes for a fair-sized listing, the concept behind the function that makes a product stack is actually fairly simple: We blend the data that belongs in the control with the HTML elements that end up containing that data. To do so, we build a single big string, one that contains the HTML and has all the proper data values in the proper places. That's all any of our controls do, but it bears repeating because people sometimes overthink what a control should do and end up causing themselves a lot of trouble.

As we've already mentioned, we use PHP in this example and on our sample web site. However, any language that can be used for web development works just as well (better, even, if you happen to be more comfortable with another language than you are with PHP). We think that idea also bears repeating, because we want you to realize that the algorithm (building a string that contains data-laden HTML) is the important part. The language used for coding controls doesn't much matter—so long as it can do the job, of course.

The function that builds a product control is called productStack. It takes two arguments: an object, called $obj, that contains the data and a string, called $treatment, that indicates whether to create a vertical or a horizontal layout. The only valid values for the $treatment argument are pcTreatment1 (for a vertical layout) and pcTreatment2 (for a horizontal layout). Any other value will lead to nasty output in the customer's browser. If we were being more cautious, we'd validate the value of the $treatment argument and fail in some graceful way (such as by displaying nothing but writing an error message to a log file).

If you read through the function, you'll see that we first create a variable named $output. We start the function by putting the opening tag of the outermost element class (an article) in the $output variable. Most of the rest of the function consists of a series of "if" statements that check the contents of the data object. If we don't get a value for a particular name within the data object, we just don't add that bit of HTML to the output string. Finally, we append the closing tag of the outermost element and echo the output to the browser, which results in the line that called the function being replaced by the HTML we built in that long string.

It's pretty simple, really. However, because the product control has a lot of possibilities—an image, multiple price values, shipping information, multiple descriptive elements, and so on—the listing can seem to be complex. Just remember that we're building a string that holds HTML by checking for the presence of each kind of data within our data object and appending more elements if we find that kind of data. Again, that's the basic algorithm for building a control.

Notice that we commented out the if statement that checks for the data that the button needs. What kind of product listing doesn't have a Buy button? (Actually, we can think of a few such use cases, but we won't go down that rabbit hole. That's complexity we don't need for this example.)

Listing 15-7 shows the PHP code that we use to create the HTML output of a product control.

Listing 15-7. The PHP Code Behind the Product Control

```php
<?php
  function productStack($obj, $treatment) {
```

```
// Start with our containing element and add a product control treatment if applicable
$output = '    <article class="productControlWrap '.$treatment.'">';
// If there's an image defined output the image tag
if($obj->img != NULL){
    $output .= '     <img src="'.$obj->img.'" alt="'.$obj->imgAlt.'" class="pcImage" />';
}
// If there's a title defined output it
if($obj->title != NULL){
    $output .= '     <h2 class="pcTitle">'.$obj->title.'</h2>';
}
// If there's a priceStack defined output it
if($obj->priceStack != NULL){
    $output .= '<div class="pcPriceStack">';
    for ($i=0; $i < sizeof($obj->{'priceStack'}); $i++) {
    // We create a series of price controls here. See chapter 14 for how price controls work.
      $output .= price(
            $obj->priceStack[$i]->{'label'},
            $obj->priceStack[$i]->{'currencySymbol'},
            $obj->priceStack[$i]->{'wholeNumber'},
            $obj->priceStack[$i]->{'remainder'},
            "return"
            );
    }
    $output .= '</div>';
}
// If there's a shipDate defined output it
if($obj->shipDate != NULL){
    // the shipDate function is an instance of our shipping control. See chapter 14.
    $output .= '     <div class="pcShippingStack">'. shipDate($obj->shipDate->shipLabel, $obj-
>shipDate->shipDate, "return") . '</div>';
}
// If there's descriptive text or bullets defined output the parent element
if($obj->descText != NULL || $obj->descBullets != NULL){
    $output .= '  <div class="pcDescWrap">';
}
// If there's descriptive text defined output it
if($obj->descText != NULL){
    $output .= '        <div class="pcDescText">';
    $output .=              $obj->descText;
    $output .= '        </div>';
}
// If descriptive bullets are defined, output them
if($obj->descBullets != NULL){
    $output .= '<ul class="pcDescBullets">';
      for ($i=0; $i < sizeof($obj->{'descBullets'}); $i++) {
        $output .= ' <li class="pcDescLI">'.$obj->descBullets[$i]->{'bulletText'}.'</li>';
      }
    $output .= '</ul>';
}
// Closing tag for the .pcDescWrap
if($obj->descText != NULL || $obj->descBullets != NULL){
```

```php
        $output .= '   </div>';
    }
    // If there's a button defined output it
    //if($obj->button != NULL){
    // We're using the button control here. See Chapter 13 for more about button controls.
    $output .= button(
                $obj->button->{'text'},
                $obj->button->{'href'},
                NULL,
                NULL,
                $obj->button->{'type'},
                NULL,
                NULL,
                NULL,
                NULL,
                "return"
                );
    //}
    $output .= '   </article>';

    echo $output;
    }
?>
```

Summary

This chapter covered another essential control for an e-commerce site. An e-commerce site has to have product listings and some way to buy those products. The product control meets both of those business goals.

We showed several key techniques in this chapter:

- using controls within controls;

- using a data object to provide values for a control;

- attaching CSS to the control's output HTML through class names;

- implementing the essential algorithm that makes a control work.

Since that algorithm is the core of how our controls work, we want to remind you of it one more time here at the close of the chapter. The essence of making a control work is building an HTML string that contains both the elements and the data needed on your web page. That string then replaces the function you put in your web page when a visitor views that page in a web browser. While it's not what Michael calls rocket surgery (one of his favorite phrases), it is a remarkably powerful way to create web pages.

CHAPTER 16

■ ■ ■

Table Control

As a front-end developer, Michael has a love-hate relationship with tables. On the one hand, tables offer a near-perfect way to display tabular data. On the other, some developers abuse tables as a layout mechanism for almost anything. Michael has frequently seen a developer (often a back-end or middleware developer pressed into doing front-end work) use nested tables just to move content a few pixels. To someone who knows what it should be, seeing that kind of thing is hugely frustrating. We're sure many readers feel the same way.

We assume that you've heard the "Tables are evil for layout" spiel before. To add fuel to that fire, we have responsive design. In addition to all the other reasons not to use tables for layout (including slower performance, an increase in HTML elements to render, and hard-to-read code), there's the added problem that tables don't respond to responsive design. Tables are fixed internally; they won't allow reordering of TD elements (as with CSS). For example, if a table with two columns (left for navigation, right for content) is used for basic page layout, the page can't easily be rearranged. The navigation can't be moved to the top or the right without creating a new page from the server (and creating a huge hit on performance).

So what about tables and performance? Having touched on a couple of performance-related points in the previous two paragraphs, let's plunge into the issue in a bit more depth. The big problem with tables in terms of client-side (i.e., browser) performance is that they often force one or more redraw operations as the browser renders them. Even if you have followed the guidelines about loading your styles at the top of the page and your scripts at the bottom and even if your tables have fairly regular content, they often trigger redraw events. Those redraw events greatly slow rendering (and consequently page-load time), because the rendering engine has to start at the top of the table each time. On the server side, if you use a different page for each layout (e.g., vertical vs. horizontal), some poor visitor turning a phone 90 degrees can cause a whole new page load. In addition to driving the visitor nuts, you've just added a whole set of HTTP requests and increased bandwidth usage, all because someone wanted to see a wider display of your information. Finally, developer performance improves if you create a control that accepts a data stream and produces a table. Hand-coding even a small table takes time, at least when compared with passing data from the database to a function and being done.

Because of the performance issues (especially developer performance in this case) and all those other concerns, we reiterate the advice of many others: don't use tables for layout. But what about the proper use of tables—for tabular data—in mobile? The problem in that context is limited horizontal space; most tables would require scrolling to the right—a web no-no, unless you're on a Windows phone. Since we're following the mobile-first paradigm, we design all our pages to look as good as they can on mobile phones. Consequently, we're going to share a technique Michael came up with to get around this problem: nested lists styled with CSS to present a table. Does that sound familiar? It's how we built our navigation in Chapter 7, though here we use different styles, of course.

Throughout this chapter, we're going to show how we built a sample table control. You can find that control on our sample site: `http://clikz.us/BookExamples/tableControl.php`

Before starting to describe how the control works, we thought we'd show you what it looks like in its two states: wide and narrow. (Again, we call each state a treatment, as with all variations of all our controls.) We'll also show a highlighted cell within the table.

Figure 16-1 shows the wide treatment of our table control. While this looks like a standard table, it's really a `div` element with a bunch of lists (`ul` elements and their `li` children) inside. It behaves and looks like a standard table. Inside the control, we show a way to convert the table to standard table elements. We provide the ability to use table elements because Internet Explorer prior to IE8 doesn't support our nested-list method of showing tabular data. We use browser detection to show the right content for IE6 and IE7.

	The Head	Top of the Stack	Don't Forget Me	Austin blog	The Best for Last
Irony mumblecore	Letterpress authentic	Salvia hella raw	Austin blog bicycle	Chambray 8-bit post-ironic	Master cleanse hoodie
Cosby sweater cred	Chambray 8-bit post-ironic	Letterpress authentic	Austin blog bicycle	Irony mumblecore	Master cleanse hoodie
Chambray 8-bit post-ironic	Letterpress authentic	Austin blog bicycle	Synth jean shorts	Cosby sweater cred	Cosby sweater cred
Salvia hella raw	Cosby sweater cred	Master cleanse hoodie	Irony mumblecore	Austin blog bicycle	Letterpress authentic
Master cleanse hoodie	Chambray 8-bit post-ironic	Irony mumblecore	Austin blog bicycle	Letterpress authentic	Salvia hella raw
Austin blog bicycle	Letterpress authentic	Salvia hella raw	Cosby sweater cred	Irony mumblecore	Chambray 8-bit post-ironic

Figure 16-1. The wide layout of our sample table

Figure 16-2 shows our hover functionality. When a visitor's mouse hovers over a cell, the entire row highlights, and the cell over which the mouse is hovering gets further highlighting (it gets darker). In highlighting both the row and the cell, details related to the choice the visitor is considering are also highlighted. As we show later in the chapter, all of this highlighting is controlled through CSS.

	The Head	Top of the Stack	Don't Forget Me	Austin blog	The Best for Last
Irony mumblecore	Letterpress authentic	Salvia hella raw	Austin blog bicycle	Chambray 8-bit post-ironic	Master cleanse hoodie
Cosby sweater cred	Chambray 8-bit post-ironic	Letterpress authentic	Austin blog bicycle	Irony mumblecore	Master cleanse hoodie
Chambray 8-bit post-ironic	Letterpress authentic	Austin blog bicycle	Synth jean shorts	Cosby sweater cred	Cosby sweater cred
Salvia hella raw	Cosby sweater cred	Master cleanse hoodie	Irony mumblecore	Austin blog bicycle	Letterpress authentic
Master cleanse hoodie	Chambray 8-bit post-ironic	Irony mumblecore	Austin blog bicycle	Letterpress authentic	Salvia hella raw
Austin blog bicycle	Letterpress authentic	Salvia hella raw	Cosby sweater cred	Irony mumblecore	Chambray 8-bit post-ironic

Figure 16-2. The wide layout with a highlighted (dark) cell

Figure 16-3 shows the narrow (and consequently much taller) treatment of our table control. Such a treatment might be useful for visitors viewing the table on a phone or other device with a limited display. The narrow view could also be useful for situations where a page designer wants to put tabular information one side of a page and other information on the other side of the page. For example, a music site might have a list of songs and the artists who perform them accompanied by a description of what the songs all have in common.

■ **Note**　As we've mentioned before, with the rapid proliferation of devices, we can't plan on just phones and desktop browsers. For all we know, someone may see our table control on a refrigerator door or the inside of a cabinet door or in places we haven't even imagined. Consequently, we think (and name our controls and treatments) in terms of layout characteristics (narrow vs. wide) rather than target devices (desktop vs. phone).

Irony mumblecore

The Head: Letterpress authentic

Top of the Stack: Salvia hella raw

Don't Forget Me: Austin blog bicycle

Austin blog: Chambray 8-bit post-ironic

The Best for Last: Master cleanse hoodie

Cosby sweater cred

The Head: Chambray 8-bit post-ironic

Top of the Stack: Letterpress authentic

Don't Forget Me: Austin blog bicycle

Austin blog: Irony mumblecore

The Best for Last: Master cleanse hoodie

Chambray 8-bit post-ironic

The Head: Letterpress authentic

Top of the Stack: Austin blog bicycle

Don't Forget Me: Synth jean shorts

Austin blog: Cosby sweater cred

The Best for Last: Cosby sweater cred

Salvia hella raw

The Head: Cosby sweater cred

Top of the Stack: Master cleanse hoodie

Don't Forget Me: Irony mumblecore

Austin blog: Austin blog bicycle

The Best for Last: Letterpress authentic

Master cleanse hoodie

The Head: Chambray 8-bit post-ironic

Top of the Stack: Irony mumblecore

Don't Forget Me: Austin blog bicycle

Austin blog: Letterpress authentic

The Best for Last: Salvia hella raw

Austin blog bicycle

The Head: Letterpress authentic

Top of the Stack: Salvia hella raw

Don't Forget Me: Cosby sweater cred

Austin blog: Irony mumblecore

The Best for Last: Chambray 8-bit post-ironic

Figure 16-3. The narrow treatment of our table control

The narrow treatment uses exactly the same HTML as the wide treatment, with the exception of changing a class name to reflect the intended treatment. We've just used CSS to pivot the table for devices with narrow displays. Speaking of HTML, let's look at the HTML behind our example.

The HTML

The HTML for our sample table is generated by the table control. As already mentioned, it consists of a `div` element whose contents are a set of unordered lists (one list per row in the wide layout, one per block in the narrow layout).

As you read the HTML, notice the class names on the `div` element. They indicate both that this `div` contains the content for a table and which treatment to use (`tableTreatment1` is the wide treatment, `tableTreatment2` is the narrow treatment). Similarly, the style names within the `ul` elements indicate whether a row is a header row or a body row. Also, the style names within the `li` elements indicate that the element is a cell and whether any given cell is the first cell. Within the `li` elements, the `data-colhead` attribute (a custom attribute) identifies the column to which a cell belongs. We use the value of the data-colhead attribute to provide header information in the narrow treatment, which enables the pivoting of the table.

■ **Note**   Listing 16-1 would be very long if all the data used on our sample site were included. Making a decent sample requires a fair bit of data, but that makes for a lot of repetition within the listing. As a result, we include just the list that defines the header row and the list that defines the first row of content. The first list defines the header row. The second list defines the first of the body rows. Since the body rows are identical in structure, varying only in content, you can see how they work by examining just one of them. To see the whole listing and to see the table in action, go to `http://clikz.us/BookExamples/tableControl.php`

Listing 16-1 shows the HTML behind the sample shown earlier in the chapter.

Listing 16-1. The HTML for our sample table

```
<div class="table tableTreatment1">
  <ul class="tr tableHead">
    <li class="td " data-colhead=""></li>
    <li class="td " data-colhead="The Head">
      The Head
    </li>
    <li class="td " data-colhead="Top of the Stack">
      Top of the Stack
    </li>
    <li class="td " data-colhead="Don't Forget Me">
      Don't Forget Me
    </li>
    <li class="td " data-colhead="Austin blog">
      Austin blog
    </li>
    <li class="td " data-colhead="The Best for Last">
      The Best for Last
    </li>
```

```
    </ul>
    <ul class="tr tableBody">
      <li class="td first" data-colhead="">
        Irony mumblecore
      </li>
      <li class="td " data-colhead="The Head">
        Letterpress authentic
      </li>
      <li class="td " data-colhead="Top of the Stack">
        Salvia hella raw
      </li>
      <li class="td " data-colhead="Don't Forget Me">
        Austin blog bicycle
      </li>
      <li class="td " data-colhead="Austin blog">
        Chambray 8-bit post-ironic
      </li>
      <li class="td " data-colhead="The Best for Last">
        Master cleanse hoodie
      </li>
    </ul>
</div>
```

The Data Object

Now that you've seen the HTML behind our sample table, let's move on to the data that went into the HTML. The table control turns the data into HTML similar to the HTML we saw in Listing 16-1. The table control expects an array of arrays, with the first of the inner arrays holding the data for the header row (notice the empty string as its first value) and the remaining inner arrays holding the data for the body rows. Of course, in a more realistic scenario, you'd get this data from a database through a function or object that queries the database and builds the list for you. Since our sample site isn't using a database (the focus is solely on the front end for this book), we use static data.

Listing 16-2 shows the data behind our sample table.

Listing 16-2. The data that goes into our sample table

```php
<?php
  $tableObj = '[
    ["","The Head","Top of the Stack","Don\'t Forget Me","Austin blog", "The Best for Last"],
    ["Irony mumblecore","Letterpress authentic","Salvia hella raw","Austin blog
bicycle","Chambray 8-bit post-ironic","Master cleanse hoodie"],
    ["Cosby sweater cred","Chambray 8-bit post-ironic","Letterpress authentic","Austin blog
bicycle","Irony mumblecore","Master cleanse hoodie"],
    ["Chambray 8-bit post-ironic","Letterpress authentic","Austin blog bicycle","Synth jean
shorts","Cosby sweater cred","Cosby sweater cred"],
    ["Salvia hella raw","Cosby sweater cred","Master cleanse hoodie","Irony mumblecore","Austin
blog bicycle","Letterpress authentic"],
    ["Master cleanse hoodie","Chambray 8-bit post-ironic","Irony mumblecore","Austin blog
bicycle","Letterpress authentic","Salvia hella raw"],
```

```
    ["Austin blog bicycle","Letterpress authentic","Salvia hella raw","Cosby sweater
cred","Irony mumblecore","Chambray 8-bit post-ironic"]
  ]';
?>
```

The Table Control

As already mentioned, we're using PHP for our sample site. However, any language that supports web development would work just as well. In our own work, we've used Java and C# and other languages over the years.

At the top of the control, we check the value of the legacyBrowser argument and set the elements that we write either to div, ul, and li (for most browsers) or to table, tr, and td (for versions of Internet Explorer prior to IE8).

Most of the rest of the control consists of a pair of nested for loops that go through the data and write the proper elements and their attributes and content. The final bit of the control echoes the HTML to the browser.

Listing 16-3 shows the PHP that constitutes the table control.

Listing 16-3. The PHP Code That Defines the Table Control

```php
<?php
function tableControl($model, $treatment, $legacyBrowser) {
  // We use ternary operator to set whether our
  // table will use conventional table tags
  // or our divs, uls, and lis since the CSS
  // for the nontraditional elements aren't supported
  // in IE7. We can use browser detection to turn
  // on traditional table elements for those browsers
  // that can't support this new method.
  $tableElement = ($legacyBrowser == TRUE ? "table" : "div");
  $trElement = ($legacyBrowser == TRUE ? "tr" : "ul");
  $tdElement = ($legacyBrowser == TRUE ? "td" : "li");

  $output = '<' . $tableElement . ' class="table ' . $treatment . '">';
  for ($i = 0; $i < sizeof($model); $i++) {
    if ($i == 0) {
      $rowClass = "tableHead";
    } else {
      $rowClass = "tableBody";
    }
    $output .= '<' . $trElement . ' class="tr ' . $rowClass . '">';
    for ($j = 0; $j < sizeof($model[$i]); $j++) {
      // Add a class of 'first' if it's the first column but not the header row.
      $first = (($j == 0 && $i > 0) ? "first" : "");
      // We're iterating through the 'td's here but also adding in the column head text as a
      // data attribute in case we
      // want it later. You can put a conditional around this and turn it on only if you require
      // it to save bytes.
      $output .= '<' . $tdElement . ' class="td ' . $first . '" data-colhead="' . $model[0][$j] .
'">' . $model[$i][$j] . '</' . $tdElement . '>';
```

```
    }
    $output .= '</' . $trElement . '>';
  }
  $output .= '</' . $tableElement . '>';
  echo $output;
}
?>
```

The actual control is pretty simple. The real work gets done by the styles. Let's look at them.

The Styles

We do all of the layout work in the CSS styles. As mentioned before, doing so provides a number of benefits. For one thing, using CSS as much as possible boosts performance for the visitor, because rendering CSS is native to the browser (rather than interpreting a script, which is much slower).

Second, we might be able to make much greater use of the cache. If a visitor has already viewed a page with a table that uses our table stylesheet, the styles are in the cache, saving a lot of bytes from going down the pipe (boosting page-load time for visitors and decreasing bandwidth costs for our fictional company). Consequently, we want to do as much work as possible through CSS. That's why the CSS styles are the largest part of our table control. We lose the benefit of caching isif the styles are assembled on the fly (as from a system that dynamically builds each page), so it pays to think about how to build our files (both HTML and CSS) such that we get the most benefit from the cache.

▓ **Note** On our sample site, the CSS styles are in a single file. We break them up into several listings so that we can explain a bit about each part.

Styles for All Treatments

Listings 16-4 through 16-6 show the rules that apply to all the treatments of the table control. If we added a third treatment, these rules would apply to that third treatment as well as to the two treatments thus far created.

Listing 16-4 sets the padding and margin for our list elements to 0 (zero) and sets the `list-style` attribute to none (to avoid getting any unfortunate bullets in our table).

Listing 16-4. The CSS That Controls the Appearance of the Table Control

```
.table ul, .table li {
  padding: 0;
  margin: 0;
  list-style: none;
}
```

Listing 16-5 shows how we set the display mode for the various elements that compose a table, so that we get a table, rows, and cells.

Listing 16-5. Setting the Display Mode for the Classes That Define Our Tables

```
/*
 * This is how we achieve our tablelike structure with these elements.
 * Basically we're just assigning the same attributes that the corresponding
 * table elements have in the 'display' property.
 */
.table {
  display: table;
}
.tr {
  display: table-row;
}
.td {
  display: table-cell;
}
```

Listing 16-6 shows how we set the borders for the tables generated by our table control.

Listing 16-6. Controlling Borders for Our Tables

```
.table, .tr, .td {
  border: 1px solid #CCC;
  border-collapse: collapse;
}
```

Styles for the Wide Treatment

Listings 16-7 through 16-24 contain the rules that define the appearance of the wide treatment for our table control.

Listing 16-7 shows how we set the width of the table and the shadow around the outside of the table. In this case, we're setting these values for the wide treatment of the table (named `tableTreatment1`).

Listing 16-7. Setting the Width and Shadow of the Table for the Wide Treatment

```
/*
 * Table Treatment 1
 */
.tableTreatment1 {
  width: 800px;
  -webkit-box-shadow: 2px 2px 2px #999999;
  -moz-box-shadow: 2px 2px 2px #999999;
  box-shadow: 2px 2px 2px #999999;
}
```

Listing 16-8 sets the appearance of the leftmost cells for the wide treatment. In particular, it sets the background to light blue and the font weight to bold.

Listing 16-8. Styling the Content of the Leftmost Cells for the Wide Treatment

```
.tableTreatment1 .first {
  background: #c8dfff;
```

```
    font-weight: bold;
}
```

Listing 16-9 shows how we style the body cells. To do so, we use one of the more rarely used CSS selectors (the nth-child selector). Doing so lets us style every other row differently and thus make the table more attractive and easier to read. We've put additional explanation in the comments.

Listing 16-9. Styling the Body Cells

```
/*
 * By using the nth-child selector (which works in all
 * modern browsers), we can give our table a striped look.
 * Normally, you'd do this on the server side or with
 * JavaScript. Alternating the colors of the rows improves
 * readability and is (we think) more attractive.
 */
```

Listing 16-10 shows how we set the color of a highlighted cell.

Listing 16-10. Changing the Color of a Highlighted Cell

```
.tableTreatment1 .tableBody.tr:nth-child(odd) {
  background: #eef3fe;
}
```

Listing 16-11 shows how we set the color of a row that the visitor's mouse hovers over. Again, we've used the nth-child selector to determine which row to highlight. Notice that we style the odd rows but never the even rows. That's because another rule (in Listing 16-14) sets the hover state for all rows. Then this rule overrides that rule (because this one is more specific) to set the hover state for the odd rows. We'll see this arrangement repeatedly throughout this set of rules, and we'll discuss a common pitfall with this kind of technique (and how to avoid it) at the end of this section.

Listing 16-11. Setting the Hover State for a Row

```
.tableTreatment1 .tableBody.tr:nth-child(odd):hover {
  /*
   * We add a hover state to the odd .tr's that are also of
   * class .tableBody. This effect highlights the row the
   * visitor is hovering over with a slightly different
   * background color. However, since we want to maintain
   * the alternating row effect, this effect will be slightly
   * different from that on the even rows.
   */
  background: #cad0f8;
}
```

Listing 16-12 shows how we make a cell in the third column become a darker green when highlighted. Notice that we use the nth-child selector to specify both odd rows and a particular column (the third).

Listing 16-12. Setting the Hover Color for the Third Column

```
.tableTreatment1 .tableBody.tr:nth-child(odd):hover .td:nth-child(3) {
  /*
   * We also use the nth-child selector to target columns.
```

```
 * In this case, we target the third column of each odd row.
 * This rule complements the next rule, which makes the
 * entire 3rd column a green color but makes the alternating
 * rows a slightly darker green color to maintain readability.
 */
background: #54d543;
}
```

Listing 16-13 shows how we make the odd rows of the third column a slightly darker green than the even rows of the third column. We again use the nth-child selector to specify both odd rows and a particular column (the third).

Listing 16-13. *Making the Odd Rows of Third Column a Slightly Darker Green*

```
.tableTreatment1 .tableBody.tr:nth-child(odd) .td:nth-child(3) {
  /*
   * To maintain the integrity of our different-color column,
   * we make the highlighted cell go to a stronger green color
   * when the visitor hovers on that row. This rule selects only
   * the odd rows in the green column.
   */
  background: #8ce981;
}
```

Listing 16-14 sets the base hover highlight effect for the body rows. Again, it's really setting the highlight effect for rows that are not otherwise specified, but the effect is to define the hover effect for even rows.

Listing 16-14. *Setting the Base Hover Highlight for Body Rows*

```
.tableTreatment1 .tableBody.tr:hover {
  background: #eeeff0;
  color: #1d80fd;
}
```

Listing 16-15 sets the hover color for cells in the third column so that the background color of a highlighted cell in that column is dark green.

Listing 16-15. *Setting the Hover Color for Cells in the Third Column*

```
.tableTreatment1 .tableBody.tr:hover .td:nth-child(3) {
  background: #76f564;
}
```

Listing 16-16 makes the third column green. Because the rules to set the odd rows of the third column to a darker green have greater specificity, this rule has the effect of setting the even rows to the lighter shade of green that we're using as the base color of the third column.

Listing 16-16. *Making the Third Column Green*

```
.tableTreatment1 .tableBody.tr .td:nth-child(3) {
  /*
   * Now we make the entire third column a slightly green
```

```
 * background color. Because the previous nth-child
 * selector has greater specificity, it will override this
 * rule in odd rows.
 */
  background: #b2ebac;
}
```

Listing 16-17 shows how we set the appearance (not including the background color) of the cells, including both header cells and body cells.

Listing 16-17. Styling the Cells (Not Including Background Color)

```
.tableTreatment1 .td {
  padding: 4px;
  font-size: 12px;
  vertical-align: middle;
}
```

Listing 16-18 shows how we set the foreground and background color of a highlighted cell. The foreground color becomes white and the background color becomes a strong shade of blue. Because the hover rule for the third column (the next rule, in Listing 16-19) has greater specificity, this rule does not apply to the third column.

Listing 16-18. Setting the Hover State for All but the Third Column

```
.tableTreatment1 .tableBody .td:hover {
  color: white;
  background: #1d80fd;
}
```

Listing 16-19 shows how we set the foreground and background color of a cell in the third column when the visitor's mouse hovers over that cell. The !important directive ensures that the cells in the third column always turn dark green when a visitor's mouse hovers over them.

Listing 16-19. The Hover Rule for the Cells in the Third Column

```
.tableTreatment1 .tableBody:hover .td:nth-child(3):hover {
  color: white;
  background: #12ba00 !important;
}
```

Listing 16-20 controls the appearance in the header row. It sets the text to white and bold, sets a dark gray text shadow, and sets a lighter gray background color. Also, for most browsers, it uses an SVG image to set the background image for the header. Finally, it sets a gradient effect for most browsers. The net effect is white text on a dark gradient background.

Listing 16-20. Styling the Table Header for the Wide Treatment

```
.tableTreatment1 .tableHead {
  color: white;
  font-weight: bold;
  text-shadow: 0 0 3px #333;
  background: #aebcbf;
  background: url(data:image/svg+xml;base64,PD94bWwgdmVyc2lvbj0iMS4wIiA/Pgo8c3ZnIHhtbG5zPSJodHRw
```

Oi8vd3d3LnczLm9yZy8yMDAwL3N2ZyIgd2lkdGg9IjEwMCUiIGhlaWdodD0iMTAwJSIgdmlld0JveD0iMCAwIDEgMSIgcHJl
c2VydmVBc3BlY3RSYXRpb2oibm9uZSI+CiAgPGxpbmVhckdyYWRpZW50IGlkPSJncmFkLXVjZ2ctZ2VuZXJhdGVkIiBncmFk
aWVudFVuaXRzPSJ1c2VyU3BhY2VPblVzZSIgeDE9IjAlIiB5MToiMCUiIHgyPSIwJSIgeTI9IjEwMCUiPgogICAgPHNob3Ag
b2Zmc2VOPSIwJSIgc3RvcC1jb2xvcjoiI2FlYmNiZiIgc3RvcC1vcGFjaXR5PSIxIi8+CiAgICA8c3RvcCBvZmZzZXQ9IjUw
JSIgc3RvcC1jb2xvcjoiIzZlNzc3NCIgc3RvcC1vcGFjaXR5PSIxIi8+CiAgICA8c3RvcCBvZmZzZXQ9IjUxJSIgc3RvcC1j
b2xvcjoiIzBhMGUwYSIgc3RvcC1vcGFjaXR5PSIxIi8+CiAgICA8c3RvcCBvZmZzZXQ9IjEwMCUiIHNOb3AtY29sb3I9IiMw
YTA4MDkiIHNOb3Atb3BhY2l0eToiMSIvPgogIDwvbGluZWFyR3JhZGllbnQ+CiAgPHJlY3QgeDOiMCIgeTOiMCIgd2lkdGg9
IjEiIGhlaWdodD0iMSIgZmlsbDOidXJsKCNncmFkLXVjZ2ctZ2VuZXJhdGVkKSIgLz4KPC9zdmc+);
```
  background: -moz-linear-gradient(top, #aebcbf 0%, #6e7774 50%, #0a0e0a 51%, #0a0809 100%);
  background: -webkit-gradient(linear, left top, left bottom, color-stop(0%, #aebcbf),
color-stop(50%, #6e7774), color-stop(51%, #0a0e0a), color-stop(100%, #0a0809));
  background: -webkit-linear-gradient(top, #aebcbf 0%, #6e7774 50%, #0a0e0a 51%, #0a0809 100%);
  background: -o-linear-gradient(top, #aebcbf 0%, #6e7774 50%, #0a0e0a 51%, #0a0809 100%);
  background: -ms-linear-gradient(top, #aebcbf 0%, #6e7774 50%, #0a0e0a 51%, #0a0809 100%);
  background: linear-gradient(to bottom, #aebcbf 0%, #6e7774 50%, #0a0e0a 51%, #0a0809 100%);
  filter: progid:dximagetransform.microsoft.gradient(startColorstr='#aebcbf',
endColorstr='#0a0809', GradientType=0);
}
```

Listing 16-21 just centers the content of each cell in the header row—simple but necessary to get attractively aligned content in the header.

Listing 16-21. *Centering the Cells in the Header Row*

```
.tableTreatment1 .tableHead .td {
  text-align: center;
}
```

Listing 16-22 shows where we turn off the filter we created in Listing 16-21 when the visitor uses IE9. IE9 doesn't need that filter, so we turn it off in this rule.

Listing 16-22. *Turning off the Filter in the Header for IE9*

```
.ie9 .tableTreatment1 .tableHead {
  filter: none;
}
```

Listing 16-23 shows how we turn off the filter and background we created in Listing 16-21 when the visitor uses IE8. Internet Explorer requires a background for each cell rather than for the whole row to be set, so we'll do that in Listing 16-24.

Listing 16-23. *Turning Off the Filter and Background for IE8*

```
.ie8 .tableTreatment1 .tableHead {
  filter: none;
  background: none;
}
```

Listing 16-24 shows how we set the background and filter for the header cells when the visitor uses IE8. IE8 won't use the background and filter definition for a row, so we have to set those values on the cells.

Listing 16-24. Setting the Background for Header Cells in IE8

```
.ie8 .tableTreatment1 .tableHead .td {
  background: #aebcbf;
  filter: progid:dximagetransform.microsoft.gradient(startColorstr='#aebcbf',
endColorstr='#0a0809', GradientType=0);
}
```

Styles for the Narrow Treatment

The narrow treatment gets styles that differ quite a bit from the styles that define the appearance of the wide treatment. For one thing, the narrow treatment creates a set of rows rather than a single row for each array in the control's data. Also, the second treatment has no highlighting for hover effects. Since touch screens (whether in phones or fridges) don't have a mouse pointer floating around, there's no point in setting hover effects. Consequently, the rules for the narrow treatment are quite a bit simpler. Listings 16-25 through 16-32 show the rules that define the narrow treatment of our table control.

Listing 16-25 shows how we set the width of the narrow table to 320 pixels.

Listing 16-25. Setting the Width of the Narrow Treatment

```
/*
 * Table Treatment 2
 */
.tableTreatment2 {
  width: 320px;
}
```

Listing 16-26 shows how we turn off borders for all the elements in the HTML when we use the narrow treatment.

Listing 16-26. Turning Off Borders for the Narrow Treatment

```
.tableTreatment2 .table, .tableTreatment2 .tr, .tableTreatment2 .td {
  border: none;
}
```

Listing 16-27 shows how we turn off the display of the header content, since we don't use header cells in the narrow treatment.

Listing 16-27. Turning Off the Header Cells for the Narrow Treatment

```
.tableTreatment2 .tableHead {
  display: none;
}
```

Listing 16-28 shows how we set the width of a row within the narrow treatment of our table control to 200 pixels.

Listing 16-28. Setting the Row Width to 200 Pixels

```
.tableTreatment2 .tr {
  width: 200px;
}
```

217

Listing 16-29 shows how we style the cells within the narrow treatment of the table control.

Listing 16-29. Styling the Cells Within the Narrow Treatment

```
.tableTreatment2 .td {
  display: block;
  float: none;
  padding: 5px;
}
```

Listing 16-30 shows how we style the first cell within each block of the narrow treatment of our table control. We use the same styling as the header row in the wide treatment. The first-child selector lets us specify just the first cell of each block within the narrow treatment.

Listing 16-30. Styling the First Cell Within Each Block for the Narrow Treatment

```
.tableTreatment2 .td:first-child {
  /*
   * By using the first-child selector, we can target
   * the first TD, which is a relevant pivot point for our data.
   */
  color: white;
  font-weight: bold;
  text-shadow: 0 0 3px #333;
  background: #aebcbf;
  background: url(data:image/svg+xml;base64,PD94bWwgdmVyc2lvbj0iMS4wIiA/Pgo8c3ZnIHhtbG5zPSJodHRw
Oi8vd3d3LnczLm9yZy8yMDAwL3N2ZyIgd2lkdGg9IjEwMCUiIGhlaWdodD0iMTAwJSIgdmlld0JveD0iMCAwIDEgMSIgcHJl
c2VydmVBc3BlY3RSYXRpbz0ibm9uZSI+CiAgPGxpbmVhckdyYWRpZW50IGlkPSJncmFkLXVjZ2ctZ2VuZXJhdGVkIiBncmFk
aWVudFVuaXRzPSJ1c2VyU3BhY2VPblVzZSIgeDE9IjAlIiB5MT0iMCUiIHgyPSIwJSIgeTI9IjEwMCUiPgogICAgPHN0b3Ag
b2Zmc2V0PSIwJSIgc3RvcC1jb2xvcj0iI2FlYmNiZiIgc3RvcC1vcGFjaXR5PSIxIi8+CiAgICA8c3RvcCBvZmZzZXQ9IjUw
JSIgc3RvcC1jb2xvcj0iIzZlNzc3NCIgc3RvcC1vcGFjaXR5PSIxIi8+CiAgICA8c3RvcCBvZmZzZXQ9IjUxJSIgc3RvcC1j
b2xvcj0iIzBhMGUwYSIgc3RvcC1vcGFjaXR5PSIxIi8+CiAgICA8c3RvcCBvZmZzZXQ9IjEwMCUiIHN0b3AtY29sb3I9IiMw
YTA4MDkiIHN0b3Atb3BhY2l0eT0iMSIvPgogIDwvbGluZWFyR3JhZGllbnQ+CiAgPHJlY3QgeD0iMCIgeT0iMCIgd2lkdGg9
IjEiIGhlaWdodD0iMSIgZmlsbD0idXJsKCNncmFkLXVjZ2ctZ2VuZXJhdGVkKSIgLz4KPC9zdmc+);
  background: -moz-linear-gradient(top, #aebcbf 0%, #6e7774 50%, #0a0e0a 51%, #0a0809 100%);
  background: -webkit-gradient(linear, left top, left bottom, color-stop(0%, #aebcbf),
color-stop(50%, #6e7774), color-stop(51%, #0a0e0a), color-stop(100%, #0a0809));
  background: -webkit-linear-gradient(top, #aebcbf 0%, #6e7774 50%, #0a0e0a 51%, #0a0809 100%);
  background: -o-linear-gradient(top, #aebcbf 0%, #6e7774 50%, #0a0e0a 51%, #0a0809 100%);
  background: -ms-linear-gradient(top, #aebcbf 0%, #6e7774 50%, #0a0e0a 51%, #0a0809 100%);
  background: linear-gradient(to bottom, #aebcbf 0%, #6e7774 50%, #0a0e0a 51%, #0a0809 100%);
  filter: progid:dximagetransform.microsoft.gradient(startColorstr='#aebcbf', endColorstr='#0a080
9', GradientType=0);
}
```

Listing 16-31 shows how we insert the value of the data-colhead attribute, a colon, and a space before the usual contents of the cell. We also set all the inserted content to have a bold font weight and a medium-dark gray color. This technique provides the equivalent of a header for each cell.

Listing 16-31. Inserting the Equivalent of a Header for Cells in the Narrow Treatment

```
.tableTreatment2 .td:before {
  /*
   * We're able to leverage the content: attr() again as we did
   * in our link control. Since our control has stored the
   * value of the column in the 'td' we can just get it from there.
   */
  content: attr(data colhead) ": ";
  font-weight: bold;
  color: #777;
}
```

Listing 16-32 shows how we override the insertion of text for the first row in each block. Since we don't want to end up with a colon and a space before a heading, we need to set the first one to the empty string ("").

Listing 16-32. Ensuring There Are No Nonsense Characters in the First Row

```
.tableTreatment2 .td:first-child:before {
  /*
   * Since we don't need the header data for the
   * first TD, we override it so we don't get the ': '.
   */
  content: "";
}
```

Adding Media Queries

We think this control goes well with media queries. It's natural to think of changing the layout from wide to narrow for visitors with narrow devices. If you want to add media queries to your table controls, the rules in Listing 16-33 show how to do so. We don't describe them individually because they are all very similar to rules we've already described. When you use this set of rules, you can add them anywhere within your CSS file that supports your table control.

```
/* Mobile Layout */
@media only screen and (max-width: 767px) {
  .tableTreatment1 {
    width: 320px;
  }
  .tableTreatment1 .table, .tableTreatment1 .tr, .tableTreatment1 .td {
    border: none;
  }
  .tableTreatment1 .tableHead {
    display: none;
  }
  .tableTreatment1 .tr {
    width: 200px;
  }
  .tableTreatment1 .td {
    display: block;
    float: none;
```

219

```css
    padding: 5px;
}
.tableTreatment1 .td:first-child {
    color: white;
    font-weight: bold;
    text-shadow: 0 0 3px #333;
    background: #aebcbf;
    background: url(data:image/svg+xml;base64,PD94bWwgdmVyc2lvbj0iMS4wIiA/Pgo8c3ZnIHhtbG5zPSJodH
RwOi8vd3d3LnczLm9yZy8yMDAwL3N2ZyIgd2lkdGg9IjEwMCUiIGhlaWdodD0iMTAwJSIgdmlld0JveD0iMCAwIDEgMSIgcH
Jlc2VydmVBc3BlY3RSYXRpbz0ibm9uZSI+CiAgPGxpbmVhckdyYWRpZW50IGlkPSJncmFkLXVjZ2ctZ2VuZXJhdGVkIiBncm
FkaWVudFVuaXRzPSJ1c2VyU3BhY2VPblVzZSIgeDE9IjAlIiB5MT0iMCUiIHgyPSIwJSIgeTI9IjEwMCUiPgogICAgPHNob3
Agb2Zmc2V0PSIwJSIgc3RvcC1jb2xvcj0iI2FlYmNiZiIgc3RvcC1vcGFjaXR5PSIxIi8+CiAgICA8c3RvcCBvZmZzZXQ9Ij
UwJSIgc3RvcC1jb2xvcj0iIzZlNzc3NCIgc3RvcC1vcGFjaXR5PSIxIi8+CiAgICA8c3RvcCBvZmZzZXQ9IjUxJSIgc3RvcC
1jb2xvcj0iIzBhMGUwYSIgc3RvcC1vcGFjaXR5PSIxIi8+CiAgICA8c3RvcCBvZmZzZXQ9IjEwMCUiIHNob3AtY29sb3I9Ii
MwYTA4MDkiIHNob3Atb3BhY2l0eT0iMSIvPgogIDwvbGluZWFyR3JhZGllbnQ+CiAgPHJlY3QgeD0iMCIgeT0iMCIgd2lkdG
g9IjEiIGhlaWdodD0iMSIgZmlsbD0idXJsKCNncmFkLXVjZ2ctZ2VuZXJhdGVkKSIgLz4KPC9zdmc+);
    background: -moz-linear-gradient(top, #aebcbf 0%, #6e7774 50%, #0a0e0a 51%, #0a0809 100%);
    background: -webkit-gradient(linear, left top, left bottom, color-stop(0%, #aebcbf),
color-stop(50%, #6e7774), color-stop(51%, #0a0e0a), color-stop(100%, #0a0809));
    background: -webkit-linear-gradient(top, #aebcbf 0%, #6e7774 50%, #0a0e0a 51%, #0a0809 100%)
;
    background: -o-linear-gradient(top, #aebcbf 0%, #6e7774 50%, #0a0e0a 51%, #0a0809 100%);
    background: -ms-linear-gradient(top, #aebcbf 0%, #6e7774 50%, #0a0e0a 51%, #0a0809 100%);
    background: linear-gradient(to bottom, #aebcbf 0%, #6e7774 50%, #0a0e0a 51%, #0a0809 100%);
    filter: progid:dximagetransform.microsoft.gradient(startColorstr='#aebcbf', endColorstr='#0a0
809', GradientType=0);
}
.tableTreatment1 .td:before {
    content: attr(data-colhead) ": ";
    font-weight: bold;
    color: #777;
}
.tableTreatment1 .td:first-child:before {
    content: "";
}
}
```

These rules produce a table similar to the narrow treatment. However, the rules within the media query actually modify the wide treatment (tableTreatment1). The result is a table that has the structure of the narrow treatment with the color scheme of the wide treatment. Figure 16-4 shows the result.

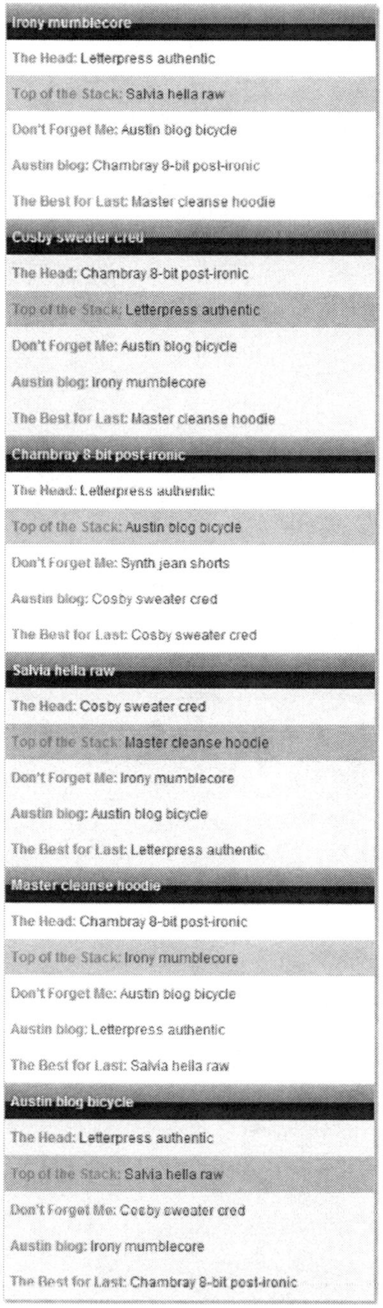

Irony mumblecore

The Head: Letterpress authentic

Top of the Stack: Salvia hella raw

Don't Forget Me: Austin blog bicycle

Austin blog: Chambray 8-bit post-ironic

The Best for Last: Master cleanse hoodie

Cosby sweater cred

The Head: Chambray 8-bit post-ironic

Top of the Stack: Letterpress authentic

Don't Forget Me: Austin blog bicycle

Austin blog: Irony mumblecore

The Best for Last: Master cleanse hoodie

Chambray 8-bit post-ironic

The Head: Letterpress authentic

Top of the Stack: Austin blog bicycle

Don't Forget Me: Synth jean shorts

Austin blog: Cosby sweater cred

The Best for Last: Cosby sweater cred

Salvia hella raw

The Head: Cosby sweater cred

Top of the Stack: Master cleanse hoodie

Don't Forget Me: Irony mumblecore

Austin blog: Austin blog bicycle

The Best for Last: Letterpress authentic

Master cleanse hoodie

The Head: Chambray 8-bit post-ironic

Top of the Stack: Irony mumblecore

Don't Forget Me: Austin blog bicycle

Austin blog: Letterpress authentic

The Best for Last: Salvia hella raw

Austin blog bicycle

The Head: Letterpress authentic

Top of the Stack: Salvia hella raw

Don't Forget Me: Cosby sweater cred

Austin blog: Irony mumblecore

The Best for Last: Chambray 8-bit post-ironic

Figure 16-4. The result of using media queries with the table control

For us, writing the CSS rules for the table control was fun. We don't often get to use those more unusual selectors, so it's nice to find a place to show how they work. Many tables probably don't need this level of complexity; making a column in the middle a different color is unusual, in our experience.

221

However, when you need to do it, it's handy to have selectors that let you specify a particular child and even a child within a child. As we said, it's fun—but then we're weird.

▪ **Caution: When Even Isn't Really Even.** We mentioned in passing that the even rows aren't specified as being even. Rather, we set a background for all the rows and then override that background for the odd rows. We could have used the even specifier to complement the odd specifier, but it would have added bytes we don't need to add. Also, it's best to avoid unneeded specifiers. In addition to saving bytes, you might encounter a situation where you use seemingly complementary specifiers and then find that some oddball case doesn't match either one of them. So it's better to set a base treatment and specify the exceptions. In this case, odd and even will do the trick. A problem arises when more than two cases exist, such as an additional value for the first item in a series as well as values for even and odd.

Summary

In this chapter, we've shown how to develop and use a table control. We demonstrated that, if you use responsive design, you can't use the usual table elements (table, tr, and td). Then we showed how to make a table without those elements by creating a set of lists within a div element. After that, we showed how to use code (PHP in this case, but it could be Java or C# or any web-capable language) to turn data into HTML that we can style such that it becomes a table. Finally, we described each of the styles that we use to turn those lists into rows and cells within our table.

Along the way, we demonstrated how to select individual rows and cells within the table. We used that effect for changing foreground and background colors. However, you could also use those selectors to create an iframe element that contains help content or more product details or whatever else you can imagine and then put the iframe element somewhere near the highlighted cell. We're certain that there are other uses for the selectors that let you specify a particular child (or set of children, in the case of the even and odd specifiers), but we'll leave them to your imagination.

CHAPTER 17

■ ■ ■

Tab Control

We've all seen lots of tabs on the web. Some of them are OK. Some stink. Naturally, we want to make a tab control that doesn't stink (and that's hopefully better than just OK), so that we can re-use it for all kinds of content while being sure it looks good and works well.

One way in which tabs on web sites often stink is that they don't track a visitor's location. Ever gone to a page, navigated to the third tab to find what you want, gone to another site, and then come back to the site with tabs, only to find that you're on the first tab again? We have, and we don't like it. Worse, some tab schemes jump back to the first tab if the visitor refreshes the page. That's annoying. On a related issue, we also want tabs to which we (and our visitors) can make links.

For a bit of flexibility in design, we want tabs that run along the top of the content (that is, horizontal tabs) and tabs that run down the left side of the content (that is, vertical tabs). In our opinion, some content just seems to make more sense with horizontal or vertical tabs. Also, we want our page designers (the folks who put all these controls together to make web pages) to have the option of horizontal or vertical tabs. As a result, we have two treatments (variations) within a control. Naturally, we want our tabs to look good. Tabs aren't the most attractive web design element ever made, but that doesn't mean they have to be square boxes with plain text in them. Consequently, we want tabs with rounded corners, a gradient background, and text that's centered both horizontally and vertically. The text has to remain properly centered when one or more tabs contain more than one line of text, too. To top it all off, we want the tabs to animate when they shrink and expand to fit their contents.

■ **Note** We can't show an animation effect in a book. To see the tabs change size in an animated way, play with the tab control on our sample site: `http://www.clikz.us/BookExamples/tabControl.php`

Last but not least, we want tabs that perform well. Unfortunately, many tab controls use tables. As we discussed in the previous chapter, tables suffer from a number of performance problems. Also, we're strict about using tables only for tabular content. However, tabs *are* tabular content. So how do we get tablelike functionality without using those poorly rendering table elements? Fortunately, CSS provides a way—through the `display` property. As you'll see in the section on the CSS listings later in the chapter, we use `display:table` to turn a list into a table and then use `display:table-cell` to turn list items into table cells. This technique provides better performance because the browser's rendering engine doesn't wait for a whole row (or worse, the whole table) to arrive before starting to render each cell. It's not a huge difference, unless you have lots of tables or, worse, tables within tables. However, these little things add up to poor performance, so we prevent all these minor performance issues whenever we can. As we've mentioned elsewhere, a much more significant performance boost accrues to the web developers. It's a lot easier to retrieve data from the database and pass it to a function (the control) than it is to make your own tabs every time you need them. Also, a control ensures consistency, which is an important issue on most web sites.

Now that we have a list of what we want our tabs to do (i.e., we have requirements for our control), we can move on to describing how we get all that to work. As we go through the chapter, we also explore some technical details that we had to implement to get everything to work right. For now, though, let's start by looking at the output. Figure 17-1 shows the horizontal treatment of our tab control.

This is a Tab	The Trigger for a Long Tab Two	Don't Forget Me	I Like Being a Tab

Skateboard banh mi direct trade fanny pack mixtape, pork belly art party. Dreamcatcher wes anderson raw denim kogi gastropub.

Thundercats ennui carles iphone, pour-over photo booth quinoa leggings stumptown PBR fanny pack cliche gluten-free.

Small batch tofu gluten-free, vinyl you probably haven't heard of them typewriter umami viral DIY four loko aesthetic.

Figure 17-1. Horizontal treatment of the tab control

For variety, the horizontal treatment uses a white background, while the vertical treatment uses a black background. You could easily use other colors. Figure 17-2 shows the tab control's vertical treatment.

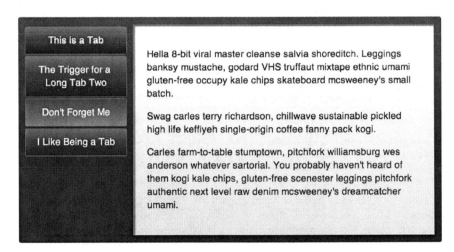

Figure 17-2. Vertical treatment of the tab control

The HTML

As usual, the control doesn't directly include HTML. Rather, a PHP function creates the HTML when the page loads. Still, it's helpful to see the HTML that the control creates to provide context for the scripting

(JavaScript) and style (CSS) information. The HTML does not change between the horizontal and vertical treatments; we control the differences in appearance entirely through CSS.

The HTML consists of a section element that has two ul children. The li children of the first list, whose class attribute includes tabTriggerLI, hold the tab labels. The li child of the first list whose class attribute includes activeTab holds the label of the currently open tab. The second ul element contains the content of the tabs (whether currently open or closed). The li elements whose class attribute includes tabContentLI contain the content for the tabs. The li element whose class attribute includes showTab holds the content of the currently open tab. Listing 17-1 shows the HTML for the tab control shown in Figures 17-1 and 17-2, opened to the first tab.

Listing 17-1. The HTML for a Tab

```
<section data-item="tab" class="tabWrap tabTreatment1" id="tabID">
  <ul class="tabTriggerUL">
    <li class="tabTriggerLI activeTab">
      <a href="#tab1" class="tabTriggerA">This is a Tab</a>
    </li>
    <li class="tabTriggerLI">
      <a href="#tab2" class="tabTriggerA">The Trigger for a
      <br>
      Long Tab Two</a>
    </li>
    <li class="tabTriggerLI">
      <a href="#tab3" class="tabTriggerA">Don't Forget Me</a>
    </li>
    <li class="tabTriggerLI">
      <a href="#tab4" class="tabTriggerA">I Like Being a Tab</a>
    </li>
  </ul>
  <ul class="tabContentUL" style="height: 215px; ">
    <li class="tabContentLI showTab" data-tabid="#tab1">
      <p>
        Skateboard banh mi direct trade fanny pack mixtape, pork belly art party. Dreamcatcher
wes anderson raw denim kogi gastropub.
      </p>
      <p>
        Thundercats ennui carles iphone, pour-over photo booth quinoa leggings stumptown PBR
fanny pack cliche gluten-free.
      </p>
      <p>
        Small batch tofu gluten-free, vinyl you probably haven't heard of them typewriter umami
viral DIY four loko aesthetic.
      </p>
    </li>
    <li class="tabContentLI" data-tabid="#tab2">
      <p>
        Carles viral yr, williamsburg letterpress ethnic gluten-free aesthetic american apparel
ennui chambray polaroid you probably haven't heard of them.
      </p>
      <p>
```

```
            Scenester hoodie tattooed food truck tofu, selvage blog sriracha polaroid hella keytar
    before they sold out +1.
        </p>
    </li>
    <li class="tabContentLI" data-tabid="#tab3">
        <p>
            Hella 8-bit viral master cleanse salvia shoreditch. Leggings banksy mustache, godard VHS
    truffaut mixtape ethnic umami gluten-free occupy kale chips skateboard mcsweeney's small batch.
        </p>
        <p>
            Swag carles terry richardson, chillwave sustainable pickled high life keffiyeh single-
    origin coffee fanny pack kogi.
        </p>
        <p>
            Carles farm-to-table stumptown, pitchfork williamsburg wes anderson whatever sartorial.
    You probably haven't heard of them kogi kale chips, gluten-free scenester leggings pitchfork
    authentic next level raw denim mcsweeney's dreamcatcher umami.
        </p>
    </li>
    <li class="tabContentLI" data-tabid="#tab4">
        <p>
            Swag carles terry richardson, chillwave sustainable pickled high life keffiyeh single-
    origin coffee fanny pack kogi.
        </p>
        <p>
            Carles farm-to-table stumptown, pitchfork williamsburg wes anderson whatever sartorial.
    You probably haven't heard of them kogi kale chips, gluten-free scenester leggings pitchfork
    authentic next level raw denim mcsweeney's dreamcatcher umami.
        </p>
    </li>
  </ul>
</section>
```

The Data

While describing the function at the heart of the control, we mentioned that the first parameter of the tabControl function is a model object. Since we're using PHP, it has to be a PHP object. In this case, it contains a JSON object. The JSON object contains a set of comma-separated values, one for each tab. Each of those values holds a comma-separated list, which contains the details of each tab. In other words, the data object consists of comma-separated lists within an outer comma-separated list.

■ **Tip** The tabcontent value contains HTML. You can use this mechanism to insert links or images or other HTML elements into a tab's content.

Listing 17-2 shows the data object that we used to create our sample tab controls.

Listing 17-2. The Data Object That Feeds Our Sample Tab Control

```php
<?php
$tabObj = '[
  {
    "triggertext" : "This is a Tab",
    "triggerid" : "#tab1",
    "tabcontent" : "<p>Skateboard banh mi direct trade fanny pack mixtape, pork belly art party.
Dreamcatcher wes anderson raw denim kogi gastropub. </p><p>Thundercats ennui carles iphone,
pour-over photo booth quinoa leggings stumptown PBR fanny pack cliche gluten-free. </p><p>Small
batch tofu gluten-free, vinyl you probably haven\'t heard of them typewriter umami viral DIY
four loko aesthetic.</p>"
  },
  {
    "triggertext" : "The Trigger for a <br>Long Tab Two",
    "triggerid" : "#tab2",
    "tabcontent" : "<p>Carles viral yr, williamsburg letterpress ethnic gluten-free aesthetic
american apparel ennui chambray polaroid you probably haven\'t heard of them. </p><p>Scenester
hoodie tattooed food truck tofu, selvage blog sriracha polaroid hella keytar before they sold
out +1. </p>"
  },
  {
    "triggertext" : "Don\'t Forget Me",
    "triggerid" : "#tab3",
    "tabcontent" : "<p>Hella 8-bit viral master cleanse salvia shoreditch. Leggings banksy
mustache, godard VHS truffaut mixtape ethnic umami gluten-free occupy kale chips skateboard
mcsweeney\'s small batch.</p><p>Swag carles terry richardson, chillwave sustainable pickled high
life keffiyeh single-origin coffee fanny pack kogi.</p><p>Carles farm-to-table stumptown,
pitchfork williamsburg wes anderson whatever sartorial. You probably haven\'t heard of them kogi
kale chips, gluten-free scenester leggings pitchfork authentic next level raw denim mcsweeney\'s
dreamcatcher umami. </p>"
  },
  {
    "triggertext" : "I Like Being a Tab",
    "triggerid" : "#tab4",
    "tabcontent" : "<p>Swag carles terry richardson, chillwave sustainable pickled high life
keffiyeh single-origin coffee fanny pack kogi.</p><p>Carles farm-to-table stumptown, pitchfork
williamsburg wes anderson whatever sartorial. You probably haven\'t heard of them kogi kale
chips, gluten-free scenester leggings pitchfork authentic next level raw denim mcsweeney\'s
dreamcatcher umami. </p>"
  }
]';
?>
```

The Control

As you're no doubt used to by now (unless you jumped to this chapter for some reason—if you did jump straight here, please read Chapter 10; it explains why we make controls), the actual control is a PHP function (called tabControl in this case). The function takes three arguments, as described in Table 17-1.

Table 17-1. *Arguments for the Tab Control*

Argument	Description
$model	The data that goes into the tab control. We call it a model because we're used to working with the MVC (Model-View-Controller) pattern.
$id	A unique identifier for this tab control. A page can have multiple tab controls. Having unique identifiers lets a script target an individual tab control.
$treatment	An indicator of whether to apply the horizontal treatment or the vertical treatment to this tab control.

The tabControl function creates an output variable into which it can write the HTML that the control generates. It then adds the opening tag of the section element with all of its attributes, including the identifier for this tab control, to the output variable. Next, the function writes the opening tag of the ul element that holds the tab control's labels to the output variable. Then a for loop writes the contents of the list (i.e., it writes the li elements that contain the labels) to the output variable. While writing the li elements, the control inserts the data, including the attributes and their values. Then the function closes the first list and starts the second list, which contains the content of the tabs. Another for loop writes the li elements (and their attributes) that contain the content of the tabs to the output variable. Then the function writes the closing tags for the second list and the section element to the output variable. Finally, the function echoes the content of the output variable (which now contains our HTML with all the data in the right places) to the browser. In the browser, our CSS and JavaScript can then interact with the HTML to produce the final tab control for our visitor to use.

■ **Note** The insertion of the id attribute enables linking to a particular tab and gets individual tabs to appear in the browser's history, so that a visitor can return to a particular tab (or the same tab if they refresh the page). Basically, the id makes browsers remember each tab as a separate location.

Listing 17-3 shows the tabControl function.

Listing 17-3. *The tabControl Function*

```php
<?php
function tabControl($model, $id, $treatment) {
  $output = '<section data-item="tab" class="tabWrap ' . $treatment . '" id="' . $id . '">';
  $output .= ' <ul class="tabTriggerUL">';
  for ($i = 0; $i < sizeof($model); $i++) {
    $output .= '   <li class="tabTriggerLI">';
    $output .= '      <a href="' . $model[$i] -> triggerid . '" class="tabTriggerA">' .
$model[$i] -> triggertext . '</a>';
    $output .= '   </li>';
  }
  $output .= ' </ul>';
  $output .= ' <ul class="tabContentUL">';
  for ($j = 0; $j < sizeof($model); $j++) {
    $output .= '   <li class="tabContentLI" data-tabid="' . $model[$j] -> triggerid . '">' .
$model[$j] -> tabcontent . '</li>';
  }
```

```
    $output .= '   </ul>';
    $output .= '</section>';

    echo $output;
}
?>
```

Creating a Tab Control

To create a tab control, you must call the tabControl function. As we described earlier, the PHP function that makes the tab control takes three arguments: the data, a unique identifier for each tab control, and the treatment (horizontal or vertical). The identifier, "tabTreatment1", indicates a horizontal tab control; "tabTreatment2" indicates a vertical tab control. A script then places the tabs in the page. Listing 17-4 shows how we created the tab controls we use as samples on our sample site and in this chapter.

Listing 17-4. Creating Our Sample Tab Controls

```
<?php tabControl(json_decode($tabObj), "tabID", "tabTreatment1"); ?>
<?php tabControl(json_decode($tabObj), "tabID2", "tabTreatment2"); ?>
<script>
$("#tabID").tab();
$("#tabID2").tab();
</script>
```

The JavaScript

Many of our controls don't use JavaScript. In the tab control, it's used for a bit of interactivity: getting the right tab to appear when a visitor clicks its trigger. We also use JavaScript to get the tab control to render correctly for IE7. In this case, we created a jQuery plug-in called tab. The plug-in provides visitors the ability to open a particular tab, either through their browser's back button, the browser's history function, or a link to a particular tab. It also adds a click event to each tab, which enables opening the tab the visitor clicked. It also controls the animation effect triggered when different tabs have content whose size differs.

Rather than try to describe the plug-in in detail here, we've commented extensively throughout the plug-in. The comments make for a long listing, but they also put the description into a more meaningful context. Listing 17-5 shows the jQuery for our tab control.

Listing 17-5. The jQuery Plug-in for Our Tab Control

```
;(function($) {

  $.fn.extend({

    //name of our plug-in
    tab : function() {

      return this.each(function() {
        // Declare some pointers relative to the element passed
        // into the plug-in.
        var tab = $(this), hash = window.location.hash,
```

```
                // Find the the .tabContentUL. We'll use this as a starting
                // selector to find
        our targeted tab content
              tabContentUL = tab.find(".tabContentUL"),
                // Grabs all the .tabContentLI's into a collection.
              tabContentLIs = tabContentUL.find(".tabContentLI"),
                // Grab a collection of tab trigger anchor tags.
              tabTriggers = tab.find(".tabTriggerA"), tabTriggerLIs = tab.find(".tabTriggerLI");
                // If a user has bookmarked this page, we want to open the
                // tab he had open when bookmarking. First we'll check to see
                // whether there's a hash left by using one of the tab
                // triggers.
              if (hash) {
                var count = 0;
                tabTriggers.each(function checkHash() {
                  // Because this variable is scoped within a function
                  // we can use 't' again to represent each tab trigger
                  // as we enumerate through the collection.
                  var t = $(this);
                  if (t.attr("href") == hash) {
                    // if the href matches the hash, add the activeTab
                    // class to the that triggers parent LI
                    t.parents(".tabTriggerLI").addClass("activeTab"),
                    // Then find the matching content tab and add
                    // the showTab class to that, displaying that tab.
                    currentTab = findTabContentLI(hash);
                    currentTab.addClass("showTab");
                    //Set the height of the tabContentUL for the bookmarked
                    // contentTab.
                    tabContentUL.height(currentTab.outerHeight(true));
                  } else {
                    // Add 1 to the count if there isn't a match
                    // to the hash. We'll use this later to trigger
                    // the first tab if we don't find a match for any
                    // of the elements.
                    count++;
                  }
                });
                // In case our page has changed since the user bookmarked it
                // or if there are two tab controls on a page with varying
                // tab trigger names, we'll handle the case where there's no
                // matches and display the first tab. So if the count shows as
                // many unmatched tabTriggers as there are tabTriggers in
                // total, we'll show the first tab.
                if (count == tabTriggers.length) {
                  showFirstTab();
                }

              } else {
                // If there's no hash, show the first tab
                showFirstTab();
```

```
}
// Add a click event to the tab targets.
$(this).find(".tabTriggerA").click(function tabTrigger() {
  // Captures the element clicked and makes it a jQuery element.
  // The $(this) here is scoped to only the .tabTriggerA that
  // was clicked.
  var t = $(this),
  // We'll resuse the href as the identifier
  // for our tab selection
  tabId = t.attr("href"),
  // Find the matching .tab1ContentLI with the same id attribute
  // as the href from the target selected.
  targetContentTab = findTabContentLI(tabId);
  // Set all the tab content areas back to the default of
  // display: none and opacity:0 by removing the showTab class
  // from all of them.
  tabContentLIs.removeClass("showTab");
  // The same as above: Remove all the 'activeTab' classes from
  // the tabTriggers to reset them.
  tabTriggerLIs.removeClass("activeTab");
  // Add a class to the LI containing the clicked tab trigger.
  // We'll use this to style the active trigger.
  t.parents(".tabTriggerLI").addClass("activeTab");

  // For our progressive enhancement, we're going to use CSS3
  // transitions to handle animating the height of our tab
  // content wrap to match its contents, as well as animating
  // the opacity to let the content fade in after the height
  // animation is complete. However if the CSS3 animation isn't
  // available we'll get the same effect by using Javascript.
  if (Modernizr.cssanimations) {

    tabContentUL.height(targetContentTab.outerHeight(true));
    targetContentTab.addClass("showTab");
  } else {
    tabContentUL.animate(
    // Declare what property to animate. In this case we're
    // animating the height of the .tabContentUL to the same
    // height as the targetContentTab plus padding (that's the
    // outerHeight()).
    {
      "height" : targetContentTab.outerHeight() + "px"
    },
    // how long to complete the animation
    300,
    // callback after animation is complete.
    function showTab() {
      targetContentTab.addClass("showTab");
    });
  }
```

```
  });
  // Because IE still has some trouble being in compliance, we'll
  // trigger a JS solution to allow for our tabs to be any height
  // and still retain  the tab style metaphor by being the same
  // height.
  if($("html").hasClass("ie")){
    equalizeTriggerHeights();
  }
  // We'll find the tallest triggerLI and set the remaining LIs to
  // that height.
  function equalizeTriggerHeights(){
    var maxHeight = 0;
    tabTriggerLIs.each(function(){
      var t = $(this);
      var tHeight = t.height();
      if(tHeight > maxHeight){
        maxHeight = tHeight;
      }
      // As long as we're in here, we'll vertically center
      // the text inside the trigger LIs. We'll accomplish
      // this centering by positioning the text 50% from the
      // top, which puts the top of the text box in the middle
      // of the vertical height of our LI. But since that would
      // look too low, we'll give the text a negative margin equal
      // to 1/2 its height; that should do that trick. However,
      // IE7 doesn't allow this trick, so we'll disable it for
      //  that browser. The reason we don't use CSS to set the
      // margin is that we don't know how high the tab will be,
      // because the tab may have more than one line of content.
      if(!$("html").hasClass("ie7")){
        var tabTrigger = t.find(".tabTriggerA");
        tabTrigger.css("margin-top", -(tabTrigger.outerHeight() / 2));
      }else {
        t.find(".tabTriggerA").css("position", "static");
        // There's a display bug when IE7 first loads, we'll
        // counteract that here.
        setTimeout(function(){ie7Fix();}, 100);
      }
    })
    tabTriggerLIs.height(maxHeight);


  }
  function ie7Fix(){
    var showTab = tab.find(".showTab");
    showTab.css("display" , "block");
    tab.find(".tabContentUL").height(showTab.outerHeight(true));
  }
  // Finds the matching content based on the selector and returns
  // the element.
  function findTabContentLI(selector) {
```

```
    selectedTabContent = tabContentUL.find(".tabContentLI[data-tabid='" + selector + "']");
    return selectedTabContent;
  }

  // Shows the first tab in the series.
  function showFirstTab() {
    var currentTab = tabContentLIs.eq(0);
    currentTab.addClass("showTab");
    tabContentUL.height(currentTab.outerHeight(true));
    tabTriggers.eq(0).parents(".tabTriggerLI").addClass("activeTab");
  }

 });
 }
});

})(jQuery);
```

Styling the Tab Control

Our standard paradigm for making a control is to make a common set of HTML elements work for all treatments; we've embraced that paradigm again for the tab control. Consequently, the differences between the various treatments depend entirely on CSS.

In the case of the tab control, we have two treatments: horizontal (indicated by classes whose names include the tabTreatment1 identifier) and vertical (indicated by classes whose names include the tabTreatment2 identifier). In addition to rules that apply to one or the other of the treatments, the tab control includes some rules that apply to all treatments. Let's start with those common rules.

Styles for All Treatments

Some rules apply to all the treatments of the tab control. At present, we have two treatments (horizontal and vertical). If we were to develop additional treatments, these rules would apply to those treatments, too. As we've done for other complex controls, we'll describe each rule individually. We've also included comments throughout the rules.

The general principle is to turn the lists within the tab control into a table. A table automatically spreads our tabs over the available area and nicely centers our tab labels. So those table elements *do* have a use.

▦ **Note** On our sample site, the CSS styles are in a single file. We break them up into individual listings so that we can explain each rule.

Listing 17-6 shows the tabWrap class, which provides a wrapper for the tab control elements. The rule has no content other than comments. It exists to let other rules (such as tabWrap ul, which we'll get to in Listing 17-7) use it as part of descendant specifiers and to provide a hook for the JavaScript to use when animating the tab control. **Consequently, it has no working content – just comments.**

Listing 17-6. Styling the Outside Wrapper of the Tab Control

```
/*
 * These rules define the generic attributes that all instances of our tab controls have.
 */
.tabWrap {
  /*
   * In order to get the tabs to fit across the whole
   * control and have the text inside the tab triggers
   * be vertically centered, we use display:table and
   * display:table-cell to set up a faux table, with the
   * UL element being the table and the LI elements
   * being the cells in the table.
   */

  /*
   * This class handles making the content tab
   * visible and thus enables our animations.
   */
}
```

Listing 17-7 shows how we style the two lists within the tab control. We set the padding and margin values to zero (0) and set the position property to relative. We'll set the position property of other elements within the lists to absolute to control the positioning of the tabs and their content within the tab control.

Listing 17-7. Styling the Lists Within the Tab Control

```
.tabWrap ul {
  padding: 0;
  margin: 0;
  position: relative;
}
```

Listing 17-8 shows how we style the list items within each list. We set the padding and margins to 0. We also set the list-style property to none, so that we don't get bullets in our output.

Listing 17-8. Styling the List Items Within the Tab Control

```
.tabWrap li {
  padding: 0;
  margin: 0;
  list-style: none;
}
```

Listing 17-9 shows how we turn the list that holds the tab labels into a table. Because we set the width to 100 percent, the tab control now fills its available space.

Listing 17-9. Turning a List into a Table

```
.tabWrap .tabTriggerUL {
  display: table;
  width: 100%;
```

}

Listing 17-10 shows how we turn each of the tab labels into a table cell. We also set padding values and both horizontal and vertical centering.

Listing 17-10. Turning a List Item into a Table Cell

```
.tabWrap .tabTriggerLI {
  display: table-cell;
  padding: 5px 20px 2px 20px;
  text-align: center;
  vertical-align: middle;
}
```

Listing 17-11 shows how we style an anchor element to be a tab label. We ensure that the anchor element is not underlined (by removing any text decoration) and turn the anchor element into a block element rather than an inline element.

Listing 17-11. Styling the Text of the Tab Label

```
.tabWrap .tabTriggerA {
  text-decoration: none;
  display: block;
}
```

Listing 17-12 shows how we style the list items that hold the content of the tabs. We ensure that the content is a block, set a thin border, and set the value of the position property to relative (we set the values of the position property of the li elements to absolute). We also set the value of the overflow property to hidden, to clear floats.

Listing 17-12. Styling the content list

```
.tabWrap .tabContentUL {
  display: block;
  border: 1px solid;
  position: relative;
  overflow: hidden;
}
```

Listing 17-13 shows how we style the content of the tabs. It includes a number of noteworthy elements. First, we set the value of the opacity property to 0, which makes the content invisible. When the visitor selects a tab, we use a transition effect to set the value of the opacity property to 1, which makes the content visible. The transition effect provides our animation. For browsers that don't support opacity, we set the value of the visibility property to hidden. When the visitor clicks on a tab, we set the value of the visibility property to visible. To position the content, we set the value of the position property to absolute and set the values of the top and left properties to 0. We also specify the transition effect for various browsers. Finally, we set the value of the z-index property to 1. In the next rule, we'll set the value of the z-index property for the visible tab to 2, ensuring that the visible tab is on top.

Listing 17-13. Styling the Content Area

```
.tabWrap .tabContentLI {
  /*
   * We're starting with an opacity of 0 as the
```

```
 * default state, and when the tab content is triggered
 * by the tab trigger, it will animate into 100% opacity.
 * We're also setting the visibility to hidden and changing
 * that to a visibility of visible on trigger selection
 * to accommodate browsers that don't handle opacity.
 */
-webkit-opacity: 0;
-moz-opacity: 0;
opacity: 0;
padding: 20px;
position: absolute;
visibility: hidden;
top: 0;
left: 0;
-webkit-transition: all 0.3s ease-out;
-moz-transition: all 0.3s ease-out;
-ms-transition: all 0.3s ease-out;
-o-transition: all 0.3s ease-out;
transition: all 0.3s ease-out;
z-index: 1;
}
```

Listing 17-14 shows how we style the active (or current) tab. As we discussed for the previous rule, the value of the opacity property for inactive tabs is 0, the value of the visibility property for inactive tabs is hidden, and the value of the z-index property for inactive tabs is 1. To make a tab visible, this rule changes all of those settings. It sets the value of the opacity property to 1, sets the value of the visibility property to visible, and sets the value of the z-index to 2. We set both visibility and opacity to accommodate browsers that don't deal with opacity. Those browsers lose the animation effect, which is tied to the opacity property, but the tabs work correctly otherwise, thanks to the visibility setting. The result is a visible tab.

Listing 17-14. Styling the Active Tab

```
.tabWrap .showTab {
  -webkit-opacity: 1;
  -moz-opacity: 1;
  opacity: 1;
  z-index: 2;
  visibility: visible;
}
```

Styles for the Horizontal Treatment

Now we come to the styles that apply to the horizontal treatment of our tab control. The value, tabTreatment1, indicates the horizontal treatment. We start by setting the width of the tab control.

Listing 17-15 shows how we set the width of the tab control for the horizontal treatment.

Listing 17-15. Setting the Width of the Horizontal Treatment

```
/*
 * Here we're making style choices for the tabTreatment1.
```

```
*/
.tabTreatment1 {
  width: 625px;
}
```

Listing 17-16 shows how we style the actual tabs (the structure around each tab label) within the tab control for the horizontal treatment. In this rule, we dictate the look of the inactive tabs. We override some of these values when a tab becomes active. Here, we specify rounded corners and create a gradient for each tab. We also set a border and the background color. Because we have to account for many different browsers, it becomes a relatively long listing.

Listing 17-16. *Styling the Tabs for the Horizontal Treatment*

```
.tabTreatment1 .tabTriggerLI {
  -webkit-border-top-right-radius: 5px;
  -webkit-border-bottom-right-radius: 0;
  -webkit-border-bottom-left-radius: 0;
  -webkit-border-top-left-radius: 5px;
  -moz-border-radius-topright: 5px;
  -moz-border-radius-bottomright: 0;
  -moz-border-radius-bottomleft: 0;
  -moz-border-radius-topleft: 5px;
  border-top-right-radius: 5px;
  border-bottom-right-radius: 0;
  border-bottom-left-radius: 0;
  border-top-left-radius: 5px;
  -moz-background-clip: padding;
  -webkit-background-clip: padding-box;
  background-clip: padding-box;
  background: blue;
  border: 1px solid #444;
  background: #fffbfb;
  background: blue;
  background: url(data:image/svg+xml;base64,PD94bWwgdmVyc2lvbj0iMS4wIiA/Pgo8c3ZnIHhtbG5zPSJodHRw
Oi8vd3d3LnczLm9yZy8yMDAwL3N2ZyIgd2lkdGg9IjEwMCUiIGhlaWdodD0iMTAwJSIgdmlldz0iDveDoiMCAwIDEgMSIgcHJl
c2VydmVBc3BlY3RSYXRpbz0ibm9uZSI+CiAgPGxpbmVhckdyYWRpZW50IGlkPSJncmFkLXVjZ2ctZ2VuZXJhdGVkIiBncmFk
aWVudFVuaXRzPSJ1c2VyU3BhY2VPblVzZSIgeDE9IjAlIiB5MT0iMCUiIHgyPSIwJSIgeTI9IjEwMCUiPgogICAgPHN0b3Ag
b2Zmc2V0PSIwJSIgc3RvcC1jb2xvcj0iI2ZmZmJmYiIgc3RvcC1vcGFjaXR5PSIxIi8+CiAgICA8c3RvcCBvZmZzZXQ9IjYl
IiBzdG9wLWNvbG9yPSIjZmZmOWY5IiBzdG9wLW9wYWNpdHk9IjEiLz4KICAgIDxzdG9wIG9mZnNldD0iMjUlIiBzdG9wLWNv
bG9yPSIjZmZlYmViIiBzdG9wLW9wYWNpdHk9IjEiLz4KICAgIDxzdG9wIG9mZnNldD0iMjUlIiBzdG9wLWNvbG9yPSIjZmVl
OGU4IiBzdG9wLW9wYWNpdHk9IjEiLz4KICAgIDxzdG9wIG9mZnNldD0iMzIlIiBzdG9wLWNvbG9yPSIjZmVlNGU0IiBzdG9w
LW9wYWNpdHk9IjEiLz4KICAgIDxzdG9wIG9mZnNldD0iMzMlIiBzdG9wLWNvbG9yPSIjZmVlMWUxIiBzdG9wLW9wYWNpdHk9
IjEiLz4KICAgIDxzdG9wIG9mZnNldD0iNTAlIiBzdG9wLWNvbG9yPSIjZmVkNWQ1IiBzdG9wLW9wYWNpdHk9IjEiLz4KICAg
IDxzdG9wIG9mZnNldD0iNTElIiBzdG9wLWNvbG9yPSIjZmRjNmM3IiBzdG9wLW9wYWNpdHk9IjEiLz4KICAgIDxzdG9wIG9m
ZnNldD0iNjYlIiBzdG9wLWNvbG9yPSIjZmNiZWJmIiBzdG9wLW9wYWNpdHk9IjEiLz4KICAgIDxzdG9wIG9mZnNldD0iOTIl
IiBzdG9wLWNvbG9yPSIjZmRhYWFiIiBzdG9wLW9wYWNpdHk9IjEiLz4KICAgIDxzdG9wIG9mZnNldD0iMTAwJSIgc3RvcC1j
b2xvcj0iI2ZkYTdhOCIgc3RvcC1vcGFjaXR5PSIxIi8+CiAgPC9saW5lYXJHcmFkaWVudD4KICA8cmVjdCB4PSIwIiB5PSIw
IiB3aWR0aD0iMSIgaGVpZ2h0PSIxIiBmaWxsPSJ1cmwoI2dyYWQtdWNnZy1nZW5lcmF0ZWQpIiAvPgo8L3N2Zz4=);
  background: -moz-linear-gradient(top, #fffbfb 0%, #fff9f9 6%, #ffebeb 25%, #fee8e8 25%, #fee4e
4 32%, #fee1e1 33%, #fed5d5 50%, #fdc6c7 51%, #fcbebf 66%, #fdaaab 92%, #fda7a8 100%);
  background: -webkit-gradient(linear, left top, left bottom, color-stop(0%, #fffbfb), color-
```

237

```
stop(6%, #fff9f9), color-stop(25%, #ffebeb), color-stop(25%, #fee8e8), color-stop(32%, #fee4e4),
 color-stop(33%, #fee1e1), color-stop(50%, #fed5d5), color-stop(51%, #fdc6c7), color-stop(66%,
#fcbebf), color-stop(92%, #fdaaab), color-stop(100%, #fda7a8));
  background: -webkit-linear-gradient(top, #fffbfb 0%, #fff9f9 6%, #ffebeb 25%, #fee8e8 25%,
#fee4e4 32%, #fee1e1 33%, #fed5d5 50%, #fdc6c7 51%, #fcbebf 66%, #fdaaab 92%, #fda7a8 100%);
  background: -o-linear-gradient(top, #fffbfb 0%, #fff9f9 6%, #ffebeb 25%, #fee8e8 25%, #fee4e4
32%, #fee1e1 33%, #fed5d5 50%, #fdc6c7 51%, #fcbebf 66%, #fdaaab 92%, #fda7a8 100%);
  background: -ms-linear-gradient(top, #fffbfb 0%, #fff9f9 6%, #ffebeb 25%, #fee8e8 25%, #fee4e4
32%, #fee1e1 33%, #fed5d5 50%, #fdc6c7 51%, #fcbebf 66%, #fdaaab 92%, #fda7a8 100%);
  background: linear-gradient(to bottom, #fffbfb 0%, #fff9f9 6%, #ffebeb 25%, #fee8e8 25%,
#fee4e4 32%, #fee1e1 33%, #fed5d5 50%, #fdc6c7 51%, #fcbebf 66%, #fdaaab 92%, #fda7a8 100%);
  filter: progid:dximagetransform.microsoft.gradient(startColorstr='#fffbfb',
endColorstr='#fda7a8', GradientType=0);
}
```

Listing 17-17 shows how we set the appearance of the active tab for the horizontal treatment. As discussed in the description of Listing 17-16, we override properties that we set in the .tabTreatment . tabTriggerLI rule (the rule described in Listing 17-16). First, we turn off the bottom border, so that the area containing the label seems to join the area containing the content. Then we change the background color to a slightly lighter color. Finally, we override the gradient settings to provide a slightly lighter gradient.

Listing 17-17. *Styling the Active Tab for the Horizontal Treatment*

```
.tabTreatment1 .activeTab {
  /*
   * We're setting the style for the selected tab
   */
  border-bottom: none;
  background: #fffbfb;
  background: url(data:image/svg+xml;base64,PD94bWwgdmVyc2lvbjOiMS4wIiA/Pgo8c3ZnIHhtbG5zPSJodHRw
Oi8vd3d3LnczLm9yZy8yMDAwL3N2ZyIgd2lkdGg9IjEwMCUiIGhlaWdodDOiMTAwJSIgdmlld0JveDOiMCAwIDEgMSIgcHJl
c2VydmVBc3BlY3RSYXRpbz0ibm9uZSI+CiAgPGxpbmVhckdyYWRpZW50IGlkPSJncmFkLXVjZ2ctZ2VuZXJhdGVkIiBncmFk
aWVudFVuaXRzPSJ1c2VyU3BhY2VPblVzZSIgeDE9IjAlIiB5MTOiMCUiIHgyPSIwJSIgeTI9IjEwMCUiPgogICAgPHN0b3Ag
b2Zmc2VOPSIwJSIgc3RvcC1jb2xvcjOiI2ZmZmJmYiIgc3RvcC1vcGFjaXR5PSIxIi8+CiAgICA8c3RvcCBvZmZzZXQ9IjYl
IiBzdG9wLWNvbG9yPSIjZmZmOWY5IiBzdG9wLW9wYWNpdHk9IjEiLz4KICAgIDxzdG9wIG9mZnNldDOiMjUlIiBzdG9wLWNv
bG9yPSIjZmZlYmViIiBzdG9wLW9wYWNpdHk9IjEiLz4KICAgIDxzdG9wIG9mZnNldDOiMjUlIiBzdG9wLWNvbG9yPSIjZmVl
OGU4IiBzdG9wLW9wYWNpdHk9IjEiLz4KICAgIDxzdG9wIG9mZnNldDOiMzIlIiBzdG9wLWNvbG9yPSIjZmVlNGU0IiBzdG9w
LW9wYWNpdHk9IjEiLz4KICAgIDxzdG9wIG9mZnNldDOiMzMlIiBzdG9wLWNvbG9yPSIjZmVlMWUxIiBzdG9wLW9wYWNpdHk9
IjEiLz4KICAgIDxzdG9wIG9mZnNldDOiNTAlIiBzdG9wLWNvbG9yPSIjZmVkNWQ1IiBzdG9wLW9wYWNpdHk9IjEiLz4KICAg
IDxzdG9wIG9mZnNldDOiNTElIiBzdG9wLWNvbG9yPSIjZmNkNGQ0IiBzdG9wLW9wYWNpdHk9IjEiLz4KICAgIDxzdG9wIG9m
ZnNldDOiMTAwJSIgc3RvcC1jb2xvcjOiI2ZjZmNmYyIgc3RvcC1vcGFjaXR5PSIxIi8+CiAgPC9saW5lYXJHcmFkaWVudD4K
ICA8cmVjdCB4PSIwIiB5PSIwIiB3aWROaDOiMSIgaGVpZ2hOPSIxIiBmaWxsPSJ1cmwoI2dyYWQtdWNnZy1nZW5lcmFOZWQp
IiAvPgo8L3N2Zz4=);
  background: -moz-linear-gradient(top, #fffbfb 0%, #fff9f9 6%, #ffebeb 25%, #fee8e8 25%, #fee4e
4 32%, #fee1e1 33%, #fed5d5 50%, #fcd4d4 51%, #fcfcfc 100%);
  background: -webkit-gradient(linear, left top, left bottom, color-stop(0%, #fffbfb), color-
stop(6%, #fff9f9), color-stop(25%, #ffebeb), color-stop(25%, #fee8e8), color-stop(32%, #fee4e4),
 color-stop(33%, #fee1e1), color-stop(50%, #fed5d5), color-stop(51%, #fcd4d4), color-stop(100%,
#fcfcfc));
  background: -webkit-linear-gradient(top, #fffbfb 0%, #fff9f9 6%, #ffebeb 25%, #fee8e8 25%, #fe
```

```
e4e4 32%, #fee1e1 33%, #fed5d5 50%, #fcd4d4 51%, #fcfcfc 100%);
  background: -o-linear-gradient(top, #fffbfb 0%, #fff9f9 6%, #ffebeb 25%, #fee8e8 25%, #fee4e4
32%, #fee1e1 33%, #fed5d5 50%, #fcd4d4 51%, #fcfcfc 100%);
  background: -ms-linear-gradient(top, #fffbfb 0%, #fff9f9 6%, #ffebeb 25%, #fee8e8 25%, #fee4e4
32%, #fee1e1 33%, #fed5d5 50%, #fcd4d4 51%, #fcfcfc 100%);
  background: linear-gradient(to bottom, #fffbfb 0%, #fff9f9 6%, #ffebeb 25%, #fee8e8 25%,
#fee4e4 32%, #fee1e1 33%, #fed5d5 50%, #fcd4d4 51%, #fcfcfc 100%);
  filter: progid:dximagetransform.microsoft.gradient(startColorstr='#fffbfb',
endColorstr='#fcfcfc', GradientType=0);
}
```

Listing 17-18 shows how we style the anchor tags that constitute the tab labels. All we do is set the color to a dark gray (we find gray to be more attractive than plain black).

Listing 17-18. Setting the Label Color for the Horizontal Treatment

```
.tabTreatment1 .tabTriggerA {
  color: #222;
}
```

Listing 17-19 shows how we style the content area of a tab. First, we set the border to a shade of gray. However, since we don't want a border at the top, we then turn off the top border. After that, we create the rounded corners, set the shadows around the content area, and set the transition that causes the animation when a visitor changes tabs. Because we have to get these settings to work on many different browsers, the code for those tasks makes for a large listing.

Listing 17-19. Styling the Content Area for the Horizontal Treatment

```
.tabTreatment1 .tabContentUL {
  border: 1px solid #444;
  border-top: none;
  -webkit-border-top-right-radius: 0;
  -webkit-border-bottom-right-radius: 3px;
  -webkit-border-bottom-left-radius: 3px;
  -webkit-border-top-left-radius: 0;
  -moz-border-radius-topright: 0;
  -moz-border-radius-bottomright: 3px;
  -moz-border-radius-bottomleft: 3px;
  -moz-border-radius-topleft: 0;
  border-top-right-radius: 0;
  border-bottom-right-radius: 3px;
  border-bottom-left-radius: 3px;
  border-top-left-radius: 0;
  -moz-background-clip: padding;
  -webkit-background-clip: padding-box;
  background-clip: padding-box;
  -webkit-box-shadow: 0 3px 3px 0 rgba(0, 0, 0, 0.4);
  -moz-box-shadow: 0 3px 3px 0 rgba(0, 0, 0, 0.4);
  box-shadow: 0 3px 3px 0 rgba(0, 0, 0, 0.4);
  /*
   * To achieve our animation for the height
   * of the content tab as it's changing content,
```

```
 * we set the transition property below. This
 * tells it to transition on all available
 * transition properties when there's a change.
 */
-webkit-transition: all 0.3s ease-out;
-moz-transition: all 0.3s ease-out;
-ms-transition: all 0.3s ease-out;
-o-transition: all 0.3s ease-out;
transition: all 0.3s ease-out;
}
```

We're going to group the next few rules, starting with Listing 17-20, because they all apply to Internet Explorer. IE6 and IE7 don't let us use the display: table-cell and display: table properties. And even IE9, which does understand the display:table types, had a problem with a complex gradient and the border of all things. Consequently, we have to use another method: floating the list items. We also set the value of the overflow property on the last list item to hidden. This technique makes the tab occupy the full width of the tab control.

Listing 17-20. Styles for Internet Explorer for the Horizontal Treatment

```
/*
 * Because even IE9 still doesn't always play well, we need
 * to take a different approach by not using the display:table and
 * display:table-cell properties. Instead, we go with a more
 * traditional approach: floating the LIs. We're also doing a bit
 * of trickery by setting the last LI to overflow:hidden and taking
 * away the float. This trick makes the tab take up the remaining
 * space so that our tabs will take up the full width of the tab
 * control.
 */
.ie .tabTreatment1 .tabTriggerLI {
  display: block;
  float: left;
  margin: 0;
  position: relative;
}
.ie .tabTreatment1 .tabTriggerUL {
  display: block;
  overflow: hidden;
}
.ie .tabTreatment1 .tabLast {
  float: none;
  overflow: hidden;
}
.ie .tabTreatment1 .tabTriggerA {
  position: relative;
  top: 50%;
  display: block;
}
```

Listing 17-21 also bundles some rules (two, in this case). If we left the filter property active for IE9, we would get a simple two-stop gradient. SVG lets us have multistop gradients. So we have to remove the filter to get the nicer gradient in IE9. We need two rules, so that we can override the filter property for all tabs and for the active tab.

Listing 17-21. Setting Filters to None for IE9 for the Horizontal Treatment

```
/*
 * We need to disable the filter property
 * for IE9 so we can use our SVG alternative.
 */
.ie9 .tabTreatment1 .tabTriggerLI {
  filter: none;
}
.ie9 .tabTreatment1 .activeTab {
  filter: none;
}
```

Styles for the Vertical Treatment

Now we come to the styles that apply to the vertical treatment of our tab control. The value `tabTreatment2` indicates the vertical treatment. We start by setting a large group of properties that apply to the whole treatment.

Listing 17-22 shows how we set a number of properties that apply to the whole treatment. We start by setting the width. Then we set the value of the overflow property to clear floats. Then we set the padding and the background color. Next, we set the gradient and create the rounded corners. As always with these properties, we have to have a number of lines for each to get the appearance we want on as many browsers as possible.

Listing 17-22. Setting Properties for the Whole Vertical Treatment

```
.tabTreatment2 {
  width: 605px;
  overflow: hidden;
  padding: 10px;
  background: #45484d;
  background: url(data:image/svg+xml;base64,PD94bWwgdmVyc2lvbjOiMS4wIiA/Pgo8c3ZnIHhtbG5zPSJodHRw
Oi8vd3d3LnczLm9yZy8yMDAwL3N2ZyIgd2lkdGg9IjEwMCUiIGhlaWdodDOiMTAwJSIgdmlld0JveDOiMCAwIDEgMSIgcHJl
c2VydmVBc3BlY3RSYXRpbzOibm9uZSI+CiAgPGxpbmVhckdyYWRpZW50IGlkPSJncmFkLXVjZ2ctZ2VuZXJhdGVkIiBncmFk
aWVudFVuaXRzPSJ1c2VyU3BhY2VPblVzZSIgeDE9IjAlIiB5MTOiMCUiIHgyPSIwJSIgeTI9IjEwMCUiPgogICAgPHNob3Ag
b2Zmc2VOPSIwJSIgc3RvcC1jb2xvcjOiIzQ1NDg0ZCIgc3RvcC1vcGFjaXR5PSIxIi8+CiAgICA8c3RvcCBvZmZzZXQ9IjEw
MCUiIHNOb3AtY29sb3I9IiMwMDAwMDAiIHNOb3Atb3BhY2l0eTOiMSIvPgogIDwvbGluZWFyR3JhZGllbnQ+CiAgPHJlY3Qg
eDOiMCIgeTOiMCIgd2lkdGg9IjEiIGhlaWdodDOiMSIgZmlsbDOidXJsKCNncmFkLXVjZ2ctZ2VuZXJhdGVkKSIgLz4KPC9z
dmc+);
  background: -moz-linear-gradient(top, #45484d 0%, #000000 100%);
  background: -webkit-gradient(linear, left top, left bottom, color-stop(0%, #45484d), color-
stop(100%, #000000));
  background: -webkit-linear-gradient(top, #45484d 0%, #000000 100%);
  background: -o-linear-gradient(top, #45484d 0%, #000000 100%);
  background: -ms-linear-gradient(top, #45484d 0%, #000000 100%);
  background: linear-gradient(to bottom, #45484d 0%, #000000 100%);
  filter: progid:dximagetransform.microsoft.gradient(startColorstr='#45484d', endColorstr='#00000
0', GradientType=0);
```

```
border: 1px solid;
-webkit-border-radius: 3px;
-moz-border-radius: 3px;
border-radius: 3px;
-moz-background-clip: padding;
-webkit-background-clip: padding-box;
background-clip: padding-box;
}
```

Listing 17-23 shows how we turn the list that holds the tab labels into a table for the vertical treatment. Because we set the width to 100 percent, the tab control now fills its available space. Unlike the rule applying to all treatments (see Listing 17-9), this rule sets the value of the float property to left, the width to 150 pixels, and the right margin to 10 pixels.

Listing 17-23. Turning a List into a Table for the Vertical Treatment

```
.tabTreatment2 .tabTriggerUL {
    display: block;
    width: 150px;
    float: left;
    height: 100%;
    margin-right: 10px;
}
```

Listing 17-24 shows how we style the actual tabs (the structure around each tab label) within the tab control for the horizontal treatment. We use this rule to dictate the look of the inactive tabs. We override some of these values when a tab becomes active. Here, we specify the padding, alignment, margins, and shadows. We also ensure that the tab appears as a block and is relatively positioned. We then set a gradient and the background color.

Listing 17-24. Styling the Tabs for the Vertical Treatment

```
.tabTreatment2 .tabTriggerLI {
    padding: 10px;
    text-align: center;
    position: relative;
    display: block;
    margin: 4px 0;
    -webkit-box-shadow: 0 0 3px rgba(255, 255, 255, 0.7);
    -moz-box-shadow: 0 0 3px rgba(255, 255, 255, 0.7);
    box-shadow: 0 0 3px rgba(255, 255, 255, 0.7);
    background: #7d7e7d;
    background: url(data:image/svg+xml;base64,PD94bWwgdmVyc2lvbjoiMS4wIiA/Pgo8c3ZnIHhtbG5zPSJodHRw
Oi8vd3d3LnczLm9yZy8yMDAwL3N2ZyIgd2lkdGg9IjEwMCUiIGhlaWdodDoiMTAwJSIgdmlld0JveDoiMCAwIDEgMSIgcHJl
c2VydmVBc3BlY3RSYXRpbz0ibm9uZSI+CiAgPGxpbmVhckdyYWRpZW50IGlkPSJncmFkLXVjZ2ctZ2VuZXJhdGVkIiBncmFk
aWVudFVuaXRzPSJ1c2VyU3BhY2VPblVzZSIgeDE9IjAlIiB5MToiMCUiIHgyPSIwJSIgeTI9IjEwMCUiPgogICAgPHN0b3Ag
b2Zmc2V0PSIwJSIgc3RvcC1jb2xvcjoiIzdkN2U3ZCIgc3RvcC1vcGFjaXR5PSIxIi8+CiAgICA8c3RvcCBvZmZzZXQ9IjEw
MCUiIHN0b3AtY29sb3I9IiMwZTBlMGUiIHN0b3Atb3BhY2l0eToiMSIvPgogIDwvbGluZWFyR3JhZGllbnQ+CiAgPHJlY3Qg
eD0iMCIgeToiMCIgd2lkdGg9IjEiIGhlaWdodD0iMSIgZmlsbD0idXJsKCNncmFkLXVjZ2ctZ2VuZXJhdGVkKSIgLz4KPC9z
dmc+);
    background: -moz-linear-gradient(top, #7d7e7d 0%, #0e0e0e 100%);
    background: -webkit-gradient(linear, left top, left bottom, color-stop(0%, #7d7e7d), color-
```

```
stop(100%, #0e0e0e));
  background: -webkit-linear-gradient(top, #7d7e7d 0%, #0e0e0e 100%);
  background: -o-linear-gradient(top, #7d7e7d 0%, #0e0e0e 100%);
  background: -ms-linear-gradient(top, #7d7e7d 0%, #0e0e0e 100%);
  background: linear-gradient(to bottom, #7d7e7d 0%, #0e0e0e 100%);
  filter: progid:dximagetransform.microsoft.gradient(startColorstr='#7d7e7d',
endColorstr='#0e0e0e', GradientType=0);
}
```

Listing 17-25 shows how we style the labels for the vertical treatment of the tab control. First, we remove the text decoration, since we don't want the text to be underlined. We then ensure the text is a block and set the color to white. Then we make sure that the text is relatively positioned and set the top distance to 50 percent.

Listing 17-25. Styling the Tab Labels for the Vertical Treatment

```
.tabTreatment2 .tabTriggerA {
  text-decoration: none;
  display: block;
  color: white;
  position: relative;
  top: 50%;
}
```

Listing 17-26 shows how we style the content area for the vertical treatment. First, we ensure that the content appears as a block. Then we set the border to a medium gray color. Next, we set the positioning to be relative. Then we prevent content from overflowing the content area, since that would look awful. Finally, we set the transition effect that provides the animation when a visitor changes tabs.

Listing 17-26. Styling the Content Area for the Vertical Treatment

```
.tabTreatment2 .tabContentUL {
  display: block;
  border: 1px solid #999;
  position: relative;
  overflow: hidden;
  /*
   * To achieve our animation for the height
   * of the content tab as it's changing content,
   * we set the transition property below. This
   * tells it to transition on all available
   * transition properties when there's a change.
   */
  -webkit-transition: all 0.3s ease-out;
  -moz-transition: all 0.3s ease-out;
  -ms-transition: all 0.3s ease-out;
  -o-transition: all 0.3s ease-out;
  transition: all 0.3s ease-out;
}
```

Listing 17-27 shows how we style the content area of a tab for the vertical treatment. We set the value of the various opacity properties to 0, set the value of the visibility property to 0, and set the z-index to 1. Those settings make the content area invisible. We'll override those values for the active tab. We also set shadows and a background gradient and a background color to control the appearance of the content area. Along the way, we set the transition values that provide the animation when a visitor changes tabs. Because we have to get these settings to work on many different browsers, the code for those tasks makes for a large listing.

Listing 17-27. Styling the Content Area for the Vertical Treatment

```css
.tabTreatment2 .tabContentLI {
  /*
   * We're starting with an opacity of 0 as the
   * default state, and when the tab content is triggered
   * by the tab trigger, it will animate into 100% opacity.
   * We're also setting the visibility to hidden and changing
   * that to a visibility of visible on trigger selection
   * to accommodate browsers that don't handle opacity.
   */
  -webkit-opacity: 0;
  -moz-opacity: 0;
  opacity: 0;
  padding: 20px;
  -webkit-box-shadow: inset 2px 2px 2px rgba(0, 0, 0, 0.6);
  -moz-box-shadow: inset 2px 2px 2px rgba(0, 0, 0, 0.6);
  box-shadow: inset 2px 2px 2px rgba(0, 0, 0, 0.6);
  position: absolute;
  visibility: hidden;
  top: 0;
  left: 0;
  -webkit-transition: all 0.3s ease-out;
  -moz-transition: all 0.3s ease-out;
  -ms-transition: all 0.3s ease-out;
  -o-transition: all 0.3s ease-out;
  transition: all 0.3s ease-out;
  z-index: 1;
  background: #ffffff;
  background: url(data:image/svg+xml;base64,PD94bWwgdmVyc2lvbjOiMS4wIiA/Pgo8c3ZnIHhtbG5zPSJodHRw
Oi8vd3d3LnczLm9yZy8yMDAwL3N2ZyIgd2lkdGg9IjEwMCUiIGhlaWdodD0iMTAwJSIgdmlld0JveD0iMCAwIDEgMSIgcHJl
c2VydmVBc3BlY3RSYXRpb2oibm9uZSI+CiAgPGxpbmVhckdyYWRpZW50IGlkPSJncmFkLXVjZ2ctZ2VuZXJhdGVkIiBncmFk
aWVudFVuaXRzPSJ1c2VyU3BhY2VPblVzZSIgeDE9IjAlIiB5MToiMCUiIHgyPSIwJSIgeTI9IjEwMCUiPgogICAgPHN0b3Ag
b2Zmc2V0PSIwJSIgc3RvcC1jb2xvcjOiI2ZmZmZmZiIgc3RvcC1vcGFjaXR5PSIxIi8+CiAgICA8c3RvcCBvZmZzZXQ9IjQ3
JSIgc3RvcC1jb2xvcjOiI2Y2ZjZmNiIgc3RvcC1vcGFjaXR5PSIxIi8+CiAgICA8c3RvcCBvZmZzZXQ9IjEwMCUiIHN0b3At
Y29sb3I9IiNlZGVkZWQiIHN0b3Atb3BhY2l0eT0iMSIvPgogIDwvbGluZWFyR3JhZGllbnQ+CiAgPHJlY3QgeD0iMCIgeToi
MCIgd2lkdGg9IjEiIGhlaWdodD0iMSIgZmlsbD0idXJsKCNncmFkLXVjZ2ctZ2VuZXJhdGVkKSIgLz4KPC9zdmc+);
  background: -moz-linear-gradient(top, #ffffff 0%, #f6f6f6 47%, #ededed 100%);
  background: -webkit-gradient(linear, left top, left bottom, color-stop(0%, #ffffff), color-
stop(47%, #f6f6f6), color-stop(100%, #ededed));
  background: -webkit-linear-gradient(top, #ffffff 0%, #f6f6f6 47%, #ededed 100%);
  background: -o-linear-gradient(top, #ffffff 0%, #f6f6f6 47%, #ededed 100%);
  background: -ms-linear-gradient(top, #ffffff 0%, #f6f6f6 47%, #ededed 100%);
  background: linear-gradient(to bottom, #ffffff 0%, #f6f6f6 47%, #ededed 100%);
  filter: progid:dximagetransform.microsoft.gradient(startColorstr='#ffffff',
endColorstr='#ededed', GradientType=0);
```

```
}
```

Listing 17-28 shows how we make a tab visible for the vertical treatment. To do so, we override the value of the opacity property to be 1, the value of the visibility property to be visible, and the value of the z-index to be 2. This collection of settings makes a tab visible.

Listing 17-28. Making a Tab Visible for the Vertical Treatment

```
.tabTreatment2 .showTab {
  -webkit-opacity: 1;
  -moz-opacity: 1;
  opacity: 1;
  z-index: 2;
  visibility: visible;
}
```

Listing 17-29 shows how we style the active tab for the vertical treatment. In this case, we just need to set the background color and the background gradient. As ever, when we want a gradient, it takes a fair bit of code, not just because we use SVG but also because we have to set it for all possible browsers.

Listing 17-29. Styling the Active Tab for the Vertical Treatment

```
.tabTreatment2 .activeTab {
  background: #444444;
  background: url(data:image/svg+xml;base64,PD94bWwgdmVyc2lvbjOiMS4wIiA/Pgo8c3ZnIHhtbG5zPSJodHRw
Oi8vd3d3LnczLm9yZy8yMDAwL3N2ZyIgd2lkdGg9IjEwMCUiIGhlaWdodD0iMTAwJSIgdmlld0JveD0iMCAwIDEgMSIgcHJl
c2VydmVBc3BlY3RSYXRpbz0ibm9uZSI+CiAgPGxpbmVhckdyYWRpZW50IGlkPSJncmFkLUVjY2VudZJhdGVkIiBncmFk
aWVudFVuaXRzPSJ1c2VyU3BhY2VPblZlZSIgeDE9IjAlIiB5MToiMCUiIHgyPSIwJSIgeTI9IjEwMCUiPgogICAgPHNob3Ag
b2Zmc2V0PSIwJSIgc3RvcC1jb2xvcjoiIzQ0NDQ0NCIgc3RvcC1vcGFjaXR5PSIxIi8+CiAgICA8c3RvcCBvZmZzZXQ9IjEw
MCUiIHN0b3AtY29sb3I9IiM5ZTllOWUiIHN0b3Atb3BhY2l0eToiMSIvPgogIDwvbGluZWFyR3JhZGllbnQ+CiAgPHJlY3Qg
eDOiMCIgeToiMCIgd2lkdGg9IjEiIGhlaWdodD0iMSIgZmlsbDOidXJsKCNncmFkLUVjY2VudZJhdGVkKSIgLz4KPC9zdmc9z
dmc+);
  background: -moz-linear-gradient(top, #444444 0%, #9e9e9e 100%);
  background: -webkit-gradient(linear, left top, left bottom, color-stop(0%, #444444),
color-stop(100%, #9e9e9e));
  background: -webkit-linear-gradient(top, #444444 0%, #9e9e9e 100%);
  background: -o-linear-gradient(top, #444444 0%, #9e9e9e 100%);
  background: -ms-linear-gradient(top, #444444 0%, #9e9e9e 100%);
  background: linear-gradient(to bottom, #444444 0%, #9e9e9e 100%);
  filter: progid:dximagetransform.microsoft.gradient(startColorstr='#444444',
endColorstr='#9e9e9e', GradientType=0);
}
```

Listing 17-30 shows how we turn off the filter for IE9 for the vertical treatment. Because IE 9 would render a much simpler two-stop gradient and we want our fancier multistop SVG gradient, we override the value of the filter property for the vertical treatment so that its value is none for IE9.

Listing 17-30. Turning Off the Filter for IE9.

```
.ie9 .tabTreatment2 .activeTab {
  filter: none;
}
```

Summary

This chapter showed how to develop and use a tab control. As with all of our controls, we use a single block of HTML, generated from data by the function that is the heart of our control. From that block, we produced two different treatments, one horizontal and light-colored and one vertical and dark-colored. We also employed our standard paradigm of using CSS3 whenever possible but providing a fallback in JavaScript for browsers that can't work with CSS3. We thus embrace the principle of progressive design and give each visitor the best experience that the visitor's browser can provide. As mentioned before, we don't try to provide an identical experience for each visitor. We think that's a false goal, because different browsers make it impossible to have a truly identical experience. Rather, we aim for a good experience on any browser.

For this control, we also created a jQuery plug-in that lets us create an address for a particular tab. That way, visitors returning to or refreshing a page get the same tab they were just on. The ability to set a unique identifier on a set of tabs also allows a page to have more than one set of tabs. The address (enabled by the id attribute) also lets us create links to a particular tab. To add a little visual interest, we also animated the transition from one tab to another. The end result of all this work is a reusable tab control that looks nice and has better functionality than most of the tab arrangements we found on various web sites.

CHAPTER 18

■ ■ ■

Form Controls

Forms are essential to many web sites, certainly to e-commerce sites. If we can't gather the visitors' information, we can't do business, and forms are the mechanism for gathering information. So we really can't complete the book without a chapter on forms.

To build the form control, we had to build two controls. A form has content, so we built a control for the form's content: the fieldset control. A fieldset contains (along with other elements) input elements, so we also needed a control for building input elements.

■ **Note** We did not make an actual form control. To create a form with our controls, we create a form element and use fieldset controls as children. We provide an example in the "Creating a Form" section later in this chapter.

As usual, we've created multiple treatments for a control—a dark treatment and a light treatment in the case of the form control. The dark treatment has a diagonal pattern that looks almost like corduroy (that was the first word out of Jay's mouth when he saw it). We'll show how to create that effect when we get to the CSS rules later in the chapter.

Within the form, there are two sets of fields. We built with the fieldset control, which we use to build a form's content, as we mentioned at the chapter's start. Further along, we'll show how to build fields for a form with the fieldset control. Because we need all the usual input elementswithin a fieldset, we'll also show how to build them with the input control.

The form control uses standard form elements, with one exception. The Submit button is an instance of our button control, described in chapter 13. Later, when we get to the code behind the form control, we'll show how we insert the button control into the form control.

Our form controls offers good performance in a number of different ways. First, we rely on CSS as much as possible. As we've mentioned in earlier chapters, browsers can more quickly render content with CSS rules than with JavaScript or any other mechanism (in fact, we don't use JavaScript at all in our form controls). Second, we use class names in our CSS rules and avoid descendant selectors, which don't perform nearly as well. Again, that's a pattern we consistently use; we think it will become more common as developers realize its benefits. Third and last, building controls to render our forms speeds up developers (including ourselves) to a great extent. Developers can much more easily call a few functions to create a form than create all the form's elements themselves.

That last item has another benefit: encapsulation. If there's a problem with a form, we know to look in the form control's code rather than in one of many individual forms. That technique greatly speeds debugging. Debugging is also much less frustrating when the problem is known to be in a small space.

Reducing frustration doesn't actually boost developers' performance, but it's nice anyway. We appreciate anything that makes our jobs less frustrating and consequently more fun.

It's often easier and more effective to show than to tell, so let's see what the two treatments look like when rendered. That way, you'll see what we mean by "dark" and "light" and also see how the fieldset control, the input control, and the button control fit within the form.

If you want to see the form controls online—screenshots are never the same as the real thing—you'll find it on our sample site: http://clikz.us/BookExamples/forms.php (we've mentioned before that this book is about the front end of web sites—HTML and CSS—so the forms on our site aren't hooked up to anything).

Figure 18-1 shows the dark treatment of the form control.

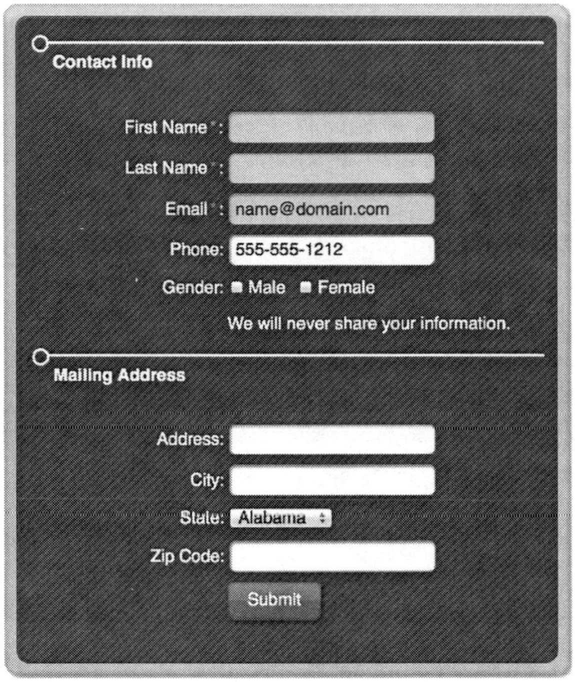

Figure 18-1. *The dark treatment of the form control*

Figure 18-2 shows the light treatment of the form control.

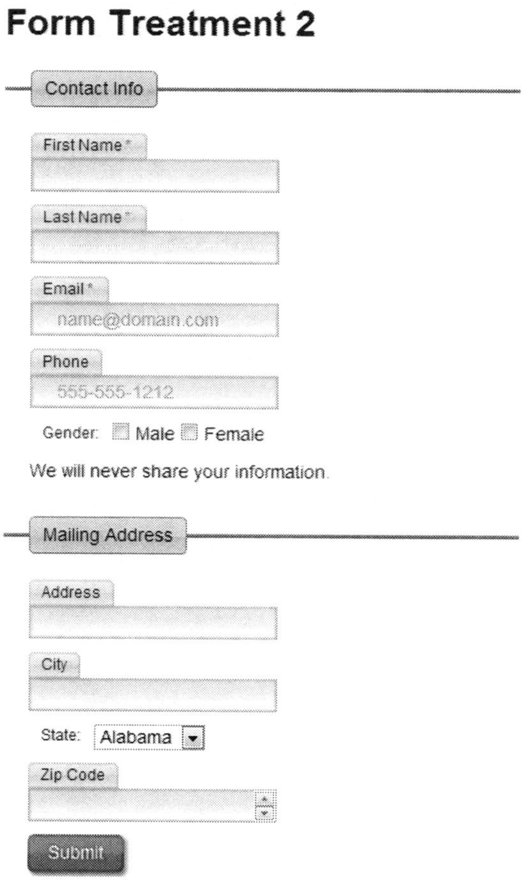

Form Treatment 2

Figure 18-2. The light treatment of the form control

Now that you've seen how they are rendered in a browser, let's move on to the HTML behind the rendered form treatments.

The HTML

As with our other controls, this one doesn't directly include HTML. Rather, a PHP function generates the HTML when the page loads. Still, we think that seeing the HTML that the control creates provides context for the style (CSS) information. Other than specifying which treatment to use as a class name, the HTML does not change from the dark to the light treatment. The CSS rules (which we'll soon get to) determine all the differences between the treatments.

The HTML consists of two fieldset elements, each of which contains a legend and a number of input elements. The fieldsets are instances of our fieldset control, and the input elements are instances of our input control. At the bottom of the second fieldset, we put in a Submit button, which is, again, an instance of our button control.

Listing 18-1 shows the HTML for the form control shown in Figures 18-1 and 18-2. Here, it specifies the dark treatment, through the fieldsetTreatment1 class name.

Listing 18-1. The HTML Behind the Two Treatments of the Form Control

```html
<fieldset class="fieldset fieldsetTreatment1">
  <legend>
    Contact Info
  </legend>
  <div class="formElement inputControl">
    <label for="id1" class="structure">First Name<span class="required">*</span></label>
    <input type="text" required="" placeholder="" id="id1" value="" name="first_name">
  </div>
  <div class="formElement inputControl">
    <label for="id2" class="structure">Last Name<span class="required">*</span></label>
    <input type="text" required="" placeholder="" id="id2" value="" name="last_name">
  </div>
  <div class="formElement inputControl">
    <label for="id3" class="structure">Email<span class="required">*</span></label>
    <input type="email" required="" placeholder="name@domain.com" id="id3" value=""
name="email">
  </div>
  <div class="formElement inputControl">
    <label for="id4" class="structure">Phone</label>
    <input type="tel" placeholder="555-555-1212" id="id4" value="" name="phone">
  </div>
  <div class="formElement inputList">
    <label class="structure">Gender</label>
    <input type="radio" name="gender" value="men" id="men_5008c8a70057f">
    <label for="men_5008c8a70057f" class="textLabel">Male</label>
    <input type="checkbox" name="gender" value="women" id="women_5008c8a700acd">
    <label for="women_5008c8a700acd" class="textLabel">Female</label>
  </div>
  <div class="formElement ">
    <div class="textMessage">
      We will never share your information.
    </div>
  </div>
</fieldset>
<fieldset class="fieldset fieldsetTreatment1">
  <legend>
    Mailing Address
  </legend>
  <div class="formElement inputControl">
    <label for="aid1" class="structure">Address</label>
    <input type="text" placeholder="" id="aid1" value="" name="address">
  </div>
  <div class="formElement inputControl">
    <label for="aid2" class="structure">City</label>
    <input type="text" placeholder="" id="aid2" value="" name="city">
  </div>
  <div class="formElement selectWrap ">
    <label class="structure">State</label>
    <select id="aid3">
```

```
        <option value="AL">Alabama</option><option value="AK">Alaska</option><option
value="AZ">Arizona</option><option value="AR">Arkansas</option>
    </select>
  </div>
  <div class="formElement inputControl">
    <label for="aid4" class="structure">Zip Code</label>
    <input type="number" placeholder="" id="aid4" value="" name="zipcode">
  </div>
  <div class="formElement buttonWrap ">
    <a title="Submit" class="button primary glass" href="#">Submit</a>
  </div>
</fieldset>
```

Since the fieldsets contain everything else, we'll start with the fieldset control.

The Fieldset Control

We make extensive use of the fieldset element in our work and in this book. Since fieldset elements can include legend elements, we've used those to name the sections within our form. Other than the fieldset and legend elements, we've used the same div and input elements that the whole web community has long been using.

As with our other sample controls for this book, the actual control is a PHP function. The function takes three arguments. Table 18-1 describes them.

Table 18-1. Arguments for the Fieldset Control

Argument	Description
$model	The data that go into the fieldset control. It's called a model because we're used to working with the MVC (Model View Controller) pattern.
$treatment	Indicates whether to apply the dark treatment or the light treatment to this fieldset control.
$echo	Indicates whether to echo the HTML built by the fieldSetControl function to the browser or return it as a string for another control to further process.

To turn the data in the model into HTML elements with all the right attribute and content values, the fieldset control first gets the data from the model. The data are in the form of a string to be decoded into a JSON object. Then the function gets the fields from the data object and puts them into a separate variable. Next, the function creates an output variable, which holds the results of the function's processing; in essence, the output variable holds a steadily growing string that contains the HTML elements with the data inserted in the right places. The output variable starts with the opening tag of the fieldset element and its class attribute. Then the function determines whether a legend value is present and, if so, adds a legend element to the output variable's string. The function then uses a for loop to read each of the fields. The for loop has several if statements to identify which kind of field is present and handle it accordingly. For each field, the function appends more HTML elements to the string in the output variable by calling the input control (which has several variations) and putting the result of that call into the output. Next, the function closes the fieldset element. Finally, it determines whether the call wants the output string to be sent (echoed) to the browser or returned to some other function and performs the corresponding action.

We'll cover details of the input control and of the data later in the chapter. For now, please accept that the data may contain a legend and must contain some fields and that each call to the input control returns an input element with the data in the right places.

■ **Note**   While Listing 18-2 may seem large, a form, with all its child elements and data, would be even larger. One of the benefits of controls (and a major motivation for using them) is that, once you have the control, using it takes less code than creating equivalent functionality from scratch.

Listing 18-2. The Fieldset Control

```
function fieldSetControl($model, $treatment, $echo) {

  $obj = json_decode($model);
  $fields = $obj -> fields;
  $output = '<fieldset class="fieldset ' . $treatment . '">';
  if ($obj -> showLegend) {
    $output .= '<legend>' . $obj -> legend . '</legend>';
  }
  for ($i = 0; $i < sizeof($fields); $i++) {
    $field = $fields[$i];
    if ($field -> formElement == "inputControl") {
      $output .= inputControl($field -> id, $field -> labelName, $field -> name, $field -> value,
$field -> type, $field -> placeholder, $field -> _class, $field -> required, $field -> optional,
$field -> _echo);
    }
    if ($field -> formElement == "inputList") {
      $output .= inputList($field -> model, $field -> labelName, $field -> name, $field -> type,
$field -> _class, $field -> _echo);
    }
    if ($field -> formElement == "inputSelect") {
      $output .= inputSelect($field -> model, $field -> id, $field -> labelName, $field -> _class,
$field -> required, $field -> _echo);
    }
    if ($field -> formElement == "html") {
      $output .= inputHTML($field -> html, $field -> _class, $field -> _echo);
    }
    if ($field -> formElement == "buttons") {
      $output .= inputButtons($field -> buttons, $field -> _class, "return");
    }
  }
  $output .= '</fieldset>';

  if ($echo != "return") {
    echo $output;
  } else {
    return $output;
  }
};
```

Now that you've seen the fieldset control, let's move along to the input control, which the fieldset control uses extensively.

The Input Control

As we observed while describing the fieldset control, the input control returns a properly formatted `input` element (or other element; see later in this section) to the fieldset control (or whatever else one calls it). It can also send its output directly to the browser, so that it can be used without the fieldset control. After all, the `fieldset` element is optional and not always useful (as when a form has just one block of fields). Again, the input control is a PHP function. As we've noted for all the other controls, both the fieldset control and the input control could readily be coded in some other language. We had to pick a language, and PHP won, mostly because we think it's easy to read.

The input control is really several related controls; that is, the input control consists of a number of functions, each of which returns a populated element. Let's start with the function called `inputControl`, which creates an `input` element.

▓ **Note**   Not all of the functions in the input control create `input` elements. That control's other functions create other elements; they exist so that we can inject other elements (notably buttons but also other elements) into forms.

The `inputControl` function takes a number of arguments and turns them into a properly populated input control. Table 18-2 describes the arguments of the `inputControl` function.

Table 18-2. *Arguments to the inputControl Function*

Argument	Description
`$id`	A unique identifier for this `input` element.
`$labelText`	The text to use as the label for the `input` element.
`$name`	The value to put in the `input` element's `name` attribute.
`$value`	The value to put in the `input` element's `value` attribute
`$type`	The value to put in the `input` element's `type` attribute.
`$placeholder`	The value to put in the `input` element's `placeholder` attribute.
`$class`	The value to put in the `input` element's `class` attribute. In addition to any class names you specify in this argument, `input` elements created by the `inputControl` function always have the following classes: `formElement` and `inputControl`
`$required`	If true, this argument causes the insertion of an asterisk into the label. The asterisk indicates to visitors that they must provide a value for this input element. It also adds the `required` attribute (with a value of `required`) to the input tag.
`$optional`	This argument can contain any other values, including custom attributes and their values.
`$echo`	If the value is `return`, send the `input` element as a string to the caller of the function. Otherwise, send the `input` element to the browser.

The input control works (as most of our controls do) by creating an output variable and, in that variable, building up a string that becomes a correctly populated element. For the most part, it takes the values of its arguments and inserts them into the corresponding attributes of the resulting input element. The $required argument needs a bit of logic to handle, as it produces two optional strings within the input element: a span that holds an asterisk and the word "required" in the element's attributes. Once the input control has all the right parts in the right places, it can either send the resulting input element to the browser or return a string containing the input element to the caller (in Listing 18-2, that's our fieldset control).

Listing 18-3. *The inputControl Function*

```
function inputControl($id, $labelText, $name, $value, $type, $placeholder, $class, $required,
$optional, $echo) {
  $output = '<div class="formElement inputControl ' . $class . '">';
  $output .= '<label class="structure" for="' . $id . '">' . $labelText;
  $output .= ($required == TRUE ? '<span class="required">*</span>' : '');
  $output .= '</label>';
  $output .= '<input type="' . $type . '" name="' . $name . '" value="' . $value . '" id="' .
$id . '" placeholder="' . $placeholder . '"';
  $output .= ($required == TRUE ? ' required = "required"' : '');
  $output .= ' ' . $optional . '/>';
  $output .= '</div>';
  if ($echo != "return") {
    echo $output;
  } else {
    return $output;
  }
}
```

The `inputList` function creates a div that contains a set of related input elements, which constitute a set of check boxes or radio buttons. Table 18-3 describes the arguments of the `inputList` function.

Table 18-3. *Arguments to the inputList Function*

Argument	Description
$model	The data that go into this input element. It's called a model because we're used to working with the MVC (Model View Controller) pattern.
$labelText	The text to use as the label for the input element.
$name	The value to put in the input element's name attribute.
$type	The value to put in the input element's type attribute.
$class	The value to put in the input element's class attribute. In addition to any classes you specify in this argument, input elements created by the inputList function always have the following classes: formElement and inputList
$echo	If the value is return, send the input element as a string to the caller of the function. Otherwise, send the input element to the browser.

As with the other functions in our controls, the `inputList` function builds a string that consists of populated HTML elements and attributes. First, the function writes the beginning tag of the div element that contains this list of input elements. Then the function writes the label element. To create the input elements, the function uses a for loop to write as many input elements (and corresponding label elements) as there are values in the $model argument. After the function writes the input elements to the output variable, it closes the div element. Finally, the function either sends the div element and all of its children to the browser or sends a string containing all those elements back to the caller.

Listing 18-4. The inputList Function

```
function inputList($model, $labelText, $name, $type, $class, $echo) {
  $obj = $model;
  $output = '<div class="formElement inputList' . $class . '">';
  $output .= '<label class="structure">' . $labelText . '</label>';
  for ($i = 0; $i < sizeof($obj); $i++) {
    $unique = uniqid($obj[$i] -> value . '_');
    $output .= '<input id="' . $unique . '" value="' . $obj[$i] -> value . '" name="' . $name .
'" type="' . $type . '">';
    $output .= '<label class="textLabel" for="' . $unique . '">' . $obj[$i] -> labeltext . '</
label>';
  }
  $output .= '</div>';
  if ($echo != "return") {
    echo $output;
  } else {
    return $output;
  }
}
```

The inputHTML function inserts arbitrary HTML elements into a form. Table 18-4 describes the arguments of the inputHTML function.

Table 18-4. Arguments to the inputHTML Function

Argument	Description
$html	The HTML element(s) to insert into the form.
$class	The value to put in the input element's class attribute. In addition to any classes you specify in this argument, input elements created by the inputHTML function always have the following class: formElement
$echo	If the value is return, send the input element as a string to the caller of the function. Otherwise, send the input element to the browser.

The simplest of the input control functions, the inputHTML function just creates a div, sets any classes specified in the $class argument, and puts the content of the $html argument into the div. It then sends the div containing the inserted HTML to the caller if the $echo argument is return or, if the $echo argument is anything else, sends the output div and its content as a string to the browser.

Listing 18-5. The inputHTML Function

```
function inputHTML($html, $class, $echo) {
  $output = '<div class="formElement ' . $class . '">';
  $output .= $html;
  $output .= '</div>';
  if ($echo != "return") {
    echo $output;
  } else {
```

```
      return $output;
  }
}
```

The `inputButtons` function inserts one or more button controls into a form. This is another example of using controls within controls, as we often do. Table 18-5 describes the arguments of the `inputButtons` function.

Table 18-5. Arguments to the inputButtons Function

Argument	Description
$model	The data that goes into the button(s). It's called a model because we're used to working with the MVC (Model View Controller) pattern.
$class	The value to put in the input element's class attribute. In addition to any classes you specify in this argument, input elements created by the inputButtons function always have the following classes: formElement and buttonWrap
$echo	If the value is return, send the input element as a string to the caller of the function. Otherwise, send the input element to the browser.

Following our usual paradigm for a control function, the `inputButtons` function first creates an output variable and writes the opening tag of `div` element (including the class information) into that output variable. Then it uses a `for` loop to run through the data and make a button control (see chapter 13) for each button specified in the incoming data. Then it closes the `div` element that contains the button controls. Finally, if the $echo argument is return, it sends the output to the caller or, if the $echo argument is anything else, sends the output as a string to the browser.

Listing 18-6. The inputButtons Function

```
function inputButtons($model, $class, $echo) {
  $output = '<div class="formElement buttonWrap ' . $class . '">';
  for ($j = 0; $j < sizeof($model); $j++) {
    $obj = $model[$j];
    $output .= button($obj -> text, $obj -> href, $obj -> id, $obj -> text, $obj -> type, NULL,
NULL, NULL, NULL, "return");
  }
  $output .= '</div>';
  if ($echo != "return") {
    echo $output;
  } else {
    return $output;
  }
}
```

The `inputSelect` function creates a list of mutually exclusive choices within a form. To do so, it creates a div that contains a `select` element. The `select` element contains as many `option` elements as exist in the data. Table 18-6 describes the arguments of the `inputSelect` function.

Table 18-6. *Arguments to the inputSelect Function*

Argument	Description
$model	The choices that go into the list. It's called a model because we're used to working with the MVC (Model View Controller) pattern.
$id	A unique identifier for this input element.
$labelText	The text to use as the label for the input element.
$class	The value to put in the input element's class attribute. In addition to any classes you specify in this argument, input elements created by the inputSelect function always have the following classes: formElement and selectWrap
$echo	If true, send the input element to the browser. If false, return the input element as a string to the caller of the function.

The inputSelect function inserts the opening tag of a div element and sets the classes on the div element. Then the function adds the label and the opening tag of the select element. Next, the function uses a for loop to go through the data in the $model argument and create an option element for each value in the data. Next, the function closes the select and div elements. Finally, if the $echo argument is return, it sends the resulting div element and the list it contains to the caller or, if the $echo argument is anything else, sends the div element and the list it contains as a string to the browser.

Listing 18-7. The inputSelect Function

```
function inputSelect($model, $id, $labelText, $class, $echo) {
  $output = '<div class="formElement selectWrap ' . $class . '">';
  $output .= '<label class="structure">' . $labelText . '</label>';
  $output .= '<select id="' . $id . '">';
  for ($i = 0; $i < sizeof($model); $i++) {
    $output .= '<option value="' . $model[$i] -> value . '">' . $model[$i] -> label .
'</option>';
  }
  $output .= '</select>';
  $output .= '</div>';
  if ($echo != "return") {
    echo $output;
  } else {
    return $output;
  }
}
```

Data Objects

Because we have two fieldset controls within our form, we need two sets of data, one for the contact information and one for the address information. In a real application, we'd get this data from a database. However, since we're sticking to the front end, we just use static data. Each block of data consists of a PHP variable that contains a JSON object. The JSON object contains three values. Table 18-7 describes the values in the JSON object that feeds a fieldset control.

Table 18-7. Data Values in the JSON Object That Holds Data for a fieldset Control

Value	Description
showLegend	Whether to include a legend element in the fieldset element.
legend	The value to use as the content of the legend element, if a legend element should be included.
fields	The other data to be included in the fieldset element. Each of these fields consists of a set of nested JSON objects that hold the data for the input elements (and other items, such as button controls) that appear within the fieldset element. The values within those JSON objects correspond to the arguments of the input control functions described earlier, in the Input Control section.

Listing 18-8 shows the content of the JSON object that provides the data for the contact block. Again, we would usually get this data from an object that gets values from a database and builds a JSON object that we would then pass to our fieldset control.

Listing 18-8. Data for the contact Block

```
$contactInfo = '{
  "showLegend" : true,
  "legend" : "Contact Info",
  "fields" : [
    {
      "formElement" : "inputControl",
      "id": "id1",
      "labelName" : "First Name",
      "name" : "first_name",
      "value" : "",
      "type" : "text",
      "placeholder" : "",
      "_class" : "",
      "required" : true,
      "optional" : "",
      "_echo" : "return"
    },
    {
      "formElement" : "inputControl",
      "id": "id2",
      "labelName" : "Last Name",
      "name" : "last_name",
      "value" : "",
      "type" : "text",
      "placeholder" : "",
      "_class" : "",
      "required" : true,
      "optional" : "",
      "_echo" : "return"
    },
    {
      "formElement" : "inputControl",
```

```
        "id": "id3",
        "labelName" : "Email",
        "name" : "email",
        "value" : "",
        "type" : "email",
        "placeholder" : "name@domain.com",
        "_class" : "",
        "required" : true,
        "optional" : "",
        "_echo" : "return"
    },
    {
        "formElement" : "inputControl",
        "id": "id4",
        "labelName" : "Phone",
        "name" : "phone",
        "value" : "",
        "type" : "tel",
        "placeholder" : "555-555-1212",
        "_class" : "",
        "required" : false,
        "optional" : "",
        "_echo" : "return"
    },
    {
        "formElement" : "inputList",
        "model": [{"value" : "men", "labeltext" : "Male"},{"value" : "women", "labeltext" :
"Female"}],
        "labelName" : "Gender",
        "name" : "gender",
        "type" : "checkbox",
        "_class" : "",
        "_echo" : "return"
    },
    {
        "formElement" : "html",
        "html" : "<div class=textMessage>We will never share your information.</div>",
        "_class" : "",
        "_echo": "return"
    }
  ]
}';
```

Listing 18-9 shows the content of the JSON object that provides the data for the address block. As we've mentioned before, we'd usually get this data from an object that gets values from a database and builds a JSON object that we'd then pass to our fieldset control.

Listing 18-9. *Data for the Address Block*

```
$addressInfo = '{
  "showLegend" : true,
```

```
"legend" : "Mailing Address",
"fields" : [
  {
    "formElement" : "inputControl",
    "id": "aid1",
    "labelName" : "Address",
    "name" : "address",
    "value" : "",
    "type" : "text",
    "placeholder" : "",
    "_class" : "",
    "required" : false,
    "optional" : "",
    "_echo" : "return"
  },
  {
    "formElement" : "inputControl",
    "id": "aid2",
    "labelName" : "City",
    "name" : "city",
    "value" : "",
    "type" : "text",
    "placeholder" : "",
    "_class" : "",
    "required" : false,
    "optional" : "",
    "_echo" : "return"
  },
  {
    "formElement" : "inputSelect",
    "id": "aid3",
    "labelName" : "State",
    "model" : [{"label": "Alabama", "value" : "AL"},{"label": "Alaska", "value" :
"AK"},{"label": "Arizona", "value" : "AZ"},{"label": "Arkansas", "value" : "AR"}],
    "_class" : "",
    "required" : false,
    "optional" : "",
    "_echo" : "return"
  },
  {
    "formElement" : "inputControl",
    "id": "aid4",
    "labelName" : "Zip Code",
    "name" : "zipcode",
    "value" : "",
    "type" : "number",
    "placeholder" : "",
    "_class" : "",
    "required" : false,
    "optional" : "",
    "_echo" : "return"
```

```
    },
    {
      "formElement": "buttons",
      "buttons" : [
        {
          "text": "Submit",
          "href": "#",
          "id" : "bid1",
          "type" : "primaryClass",
          "_echo" : "return"
        }
      ]
    }
  ]
};';
```

Creating a Form

As noted at this chapter's outset, we didn't make an actual form control. Rather, we made controls that provide the content of a form. So to make a form, we create an ordinary form element and then use our controls. The example we use throughout this chapter has two fieldset controls within the form element. We could have also used input controls within the form element. We didn't need to do that in the example, though. Instead, the input controls are within the fieldset controls. Our sample also uses two forms, one for the dark treatment and one for the light treatment. Listing 18-10 shows how we create the forms we used as a sample.

Listing 18-10. *Creating Our Sample Forms*

```
<div style="margin-bottom: 40px">
  <h1>Form Treatment 1</h1>
  <form class="form formTreatment1">
    <?php fieldSetControl($contactInfo, "fieldsetTreatment1"); ?>
    <?php fieldSetControl($addressInfo, "fieldsetTreatment1"); ?>
  </form>
</div>
<div style="width: 400px;">
  <h1>Form Treatment 2</h1>
  <form class="form formTreatment2">
    <?php fieldSetControl($contactInfo, "fieldsetTreatment2"); ?>
    <?php fieldSetControl($addressInfo, "fieldsetTreatment2"); ?>
  </form>
</div>
```

The CSS

As is true of all our controls, the differences between the treatments occur entirely within the CSS rules that drive the presentation of the different treatments. Other than specifying the name of the treatment (fieldsetTreatment1 for the dark treatment, fieldsetTreatment2 for the light treatment), the function and the data don't vary at all between the treatments. As usual, we'll comment on most of the CSS rules individually, though we may lump together some of the more obvious rules.

Listing 18-11 shows how we set the margins and padding values to zero (0) on the fieldset element so that those settings carry through to all elements within the fieldset control.

Listing 18-11. *Removing the Margins and Padding*

```
.fieldset {
  margin: 0;
  padding: 0;
}
```

Listing 18-12 shows how we insert colons after labels.

Listing 18-12. *Inserting Colons After Labels*

```
.fieldset label.structure:after {
  content: ":";
}
```

Listing 18-13 shows how we set the asterisk we use to show that an item is required to red and set a bit of padding to keep the asterisk from running into the text of the label.

Listing 18-13. *Styling the Required Asterisks*

```
.required {
  color: red;
  padding: 2px;
}
```

Listing 18-14 shows how we style the form for the dark treatment. In essence, this rule styles the box that holds all the content in the form. Because formTreatment1 has a dark background image, we set the text to white. Then we set the text shadow, the padding, the border radius (to create rounded corners), the box shadow, and the border. Along the way, we set the background clipping (a CSS 3 attribute) to padding-box, which keeps the background out of the border. We also ensure that the form appears as a block and set the width to 400 pixels. We also set the value of the position property to relative, because we later set elements within the form with absolute positioning. Finally, we set the background image to the small (7 pixels on a side) image that gives us the "corduroy" effect.

Listing 18-14. *Styling the form Element for the Dark Treatment*

```
.formTreatment1 {
  color: white;
  text-shadow: 0 0 2px black;
  padding: 20px;
  -webkit-border-radius: 10px;
  -moz-border-radius: 10px;
  border-radius: 10px;
  -moz-background-clip: padding;
  -webkit-background-clip: padding-box;
  background-clip: padding-box;
  -webkit-box-shadow: inset 1px 1px 1px #777777;
  -moz-box-shadow: inset 1px 1px 1px #777777;
```

```
    box-shadow: inset 1px 1px 1px #777777;
    border: 1px solid rgba(0, 0, 0, 0.2);
    background: #CCC;
    display: block;
    position: relative;
    width: 400px;
    background: #ffffff url(/images/background_stripped.png);
}
```

Listing 18-15 shows how we wrap an additional border around the form to provide a bit more visual appeal. To do so, we use the before pseudo selector, set the value of the position property to absolute, and then set the values of both the top property and the left property to -10 pixels. By then setting the padding and the border to 10 pixels and creating a 10-pixel shadow, we get a 10-pixel-wide wrapper around the form. To make the wrapper visible, we also set its z-index value to 1.

Listing 18-15. Adding a 10-Pixel Wrapper Around the Form

```
.formTreatment1:before {
    content: "";
    width: 100%;
    height: 100%;
    display: block;
    z-index: -1;
    position: absolute;
    padding: 10px;
    background: #CCC;
    left: -10px;
    top: -10px;
    -webkit-border-radius: 10px;
    -moz-border-radius: 10px;
    border-radius: 10px;
    -moz-background-clip: padding;
    -webkit-background-clip: padding-box;
    background-clip: padding-box;
    -webkit-box-shadow: inset 0px 0px 4px rgba(0, 0, 0, 0.4), inset 0 10px 2px rgba(255, 255, 255,
0.4), 2px 2px 2px rgba(0, 0, 0, 0.4);
    -moz-box-shadow: inset 0px 0px 4px rgba(0, 0, 0, 0.4), inset 0 10px 2px rgba(255, 255, 255,
0.4), 2px 2px 2px rgba(0, 0, 0, 0.4);
    box-shadow: inset 0px 0px 4px rgba(0, 0, 0, 0.4), inset 0 10px 2px rgba(255, 255, 255, 0.4),
2px 2px 2px rgba(0, 0, 0, 0.4);
}
```

Listing 18-16 shows how we disable the wrapper for Internet Explorer versions prior to IE9. The older browser versions don't render the wrapper properly; preferring nothing to a mess, we turn off the wrapper for those versions.

Listing 18-16. Turning Off the Wrapper for Versions of Internet Explorer prior to IE9.

```
.lt-ie9 .formTreatment1:before {
    display: none;
}
```

Listing 18-17 shows how we style a fieldset control for the dark treatment (identified by fieldsetTreatment1). Since we use it as an outer element around other elements (mostly input elements and anchor elements that serve as buttons), we want the padding value to be 0 and want the position value to be relative. We also set the border value to none and add a 10-pixel bottom margin (to keep the fieldset away from any following elements).

Listing 18-17. Styling the Dark Fieldset Treatment

```
.fieldsetTreatment1 {
  padding: 0px;
  position: relative;
  border: none;
  margin-bottom: 10px;
}
```

Listing 18-18 shows how we style the legend element within a fieldset. We set the left padding value to 10 pixels to give the text a bit of an indent. We also set the top and bottom padding values to 5 pixels to keep the text from running into other elements. We can ignore the right padding value, so we set it to 0. We also create a solid white line over the text to provide a boundary between the fieldset control and whatever may precede it. (While the line is defined in the style that applies to the legend element, it has the effect of making a top boundary for the fieldset control because the legend element is the first element within the fieldset control.) Because we don't want the legend element to ever be anything but a block, we set the value of the display property to block and add the !important specifier. We also set the font weight to bold (what good is a legend folks can't see?) and set the bottom margin to 20 pixels to avoid crowding the fields. We like white space (or corduroy space, in this case). We also set the position value to relative; we explain why we need this setting in the description of the next rule.

Listing 18-18. Styling the legend Element

```
.fieldsetTreatment1 legend {
  padding: 5px 0 5px 10px;
  font-weight: bold;
  border-top: 2px solid white;
  display: block !important;
  width: 100%;
  margin-bottom: 20px;
  position: relative;
}
```

Listing 18-19 shows how we get the circle (Jay calls it a knob) on the left end of the line. To create that apparently empty circle (it isn't empty, really, but it seems to be), we applied both before and after pseudo selectors to the legend element. The before pseudo selector creates a circle 14 pixels in diameter by creating a rounded border, setting the position value to absolute, setting the top and left values to -7 pixels, and setting the width and height to 14 pixels. Because we set the background color to white, we get a white circle. If we did nothing more, we'd have a circle filled with white. Remember setting the position property on the legend element to relative? If we didn't set the value to relative, the line would seem to connect to the circle with an offset rather than at the center of the circle. We show how we got a seemingly empty circle in the next rule.

Listing 18-19. Adding the Circle to the Left End of the Line Above the legend Element

```
.fieldsetTreatment1 legend:before {
  content: '';
```

```
  width: 14px;
  height: 14px;
  position: absolute;
  top: -7px;
  left: -7px;
  background: white;
  -webkit-border-radius: 100%;
  -moz-border-radius: 100%;
  border-radius: 100%;
  -moz-background-clip: padding;
  -webkit-background-clip: padding-box;
  background-clip: padding-box;
}
```

Listing 18-20 shows how we make the circle at the end of the line above the legend element seem hollow. In the legend:before pseudo selector listing, we showed how to make a circle at the end of the line above the legend element. As mentioned in the description of Listing 18-20, we would have a solid white circle if we didn't do something further. We take care of that problem in the legend:after pseudo selector. To create a circle that seems to be stroked but not filled (or to put it another way, that appears to be empty), we add another circle that has our corduroy image as its background. This time, we make a circle that's 10 pixels wide. Because the other circle is 14 pixels wide, we get the appearance of a circle with a 2-pixel stroke and no fill. The trick to getting the circles to line up is using absolute positioning and negative offsets for the left and top properties. That way, both circles' centers are at the same location. Also, because the circle appears to have a stroke of 2, the line that constitutes the circle is the same width as the line above the legend text.

That's a lot of styling to get a knob on the end of a line. We think it's worth the time and bandwidth, though, to provide a touch of pizzazz to our forms.

Listing 18-20. *Making a Circle Seem to Be Empty*

```
.fieldsetTreatment1 legend:after {
  content: '';
  width: 10px;
  height: 10px;
  position: absolute;
  top: -5px;
  left: -5px;
  background: url(/images/background_stripped.png);
  -webkit-border-radius: 100%;
  -moz-border-radius: 100%;
  border-radius: 100%;
  -moz-background-clip: padding;
  -webkit-background-clip: padding-box;
  background-clip: padding-box;
}
```

Listing 18-21 shows how we set the padding for the form elements. We set the top and bottom padding for all form elements to 4 pixels and set the left and right padding to 0.

Listing 18-21. Setting the Padding for form Elements

```
.fieldsetTreatment1 .formElement {
  padding: 4px 0;
}
```

Listing 18-22 shows how we style the label for a form element. We set the width to 150 pixels to provide ample room for most labels. Longer labels wrap to two lines, which should be rare and not look bad when it happens. We also set the alignment to right to keep the label next to the field to which it belongs. Then we set the right padding value to 4 pixels, since we don't want the label to crowd its field. Finally, we set the value of the display property to inline-block, because we can't set a width value otherwise.

■ **Tip** If you have to support labels in multiple languages, consider putting the labels above the fields. Compared with most other languages, English is pretty succinct. The same label in French or another language may be much longer. Also, English uses shorter words than many other languages. Sometimes, the same label in German is a single word and is so long that it overflows the label space before a word break. Though it's rare, we've encountered it in work for multinational clients, and it's no fun to rearrange labels at the last minute because of this kind of issue. The light treatment puts the labels above the fields, so we could use that treatment for international sites.

Listing 18-22. Styling the Labels for form Elements

```
.fieldsetTreatment1 label.structure {
  width: 150px;
  text-align: right;
  padding-right: 4px;
  display: inline-block;
}
```

Listing 18-23 shows how we style input elements for the dark treatment. In keeping with our general theme of rounded corners, we create rounded corners for our input elements by setting the various border-radius values (we need several values to accommodate different browsers). Then we set the background-clip value to padding-box to keep the field out of the corners. Next, we set a 1-pixel medium-gray border. After that, we set the padding to 4 or 5 pixels, depending on the side (some experimentation made us think these values look the best, in case you're wondering why we have different values). Finally, we set the box-shadow values to provide a feeling of depth.

Listing 18-23. Styling input Elements for the Dark Treatment

```
.fieldsetTreatment1 .inputControl input {
  -webkit-border-radius: 5px;
  -moz-border-radius: 5px;
  border-radius: 5px;
  -moz-background-clip: padding;
  -webkit-background-clip: padding-box;
  background-clip: padding-box;
  border: 1px solid #999;
  padding: 5px 5px 4px 4px;
  -webkit-box-shadow: inset 1px 1px 1px #999999;
  -moz-box-shadow: inset 1px 1px 1px #999999;
```

```
  box-shadow: inset 1px 1px 1px #999999;
}
```

Listing 18-24 shows how we set the margins for check boxes and radio buttons. We set the right margin to 3 pixels, so that we get a little separation between the check box or radio button and its label. Because different browsers handle the spacing around check boxes differently, we also set the padding to 0 (we use the margin to get the spacing we want).

Listing 18-24. *Setting the Margins for Check Boxes and Radio Buttons*

```
.fieldsetTreatment1 .inputList input[type="checkbox"], .fieldsetTreatment1 .inputList
input[type="radio"] {
  margin: 0 3px 0 0;
  padding: 0;
}
```

Listing 18-25 shows how we set the right padding of the label for a check box or radio button to 10 pixels to give some space between the label and the next check box or radio button.

Listing 18-25. *Setting the Right Padding for the Label of a Check Box or Radio Button*

```
.fieldsetTreatment1 .inputList .textLabel {
  padding-right: 10px;
}
```

Listing 18-26 shows how we set the right padding for the last check box or radio button within an input list to 0. This setting prevents accidental wrapping when the last label gets close to the right edge of the list's content area. While not strictly necessary, it's good practice to include it.

Listing 18-26. *Setting the Right Padding for the Last Label of a Check Box or Radio Button to 0*

```
.fieldsetTreatment1 .inputList .textLabel:last-child {
  padding-right: 0;
}
```

Listing 18-27 shows how we get text elements inserted into the fieldset to line up with the fields in the fieldset. Because the labels have a width of 150 pixels (see Listing 18-22) and 4 pixels of padding and because that padding overlaps the edge of the field by 1 pixel (because of the border we put on the field), we get a value of 153 pixels for the left padding of a text element within the fieldset.

Listing 18-27. *Lining Up the Text Messages with the Fields*

```
.fieldsetTreatment1 .textMessage {
  padding-left: 153px;
}
```

Listing 18-28 shows how we get buttons to line up with the field elements. The same issues that dictate 153 pixels in Listing 18-26 apply here. Basically, after calculating the width of the labels and their padding, combined with how the edges of the fields work, we end up at 153 pixels.

Listing 18-28. *Lining Up the Buttons with the Fields*

```
.fieldsetTreatment1 .buttonWrap {
  padding-left: 153px;
}
```

Listing 18-29 shows how we style the fieldset for the light treatment (fieldsetTreatment2). First, we set a 3-pixel medium-gray top border. Then we set 15 pixels of padding on top to provide space between the top border and the fieldset's content. Next, we set a bottom border of 20 pixels to provide space between the bottom of the fieldset and whatever content may follow the fieldset. Finally, we set the left padding to 20 pixels to indent the elements within the fieldset. The top border appears behind the legend element because the edge of the fieldset crosses the middle of the legend element (as intended by its designers). We could change it by playing with padding values, but we like it as is.

Listing 18-29. Styling the Fieldset for the Light Treatment

```
.fieldsetTreatment2 {
  border-top: 3px solid #777;
  padding-top: 15px;
  margin-bottom: 20px;
  padding-left: 20px;
}
```

Listing 18-30 shows how we style the legend element within the light treatment of the fieldset control. We create a solid 1-point medium-gray border. Then we set the left margin to 0 pixels. Next, we set the top and bottom padding to 4 pixels and the left and right padding to 10 pixels to get the text away from the border. Then we specify rounded corners and set the background-clip property to padding-box, which keeps the background from going behind the border. Finally, we set the background to a gradient, which we define with an SVG image for IE9. Specifying the gradient so that it works in as many browsers as possible requires a bunch of properties.

Listing 18-30. Styling the Legend for a Fieldset with the Light Treatment

```
.fieldsetTreatment2 legend {
  border: 1px solid #777;
  margin-left: 0px;
  padding: 4px 10px;
  -webkit-border-radius: 4px;
  -moz-border-radius: 4px;
  border-radius: 4px;
  -moz-background-clip: padding;
  -webkit-background-clip: padding-box;
  background-clip: padding-box;
  background: #cfeaf7;
  background: url(data:image/svg+xml;base64,PD94bWwgdmVyc2lvbjOiMS4wIiA/Pgo8c3ZnIHhtbG5zPSJodHRw
Oi8vd3d3LnczLm9yZy8yMDAwL3N2ZyIgd2lkdGg9IjEwMCUiIGhlaWdodDOiMTAwJSIgdmlld0JveD0iMCAwIDEgMSIgcHJl
c2VydmVBc3BlY3RSYXRpbz0ibm9uZSI+CiAgPGxpbmVhckdyYWRpZW50IGlkPSJncmFkLXVjZ2ctZ2VuZXJhdGVkIiBncmFk
aWVudFVuaXRzPSJ1c2VyU3BhY2VPblVzZSIgeDE9IjAlIiB5MTOiMCUiIHgyPSIwJSIgeTI9IjEwMCUiPgogICAgPHNOb3Ag
b2Zmc2VOPSIwJSIgc3RvcC1jb2xvcjOiI2NmZWFmNyIgc3RvcC1vcGFjaXR5PSIxIi8+CiAgICA8c3RvcCBvZmZzZXQ9IjUw
JSIgc3RvcC1jb2xvcjOiI2JkZGRlZCIgc3RvcC1vcGFjaXR5PSIxIi8+CiAgICA8c3RvcCBvZmZzZXQ9IjUxJSIgc3RvcC1j
b2xvcjOiI2I3ZDFlMiIgc3RvcC1vcGFjaXR5PSIxIi8+CiAgICA8c3RvcCBvZmZzZXQ9IjEwMCUiIHNOb3AtY29sb3I9IiNj
YWUxZjciIHNOb3Atb3BhY2l0eTOiMSIvPgogIDwvbGluZWFyR3JhZGllbnQ+CiAgPHJlY3QgeDOiMCIgeTOiMCIgd2lkdGg9
IjEiIGhlaWdodDOiMSIgZmlsbD0iIdXJsKCNncmFkLXVjZ2ctZ2VuZXJhdGVkKSIgLz4KPC9zdmc+);
  background: -moz-linear-gradient(top, #cfeaf7 0%, #bddded 50%, #b7d1e2 51%, #cae1f7 100%);
  background: -webkit-gradient(linear, left top, left bottom, color-stop(0%, #cfeaf7),
color-stop(50%, #bddded), color-stop(51%, #b7d1e2), color-stop(100%, #cae1f7));
  background: -webkit-linear-gradient(top, #cfeaf7 0%, #bddded 50%, #b7d1e2 51%, #cae1f7 100%);
  background: -o-linear-gradient(top, #cfeaf7 0%, #bddded 50%, #b7d1e2 51%, #cae1f7 100%);
```

```
background: -ms-linear-gradient(top, #cfeaf7 0%, #bddded 50%, #b7d1e2 51%, #cae1f7 100%);
background: linear-gradient(to bottom, #cfeaf7 0%, #bddded 50%, #b7d1e2 51%, #cae1f7 100%);
filter: progid:dximagetransform.microsoft.gradient(startColorstr='#cfeaf7', endColorstr='#cae1f
7', GradientType=0);
}
```

Listing 18-31 shows how we style a form element (input element, text element, or button) within the light treatment of the fieldset control. We set the top and bottom padding to 5 pixels and the left and right padding to 0. The top and bottom padding keeps the form elements from running into one another. We also set the value of the overflow property to hidden, so that stray text won't go outside the form element.

Listing 18-31. Styling a form Element Within the Light Treatment

```
.fieldsetTreatment2 .formElement {
  padding: 5px 0;
  overflow: hidden;
}
```

Listing 18-32 shows how we style the labels for form elements in the light treatment of the fieldset control. First, we ensure that the display value is block. Then we specify rounded corners and set the value of the background-clip property to padding-box to keep the background out of the border. Then we specify a background image with SVG to create a gradient behind the label. As ever, creating a cross-browser gradient takes a lot of properties. Then we set the text color to a dark gray. Next, we set the value of the float property to left to keep the background and border from going across the whole content area. Because we set the float value to left, we have to set the value of the clear property to both, so that the label stays on its own line. Then we set most of the padding values to 10 pixels to provide plenty of space between the label text and the border. However, we set the bottom padding to just two pixels to reinforce the connection between the label and the field. Also to reinforce that connection, we create a shadow on the bottom of the label's content area, which makes it seem that the label and the field are not just touching but are attached to one another.

Listing 18-32. Styling the Labels for form Elements in the Light Treatment

```
.fieldsetTreatment2 .structure {
  display: block;
  -webkit-border-top-right-radius: 5px;
  -webkit-border-bottom-right-radius: 0;
  -webkit-border-bottom-left-radius: 0;
  -webkit-border-top-left-radius: 5px;
  -moz-border-radius-topright: 5px;
  -moz-border-radius-bottomright: 0;
  -moz-border-radius-bottomleft: 0;
  -moz-border-radius-topleft: 5px;
  border-top-right-radius: 5px;
  border-bottom-right-radius: 0;
  border-bottom-left-radius: 0;
  border-top-left-radius: 5px;
  -moz-background-clip: padding;
  -wcbkit-background-clip: padding-box;
  background-clip: padding-box;
  background: #f6f8f9;
  background: url(data:image/svg+xml;base64,PD94bWwgdmVyc2lvbjOiMS4wIiA/Pgo8c3ZnIHhtbG5zPSJodHRw
```

```
Oi8vd3d3LnczLm9yZy8yMDAwL3N2ZyIgd2lkdGg9IjEwMCUiIGhlaWdodD0iMTAwJSIgdmlld0JveD0iMCAwIDEgMSIgcHJl
c2VydmVBc3BlY3RSYXRpbz0ibm9uZSI+CiAgPGxpbmVhckdyYWRpZW50IGlkPSJncmFkLXVjZ2ctZ2VuZXJhdGVkIiBncmFk
aWVudFVuaXRzPSJ1c2VyU3BhY2VPblVzZSIgeDE9IjAlIiB5MT0iMCUiIHgyPSIwJSIgeTI9IjEwMCUiPgogICAgPHN0b3Ag
b2Zmc2V0PSIwJSIgc3RvcC1jb2xvcj0iI2Y2ZjhmOSIgc3RvcC1vcGFjaXR5PSIxIi8+CiAgICA8c3RvcCBvZmZzZXQ9IjUw
JSIgc3RvcC1jb2xvcj0iI2U1ZWJlZSIgc3RvcC1vcGFjaXR5PSIxIi8+CiAgICA8c3RvcCBvZmZzZXQ9IjUxJSIgc3RvcC1j
b2xvcj0iI2Q3ZGVlMyIgc3RvcC1jb2xvcj0iI2Y1Zjdm OSIgc3RvcC1vcGFjaXR5PSIxIi8+CiAgICA8c3RvcCBvZmZzZXQ9IjEwMCUiIHN0b3AtY29sb3I9IiNm
NWY3ZjkiIHN0b3Atb3BhY2l0eT0iMSIvPgogIDwvbGluZWFyR3JhZGllbnQ+CiAgPHJlY3QgeD0iMCIgeT0iMCIgd2lkdGg9
IjEiIGhlaWdodD0iMSIgZmlsbD0idXJsKCNncmFkLXVjZ2ctZ2VuZXJhdGVkKSIgLz4KPC9zdmc+);
    background: -moz-linear-gradient(top, #f6f8f9 0%, #e5ebee 50%, #d7dee3 51%, #f5f7f9 100%);
    background: -webkit-gradient(linear, left top, left bottom, color-stop(0%, #f6f8f9), color-
stop(50%, #e5ebee), color-stop(51%, #d7dee3), color-stop(100%, #f5f7f9));
    background: -webkit-linear-gradient(top, #f6f8f9 0%, #e5ebee 50%, #d7dee3 51%, #f5f7f9 100%);
    background: -o-linear-gradient(top, #f6f8f9 0%, #e5ebee 50%, #d7dee3 51%, #f5f7f9 100%);
    background: -ms-linear-gradient(top, #f6f8f9 0%, #e5ebee 50%, #d7dee3 51%, #f5f7f9 100%);
    background: linear-gradient(to bottom, #f6f8f9 0%, #e5ebee 50%, #d7dee3 51%, #f5f7f9 100%);
    filter: progid:dximagetransform.microsoft.gradient(startColorstr='#f6f8f9', endColorstr='#f5f7f
9', GradientType=0);
    color: #333;
    float: left;
    clear: both;
    padding: 2px 10px 2px 10px;
    -webkit-box-shadow: inset 0 0 3px rgba(0, 0, 0, 0.4);
    -moz-box-shadow: inset 0 0 3px rgba(0, 0, 0, 0.4);
    box-shadow: inset 0 0 3px rgba(0, 0, 0, 0.4);
    font-size: 12px;
}
```

Listing 18-33 shows how we prevent extraneous text from being inserted into the labels. Because the .fieldset label.structure:after rule (see listing 18-12) inserts a colon, we need to override that rule here to prevent colons from being inserted into the labels in the light treatment.

Listing 18-33. *Block Extraneous Text for form Element Labels in the Light Treatment*

```
.fieldsetTreatment2 label.structure:after {
  content: "";
}
```

Listing 18-34 shows how we style an input element within the light treatment. This style applies to the input elements created by the inputControl function (see "The Input Control" section earlier on). In many ways, the style for the input element is the same as the style for its label (see Listing 18-31). We set the float value to left and the clear value to both to keep the element from taking more space than it should but still keep it on its own line. We also set a gradient fill. The padding values are different, though. We set top and bottom padding values of 4 pixels and left and right padding values of 20 pixels to keep the values that visitors enter well away from the borders. We also didn't set a shadow within the field; it would be unattractive and just distract visitors.

Listing 18-34. *Styling an input Element Within the Light Treatment*

```
.fieldsetTreatment2 .inputControl input {

  border: 1px solid #BBB;
  padding: 4px 20px;
```

```
  clear: both;
  float: left;
  -webkit-box-shadow: inset 0 0 3px rgba(0, 0, 0, 0.4);
  -moz-box-shadow: inset 0 0 3px rgba(0, 0, 0, 0.4);
  box-shadow: inset 0 0 3px rgba(0, 0, 0, 0.4);
  background: #EEE;
  background: #e5e5e5;
  background: url(data:image/svg+xml;base64,PD94bWwgdmVyc2lvbjoiMS4wIiA/Pgo8c3ZnIHhtbG5zPSJodHRw
Oi8vd3d3LnczLm9yZy8yMDAwL3N2ZyIgd2lkdGg9IjEwMCUiIGhlaWdodDoiMTAwJSIgdmlld0JveDoiMCAwIDEgMSIgcHJl
c2VydmVBc3BlY3RSYXRpb2oibm9uZSI+CiAgPGxpbmVhckdyYWRpZW50IGlkPSJncmFkLXVjZ2ctZ2VuZXJhdGVkIiBncmFk
aWVudFVuaXRzPSJ1c2VyU3BhY2VPblVzZSIgeDE9IjAlIiB5MToiMCUiIHgyPSIwJSIgeTI9IjEwMCUiPgogICAgPHNvb3Ag
b2Zmc2V0PSIwJSIgc3RvcC1jb2xvcjoiI2U1ZTVlNSIgc3RvcC1vcGFjaXR5PSIxIi8+CiAgICA8c3RvcCBvZmZzZXQ9IjEw
MCUiIHNvb3AtY29sb3I9IiNmZmZmZmYiIHNvb3Atb3BhY2loeToiMSIvPgogIDwvbGluZWFyR3JhZGllbnQ+CiAgPHJlY3Qg
eDoiMCIgeToiMCIgd2lkdGg9IjEiIGhlaWdodDoiMSIgZmlsbDoidXJsKCNncmFkLXVjZ2ctZ2VuZXJhdGVkKSIgLz4KPC9z
dmc+);
  background: -moz-linear-gradient(top, #e5e5e5 0%, #ffffff 100%);
  background: -webkit-gradient(linear, left top, left bottom, color-stop(0%, #e5e5e5),
color-stop(100%, #ffffff));
  background: -webkit-linear-gradient(top, #e5e5e5 0%, #ffffff 100%);
  background: -o-linear-gradient(top, #e5e5e5 0%, #ffffff 100%);
  background: -ms-linear-gradient(top, #e5e5e5 0%, #ffffff 100%);
  background: linear-gradient(to bottom, #e5e5e5 0%, #ffffff 100%);
  filter: progid:dximagetransform.microsoft.gradient(startColorstr='#e5e5e5', endColorstr='#ffff
f', GradientType=0);
}
```

Listing 18-35 shows how we style the labels for check boxes and radio buttons (which match the inputList class) and lists (which match the selectWrap style).

■ **Note**   This style applies to the label for the whole input element, not the labels for the individual choices (check boxes or radio buttons) within the element.

Because these labels don't need backgrounds or shadows (also because those properties have been set in various ancestor elements), we set those properties to none. We also set the line-height value to 14 pixels to provide enough space for the label's text.

Listing 18-35. *Styling the Labels for list and select input Elements*

```
.fieldsetTreatment2 .inputList .structure, .fieldsetTreatment2 .selectWrap .structure {
  background: none;
  -webkit-box-shadow: none;
  -moz-box-shadow: none;
  box-shadow: none;
  line-height: 14px;
  filter: none;
}
```

Listing 18-36 shows how we insert a colon after the text of a label for check boxes and radio buttons (which match the inputList class) and lists (which match the selectWrap style).

■ **Note**   As in the `.fieldsetTreatment2 .inputControl` input style (see Listing 18-33), this style applies to the label for the whole `input` element, not the labels for the individual choices (check boxes or radio buttons) within the element.

Listing 18-36. Inserting a Colon after a Label for list and select input Elements

```
.fieldsetTreatment2 .inputList .structure:after, .fieldsetTreatment2 .selectWrap .structure:after
{
  content: ":";
}
```

Listing 18-37 shows how we ensure enough space between check boxes and radio buttons (the `inputList` class) and add left and right padding to options in lists (the `selectWrap` class). In all of those cases, we set the top and bottom padding to 0 and set the left and right padding to 5 pixels.

Listing 18-37. Styling the Contents of Lists and the Labels of Radio Buttons and Check Boxes

```
.fieldsetTreatment2 .inputList .textLabel, .fieldsetTreatment2 .selectWrap .textLabel {
  padding: 0 5px;
}
```

Listing 18-38 shows how we make sure that the selection arrow for `select` elements has a white background in Internet Explorer. Without this rule, the selection arrow appears to get into the border of the selection box.

Listing 18-38. Making Sure the Selection Arrow Has White Background in Internet Explorer

```
.ie select {
  background: white;
}
```

Making Shortcut Controls

We want to end the descriptions of our controls with a helpful tip. If you embrace the idea of using controls, you can make functions that specify some of the arguments you'd generally pass to the control. This technique lets you make "shortcut controls" so that you (and your coworkers or customers who use your controls) need to do less typing to use a control. We made a few examples that apply to the input control, but you can make similar shortcut controls for all the controls we've presented in this book. Another benefit of these shortcut controls is that you can ensure that the same `text` (and other) elements appear in your commonly used controls, providing greater consistency across your sites. Consequently, you get fewer bugs being reported from your test team and your customers. That's always a good thing.

Let's start with a control that makes an e-mail `input` element. Since we can provide some of the values, we get a function that takes five arguments rather than the ten arguments. Listing 18-38 shows a function that calls the `inputControl` function to create an e-mail input field.

Listing 18-39. An e-Mail Input Control

```
function emailInput($id, $name, $value, $class, $echo) {  $output = inputControl($id, "Email",
$name, $value, "email", "name@domain.com", $class, TRUE, null, "return");  if ($echo !=
"return") {    echo $output;  } else {    return $output;  }
}
```

Listing 18-40 shows a shortcut control for creating a password input element. In this case, we can trim the arguments down to just four.

Listing 18-40. A Password Input Control

```
function passwordInput($id, $name, $class, $echo) {  $output = inputControl($id, "Password",
$name, null, "password", "Type a Unique Password", $class, TRUE, "return");  if ($echo !=
"return") {    echo $output;  } else {    return $output;  }
}
```

Listing 18-41 shows a shortcut control for creating an input element that lets a visitor reenter a password.

Listing 18-41. A Control for Reentering a Password

```
function reenterPasswordInput($id, $name, $class, $echo) {  $output = inputControl($id, "Reenter
Password", $name, null, "password", "Retype Password Exactly", $class, TRUE, "return");  if
($echo != "return") {    echo $output;  } else {    return $output;  }
}
```

We hope you can see from the examples how you can easily make your own library of shortcut controls.

Summary

This large chapter covered how to make controls that make the elements within a form. We provided two treatments, light and dark. While we called them light and dark after their most striking visual characteristics, they have other important distinctions. From a usability standpoint, the most important is that the dark treatment has labels on the same lines as the input elements, while the light treatment has labels above the input elements. As we mentioned in the body of the chapter, this distinction might make the light treatment more suitable for web sites frequented by international visitors.

We also showed how to use the before and after pseudo selectors to create two effects: a wrapper around an element (we added one around the dark treatment of the form element) and an empty circle (really a circle within a circle) to the left of a line. We find that the before and after pseudo selectors aren't much used, so we thought we'd show some tricks with them.

Along the way, we showed a technique that you can use with all of our controls (and your own controls, if you start writing controls): making shortcut controls. Shortcut controls are really just controls that call other controls with some of the arguments specified. With some careful planning, you can build a large library of shortcut controls from a much smaller set of more general controls. The trick to making that paradigm work is to make your base controls as extensible as possible. If that sounds like object-oriented programming, you're right. Making a large set of objects from a small set of base objects is a common task in object-oriented programming.

Finally, we want to reemphasize a key point: properly structured HTML and CSS offer tremendous reuse potential and flexibility of design. We can quickly repurpose any of our controls for a use we didn't anticipate just by creating another treatment (which is really just a set of CSS classes and the name of the treatment in the control). Even if you don't embrace the idea of controls, remember to write your HTML such that it can be very differently styled with a different stylesheet. That way, you can "future-proof" your work as much as possible.

Index

CPSIA information can be obtained at www.ICGtesting.com
Printed in the USA
LVOW110436231012

304026LV00004B/2/P